The Nerves of Government

THE
Nerves
OF
Government

MODELS OF POLITICAL
COMMUNICATION AND CONTROL

Karl W. Deutsch

Professor of Political Science, Yale University

THE FREE PRESS, NEW YORK
COLLIER-MACMILLAN LTD., LONDON

To the memory of my father,

Martin M. Deutsch
who first taught me the
importance of vision
and communication

PREFACE

This book offers an interim report from an enterprise of thought that is still continuing. The enterprise is to develop eventually a theory of politics, both national and international. This differs from the history of past political ideas, somewhat as the search for an adequate economic theory differs from the study of the history of economic thought.

Such a theory should develop appropriate analytic concepts and models, so as to aid the economy and power of our thinking about politics. It should suggest what facts are likely to be most relevant, and help us to order these facts into meaningful contexts. It should show the probable trend of future political developments, if present policies should be continued, and it should show the probable consequences of particular political actions or decisions. It should help us to appraise the significance of particular institutions, and of the actual patterns of political behavior that may differ greatly from whatever the formal laws and institutions would have led us to expect. In short, it should be as unblinkingly realistic as any social scientist's commitment to truth and to reality could make it.

Finally, however, such a theory should link the "is" and the "ought." It should show the effect of specific facts and policies on the main values that men have held in Western culture; and it should show the significance of some of our major values for specific policy choices. Beyond this, it should show which policies are likely to prove compatible with the pursuit of a wider range of values, and what values are likely to prove in political practice more compatible with others. Ultimately, a mature theory of this kind should help us to identify viable, growing, and creative patterns of political values and political action.

There is no such theory today. There are current political ideologies and philosophies, some of them with the claim to be "perennial." There are important theories and insights in different fields of social science. There are relevant elements in the findings and the philosophy of the natural sciences—elements that could help us in our task. There is the great tradition of classic political theory, from the ancients down to our own time, and there are important and impressive attempts at synthesis by contemporary writers.[1] Yet it seems clear that there is still before us a continuing task of producing and developing a theory of politics that will be comprehensive, coherent, relevant, and, one hopes, increasingly effective.

The development of such a body of thought, comparable to such bodies of knowledge as economic theory, the theories of evolution and genetics in biology, or, to take an extreme case, theoretical physics, will be the result of many steps and the product of many minds. Some individual contributions will be more fundamental or more comprehensive, and thus will loom larger than others, but even those will be limited contributions to the joint and continuing work of many, both from the living and from the dead.

The present book presents at most some elements for such a contribution. It offers a certain body of considerations and ideas that might be relevant to this task of reorganization and reinterpretation of political thought and to the building of a more specific and comprehensive theory of politics in the future.

In the main, these pages offer notions, propositions, and models derived from the philosophy of science, and specifically from the theory of communication and control—often called by Norbert Wiener's term "cybernetics"—in the hope that these may prove relevant to the study of politics, and suggestive and useful in the eventual development of a body of political theory that will be more adequate—or less inadequate—to the problems of the later decades of the twentieth century. Suggestions as to the possible significance of this material for political research or policy analysis are made frequently throughout the text, but the more specific discussion and documentation are limited, in the main, to the material from communication theory and the philosophy of science. The references to works on political theory proper, and generally to the writings of political scientists, are relatively brief and scanty. A proper and full discussion of the possible connections between communication theory and the great body of political thought and research would have gone far beyond the frame of this preliminary volume.

All that is offered here, in addition to a body of ideas or suggestions, is a point of view. It is this point of view that has given the title to this book. Men have long and often concerned themselves with the power of governments, much as some observers try to assess the muscle power of a horse or an athlete. Others have described the laws and institutions of states, much as anatomists describe the skeleton or organs of a body. This book concerns itself less with the bones or muscles of the body politic than with its nerves— its channels of communication and decision.

This book suggests that it might be profitable to look upon government somewhat less as a problem of power and somewhat more as a problem of steering; and it tries to show that steering is decisively a matter of communication. It tries to suggest some of the implications of this viewpoint for the analysis of governmental institutions, of political behavior, and of political ideas, and it points to some areas of empirical research on politics that might deserve a higher priority of attention than they have often received in the past.

Farther than this the present volume does not propose to go. Another volume might be filled with examples of some of the types of empirical research to which this viewpoint already has given rise. Some of this work has dealt with the changing tides among nations —the flows of communications and transactions among countries as well as within them. Related research has concerned itself with the changing balance between the demands and burdens put upon the attention and decision-making capabilities of governments and the level of those capabilities and resources themselves. Concerns of this type have led to studies of the integration, or else of the breakup, of large political communities, as well as of the strengthening or decline of an alliance between two or more countries.[2] In principle, studies of this type could be developed not only at the level of national and international politics but also on the level of municipal politics and of the political problems of metropolitan areas.[3]

Pursued in another direction, the viewpoint of communications has suggested an interest in the genesis of failures of political or military intelligence, and in the conditions that might increase or reduce the probability of such failures in the future.[4] Another related line of research has sought for the background conditions, group memories, and communication patterns bearing on the strength of popular attitudes of isolationism or internationalism in the United States.[5]

Beyond such a range of examples of empirical research, related to this viewpoint of communications, however, the main intellectual task still remains to be done. That task would be to relate the new intellectual resources of communications theory more closely and systematically to three bodies of thought. First among these would have to stand the great classic body of political theory with its orientation toward both facts and values. This body would also include the classic tradition of international politics and diplomacy, as presented in the writings of Hans Morgenthau, George Kennan, William T. R. Fox, and others, and the creative continuation of full-scale political and social theory in our own time, by such thinkers as Carl J. Friedrich, Harold Lasswell, Talcott Parsons, and David Easton. Side by side with this body of ideas, and calling for some intellectual integration with it, there is the continuing development of the theory of communications and control, as in the thought of Norbert Wiener, and of the theory of games and decisions, beginning with the classic theory of games of John von Neumann and Oskar Morgenstern, and the continuing contributions and applications by such writers as Anatol Rapoport, Thomas C. Schelling, Martin Shubik, and others. Finally, there is the impressive body of highly relevant and methodologically mature research on international communications, by such men as Paul F. Lazarsfeld, Daniel Lerner, Charles E. Osgood, Ithiel de Sola Pool, and Hans Speier, and the fundamentally significant and theoretically sophisticated empirical research on comparative political behavior, by such investigators as Gabriel A. Almond, Robert A. Dahl, and their associates.

To take any serious account of all these contributions—and of several significant others that space limitations prevent me from mentioning—will be a task for years to come. The present book, by presenting some conceptual tools and a possible viewpoint, can hope at most to get a relevant discussion started. If this first-stage volume succeeds in eliciting some early criticisms and suggestions from colleagues, so as to aid in the later stages of this undertaking, or if it should provoke others to do better, it will have served its purpose.

The foregoing lines will already have indicated some of my indebtedness to others. Not all those whose ideas have been most significant for my thinking are specifically referred to in the footnotes of the text. Even the list of names inevitably must be incomplete. To Rupert Emerson, Carl Friedrich, Harold Lasswell, Talcott Parsons, and Norbert Wiener, I owe more intellectual benefits, stimulation, and challenge than I can readily describe. Many others—among them Gabriel Almond, Samuel Beer, Robert Dahl, Harry Eckstein, Philipp Frank, Stuart Hughes, Daniel Lerner, Seymour Martin Lipset, Roy Macridis, Ithiel de Sola Pool, Anatol Rapoport, and David Riesman—have influenced my thought at some time or on some points. None of all these should be blamed for anything I have written in this book, but if anything in it should be found useful, my thanks are owed to them.

Organizations, too, have a strong claim on my indebtedness. The present book has been completed with the support of the Carnegie Corporation and the Stimson Fund of Yale University. Earlier work was stimulated and aided by the Social Science Research Council, through its Inter-University Seminar on Comparative Politics in 1952, and by the Center for Advanced Study in the Behavioral

Sciences, where I was a Fellow in 1956. The libraries of Yale, Harvard, Princeton, Stanford, and Northwestern universities, as well as of the Massachusetts Institute of Technology, all have aided me with conspicuous patience and efficiency. I am also indebted for their cooperation to the editors of the proceedings of the Conference on Science, Philosophy and Religion, and of the journals *Philosophy of Science, Philosophy and Phenomenological Research, American Journal of Orthopsychiatry, Public Opinion Quarterly,* and *Canadian Journal of Economics and Political Science,* all of which have published earlier drafts of materials for some of the chapters of this book. The excellent editorial and research assistance of Leroy N. Rieselbach and Richard L. Merritt, and the skillful and unfailing editorial and secretarial aid of Mrs. Janice Marquis and Mrs. Elizabeth M. Baskin, were crucial in preparing the present volume for the press.

Any book searching for elements of a new political theory implies a commitment to the future. Accordingly, a special word of thanks is owed to my family, whose members provided both distractions from, and motivations for, the writing of this book.

CONTENTS

xiii

PART I

The Search for
Models of Society
and Politics

I

Tools for Thinking:
The General Nature of
Theory and Models

The history of many fields of science shows a characteristic pattern. There is a time in which the science goes through a philosophic stage in its development; the emphasis is on theory, on general concepts, and on the questioning of the fundamental assumptions and methods by which knowledge has been accumulated. At the end of such a philosophic stage often stands an agreement on some basic assumptions and methods—though not necessarily on all of them—and a shifting of interest to the application of these methods to the gathering of detailed facts. The philosophic stages in the development of science define the main lines of interest; in the empirical stages these interests are followed up. Philosophic stages in the development of a particular science are concerned with strategy; they select the targets and the main lines of attack. Empirical stages are concerned with tactics; they attain the targets, or they accumulate experience indicating that the targets cannot be taken in this manner and that the underlying strategy was wrong.[1]

In any case, every empirical stage ends with the need for a revision of fundamental concepts and underlying strategy. If these were inadequate, the revision must come soon. If they were adequate for a time, the revision must nevertheless come later, for the very success of the concepts, methods, and interests adopted will lead in time to an accumulation of data and problems that will point beyond the interests and methods by which they were discovered. In the end, every empirical stage will have bitten off more facts than it can chew, and scientists will have to turn to a new philosophic stage for more powerful analytic equipment.

The test of this conceptual equipment must be twofold: it must be operational, that is, it must lead to inferences capable of being confirmed or refuted by repeatable physical operations; and it must be fruitful, that is, it must lead to new observations and experiments, and eventually to further developments in theory.[2] The stage of philosophic or conceptual emphasis must again lead to empirical progress, and the progress eventually leads once more to new fundamental problems.

The social sciences today perhaps are approaching another "philosophic crisis"—an age of re-examination of concepts, methods, and interests, of search for new symbolic models and/or new strategies in selecting their major targets for attack. At the same time, their data have increased in quantity, and selection has become ever more imperative. To understand and describe in full detail the political process even in a single country may well take the work of a lifetime. To do the same for several countries means to multiply the amount of possible data to be looked for and of possible questions to be asked.

Clearly, selection is of the essence. What are the data most worth getting? What are the questions most worth asking? What are the propositions most worth verifying or disproving? Our answers to these questions will determine the shape of any investigation and may do much to determine the value of the outcome. But to say that we must choose our questions is another way of saying that we must choose our concepts or models.

We obtain the answers to these questions by our preliminary "understanding" of the situation we propose to study. But we could perhaps obtain better answers if we had a better critical grasp of the vague process of "understanding" to which we commit so much of our professional fortunes.[3]

This process of understanding, from its early stages to the final theory or strategy of inquiry, is carried on by means of symbolic models that all of us use in our thinking. It may be worth our while to gain a clearer picture of this process of choosing models and of using them, and we may end with more and sharper intellectual tools than were available to past generations. To be sure, a master sometimes may accomplish more with crude tools than could a novice with better technical equipment. Even so, there may be some usefulness in a brief survey of the nature of conceptual models, and a discussion of a few more recently developed models of this kind in terms of their possible usefulness to comparative political studies.

KNOWLEDGE AND MODELS IN SOCIAL SCIENCE

To discuss some of the recent models in the field of political science, we must recall briefly the role of any model in the pursuit of knowledge. In order to "know" a process, we must use symbols that we match in some way against the distribution of some aspects of the process we study, much as we match the distributions of symbols on a map against the distributions of coastlines, rivers, or roads in the landscape to be pictured. To know thus always means to omit and to select. In this sense, no knowledge is completely "objective."

But to know also means to match our standards of selection, explicit or implied, against the practical requirements of the action for which this knowledge is to be used. If we want to drive a car, we can omit offshore sandbanks from our map, but we must not omit roads. (If we want to sail a boat, some of the sandbanks may have to be included.) In this sense, no knowledge can be completely "nonobjective," if it is to be applied.

Knowledge depends on four things:

1. the selective interests of the knower;
2. the actual characteristics of the situation to be known;
3. the selective operations by which these characteristics can in fact be experienced or measured; and

5

4. the system of symbols and physical facilities by which the data selected in stages 1 and 3 are recorded and used for later application.

Knowledge is thus a process in which subjective and objective elements inevitably meet. Its first stage is subjective: the interests and needs of the knower. Its second stage—the existing characteristics of the situation—is objective to the extent that these characteristics are not significantly changed by the effects of observation. The third and fourth stages involve both elements: an objectively existing repertory of available measuring operations, and of encoding and recording facilities; and a set of subjective choices of items from this available repertory for use in actual operations. Moreover, the selection, in terms of interest or the asking of questions (stage 1), and in terms of measurability or the getting of relevant data for answers (stage 3), need not coincide: we may be interested in things for which we may at present have no operations of measurement. We may be interested, as it were, in color, but may find ourselves limited by our equipment to line drawings or black-and-white photography.

Pictures, photographs, and maps are simple models of situations in space. Various geopolitical maps and crude diagrams of political or social structures have been used by social scientists for a number of years.

Sometimes we are interested in mapping the performance of some thing or process over time. Here, again, the success of such mapping or diagraming over time will depend on the four stages of the process of knowing: the criteria of interest selected, the actual characteristics of the process to be studied, the operations of measurement employed, and the symbols and symbol systems used for recording and using the results. Curves of the growth of population, of production in particular industries or of votes for a particular party, or of membership in labor unions, are examples of such mapping over time.

Maps, as well as time diagrams, can do more than summarize existing knowledge. They can suggest ways of looking for new knowledge, and help to predict regularities that may or may not be confirmed by later experience or measurement. We can do these things through the operation of *prediction*. This operation consists in noting the pattern of the distribution of a set of known data, and extending tentatively a similar pattern into some area of space, or some period of time, from which we have as yet no firsthand data. In this manner we may guess at least something of the features of an unexplored country by noting the distribution of rivers and mountains leading to the edges of the "white patch" on our map. Nineteenth-century explorers did use such reasoning to guide their search for the sources and tributaries of the river Nile.

In making predictions over time, we must similarly collect series of selected data for the past, abstract from them some pattern, and extend or "extrapolate" that pattern tentatively into the future. As in the case of the map, this procedure may yield two kinds of predictions: (1) general predictions of interest (for example, does the future seem likely to contain data of interest to us, in terms of our criteria of interest assumed at the outset?); and (2) specific predictions of distribution (for example, what relevant events seem likely to occur in the future, and when do they seem likely to occur?). General predictions of interest are related to the *heuristic* functions of models; they tell us where to go to look for *something* interesting. Specific predictions of distributions are predictive in the narrower sense of the word; they tell us just what we should expect to find. Heuristic as well as predictive forecasts—for example, of future population growth, of anticipated market changes or needs for raw materials, of business cycles, or of changes in military potential or political stability—are all well known to social scientists.

By extending several time series tentatively into the future, side by side, we may make a guess as to what might happen if the peaks or valleys of several such series, let us say, of industrial strikes and agrarian unrest, or exports and domestic credits, should happen to coincide at some date in the future, even if they did not do so in the past. Natural scientists can predict in this manner the likelihood of rip tides, when the time of flood, the phase and position of the moon, and a strong onshore wind may combine to maximum effect. Students of social and political science might similarly become able to appraise the likelihood of rip tides of social change, when several normally separate processes making for social stress might coincide so as to exercise their greatest force. Thus, if in each of, say, one hundred countries there were at work three mutually independent stress-producing processes—such as agrarian revolts, industrial unrest, and foreign military conflict—and if each of these processes should tend to become acute, or to reach a peak about once every ten years, then the chances would be better than even that these three peaks would coincide, and the "rip-tide effect" would shake or even overthrow the government in at least one of these countries within the next ten years.

Our discussion of the nature of knowledge has clear implications for the functions of models. We may think of models as serving, more or less imperfectly, four distinct functions: the organizing, the heuristic, the predictive, and the measuring (or mensurative).

By the *organizing* function is meant the ability of a model to order and relate disjointed data, and to show similarities or connections between them that had previously remained unperceived. To make isolated pieces of information fall suddenly into a meaningful pattern is to furnish an esthetic experience; Professor Paul Lazarsfeld once described it as the "Aha!-experience" familiar to psychologists.[4] Such organization may facilitate its storage in memory, and perhaps even more its recall.

If the new model organizes information about unfamiliar processes in terms of images borrowed from familiar events, we call it an *explanation*. The operational function of an explanation is that of a training or teaching device that facilitates the transfer of learned habits from a familiar to an unfamiliar environment. If it actually does help us to transfer some familiar behavior pattern to a new problem, we may feel that the explanation is "satisfactory," or even that it "satisfies our curiosity," at least for a time. Such an explanation might be subjectively satisfying without being predictive; it would satisfy some persons but not others, depending on each person's memories and habits. Since it yields no predictions that can be tested by physical operations, it would be rejected by some scien-

8

tists as a "mere explanation" that would be operationally meaningless.[5]

Certainly, such "mere explanations" are models of a very low order. It seems, however, that explanations almost invariably imply some predictions. Moreover, even if these predictions cannot be verified by techniques practicable at the present time, they may yet serve as *heuristic* devices leading to the discovery of new facts and new methods.[6] This heuristic function of making discoveries more probable has already been discussed above. Here, it is mainly important for us to remember that the heuristic function of a model may be independent to a considerable degree from its orderliness or organizing power, as well as from its predictive and mensurative performance.

Little need be added to our earlier discussion of the *predictive* function of a model, beyond the well-known requirement of verifiability by physical operations. There are different kinds of prediction, however, that form something of a spectrum. At one extreme we find simple yes-or-no predictions; at higher degrees of specificity we get qualitative predictions of similarity or matching, where the result is predicted to be of this kind or of that kind, or of this particular delicate shade; and at the other extreme we find completely quantitative predictions that may give us elaborate time series that may answer the questions of "When?" and "How much?"[7]

At this extreme, models become related to measurement. If the model is related to the thing modeled by laws that are not clearly understood, the data it yields may serve as indicators. If it is connected to the thing modeled by processes clearly understood, we may call the data obtained with its help a *measure*—and measures again may range all the way from simple rank orderings to full-fledged ratio scales.[8]

The effectiveness of our predictions will depend in all cases upon the four elements of the process of knowledge we listed earlier. One of these elements is never completely under our control: the actual structure of the process that we are trying to know in the present and to predict for the future. If this structure happens to have sufficiently large discontinuities in its performance, all our guesses and extrapolations may remain mistaken.

The other three elements of knowledge, however, are under our control to a greater degree. Our selective interests develop with our increasing experience and knowledge, and with our expanding range of needs and of things we are able to do. Our operations of observation and measurement develop with the growth of our technology, and with the introduction of new instruments or methods of inquiry in the social as well as in the natural sciences. Finally, the range and effectiveness of our symbols and symbol systems increase, and accompany increases in our power to select and abstract, to store and recall, to analyze and recombine the sets of data we obtain, to extend them for prediction, to transfer them easily for communication, to submit them to operational tests for verification, and to apply them to behavior. Progress in the effectiveness of symbols and symbol systems is thus basic progress in the technology of thinking and in the development of human powers of insight and action.

A *symbol* is an order to recall from memory a particular thing or event, or a particular set of things or events. Any physical work or event that functions repeatedly as such a command can thus function as a symbol. If we use several symbols, so as to be able to recall several different things, we must connect our symbols with some operating rules. Together, the set of symbols and the set of operating rules form a *symbol system* or a *model*.

Any language is such a symbol system. Roughly speaking, it is a set of socially standardized words, or shorter sound patterns or "phonemes" with a set of rules of grammar and syntax, which specify their combinations. A system of geometry or arithmetic, a logical calculus, a game like chess or poker, or a model, physical or abstract, of some process, or a "conceptual scheme" in a natural or social science are all symbol systems of this kind.[9]

If the system has been chosen for purposes of play, as in choosing a game, the symbols or rules adopted need only be such as to give the player such thrills or challenges for his talents as he desires. If the system has been chosen for purposes of knowledge of the existing world, as in scientific models and conceptual schemes, and in applied mathematics, then it is desirable that the symbols and rules should match as well as possible the distributions and sequences of events in the process of which knowledge is desired. If the model actually matches the reality, then the outcome of operations on the model may be used to predict the outcome of operations in reality, where such operations might be difficult or costly.

Models can be formal or material. In the case of formal models, such as mathematical or geometric models, both symbols and rules are themselves abstract, and are recorded by means of signs that can be set down on paper. Some models of this kind may be quite unsuited to visual representation. The "consumption function" and the "production function" in John Maynard Keynes' system of economics give precise quantitative predictions that can be represented on a graph, but the mathematical model from which this graph is derived is almost as difficult to imagine visually as are some of the mathematical models used in quantitative physics.

Other formal models may seem more familiar to us, since they are at least loosely connected with some familiar pictures from everyday experience—even though these pictures may fail to give the content of the models much precision. In this manner, the Ionian philosophers transferred the familiar models of "law" and "cause" from social life into the world of nature,[10] but the precise formal content of the concept of "strict causality" in either nature or society remained a subject of discussion for many centuries.

In the case of material models, symbols may be tangible objects (as in the parts of a model airplane) or unseen processes (as electric currents in a network analyzer). The operating rules are then given by the physical properties of the resulting system.

In all cases, models must be tested for their *relevance:* do they match those aspects of the empirical process in which we are interested to a degree of accuracy sufficient for our purposes? Whether or not a model matches reality must be established by some *critical process,* that is, some physical process, simple or complex, that has one kind of outcome if the matching is close enough, and another outcome if it is not.[11]

It seems clear, from what has been said thus far, that we all use models in our thinking all the time, even though we may not stop to notice it. When we say that we "understand" a situation, political or otherwise, we say, in effect, that we have in our mind an abstract model, vague or specific, that permits us to parallel or predict such changes in that situation of interest to us.

When we say that we "understand" a person, we may mean one of two things. Either we mean that we understand his *situation*, and can "put ourselves into his place," that is, that we have a model of the conditions under which he is acting that permits us to conclude that we, with our memories and values, would act very similarly in that situation as he does with his memories and his values. Or we mean that we understand his *outlook;* that is, we can imagine a model of his mind, with his memories and values, that is sufficiently accurate for us to predict—and perhaps to experience emotionally by empathy—how he would act with his mind and his personality under conditions in which we ourselves might act quite differently.

The first type of understanding, which built models of different situations but treated human nature as essentially uniform, was prominent in the political science of Hobbes and Locke. The search for the second type of understanding, which seeks for models of different personality, culture, and value patterns so as to retrace or predict their choice of goals and goal-oriented actions, has become prominent in the "understanding sociology" (*verstehende Soziologie*) of Max Weber and in the work of modern anthropologists.[12]

This kind of understanding of individuals and groups "from the inside," as it were, can again be visualized in two broad ways: as a rational reconstruction of the personality, culture, or cognitive map of the actors concerned, or an act of empathy or role-playing, that is, an emotional simulation of their feelings by an imaginative manipulation of our own minds. This type of understanding by empathy has been stressed and elaborated by Wilhelm Dilthey and his followers,[13] but its basic idea is simple: can we in our imagination feel as the other person feels, value what he values, experience his inner tensions as if they were our own—regardless of whether we approve

12

or disapprove of his purposes? This is the understanding of what the sociologist Talcott Parsons would call the "evaluative" and the "cathectic" aspects of the other person's actions.[14]

If we suggest that understanding of impersonal situations, as well as personal actions, is possible by means of models, and perhaps only by means of models, we are apt to meet with two kinds of objections.

The first objection is based on the fact of uncertainty. Since many events in politics and social life are uncertain until the moment they occur, would not a prediction based on models introduce an unwarranted bias in favor of some assumed strict causality or determinism? This objection, where it still persists, is based on ignorance or, more charitably put, on a preoccupation with obsolete models. There is no need to put more "causality" or "determinism" into our symbolic models than we have reason to expect to find in the situations we intend to investigate with their aid. Models can be set up in terms of probability, and they can be revised in line with the probability distributions found in the empirical data. Our entire discussion of prediction was in terms of a repeatable operation, and not in terms of any construct of "causality." The pitfalls of the notion of causality have been pointed out for the natural sciences by P. W. Bridgman[15] and for the social sciences by R. M. MacIver.[16] Political scientists can very well seek out and test possible regularities and probabilities without becoming entangled in the metaphysics of any absolute causality concept.

The second objection comes from a seemingly opposite viewpoint. The most important events, it claims, are not merely uncertain; they are unique. They can, therefore, be indicated by symbols, but not described by them, regardless of their arrangement in any system, language, or model whatever. Such events are thus ineffable. At most (and only if we exempt the nerve cells of the human brain from the limitations of all other symbol-carrying structures), they can be understood by solitary individuals through incommunicable intuition. In a less extreme version of this argument, comparability is not denied, but is limited to the unimportant aspects of each situation, leaving intact the "essential uniqueness" of each historical event.

This theory of uniqueness rests on unexamined assumptions regarding the nature of knowledge. As we have seen, no knowable object can be completely unique: if it were radically unique it could be neither observed nor recorded, nor could it be known. Any object or event that can interact with others sufficiently to make a relevant difference to their outcome must have sufficient structural similarities to permit such interaction. Anything that can interact with events important for us must have some structural similarities with them, and to a lesser extent with us; and once it has structure, there seems to be no a priori reason why it could not be matched by suitable symbols. Of course, our current models of many particular events may be too crude to permit the effective mapping of the probabilities involved, or the effective prediction of any probable results that would be important for us. But to conclude from this that these events cannot be effectively paralleled for such purposes by any symbol system requires either metaphysical convictions or a sweeping prediction of the entire future course of social science.

In current social science, our problems are more practical. All political processes and institutions we observe contain combinations of similarities and differences, and thus become accessible to our knowledge. Indeed, it is only against a background of similarities that differences can be recognized. It is only later, as a second step, that new symbols can be assigned to those groups of aspects that remain different from those previously familiar, and different from each other, and that these new data become part of our experience. In the course of this process, political scientists—like other men—must use comparisons of the relatively simple and familiar as stepping-stones to the gradual conquest of the relatively complex and unique.

This is in fact what they have done. From the comparative study of universal traits, anthropologists have gone on to the first steps in the study of particular configurations of culture. Psychologists have used general schemes, such as those proposed by Sigmund Freud, Abraham Kardiner, and others, as the background against which they could try to evaluate the particular personality problems of individual patients. Economists began their work with the search for uniform laws governing the relations between supply and demand, or the changes in the wealth of nations, and are now gradually progressing to the study of the "propensity to consume" (J. M. Keynes) or "propensity to innovate" (W. W. Rostow) in particular periods and countries;[17] and of the performance, stability, and growth of particular national or regional economies.

THE STUDY OF POLITICAL SYSTEMS

Political scientists are finding themselves to an increasing degree moving in the same direction. In recent years they have been less often asked to compare merely the technical details of single political institutions or devices, such as "ministerial responsibility," "proportional representation," "judicial review," or "the power of dissolution," in several countries. More often they have been asked to say how a particular law or institution of this kind was functioning in the context of a particular political and social system, or how it could be expected to function if transferred into the context of some other system. Such questions of comparative political science have thus tended indirectly to become questions concerning the partial or over-all performance of the entire political systems of different countries.

Increasingly often political scientists also are asked direct questions about political system characteristics and system performance. What are the prospects for political stability in a country? What are the present political and military capabilities of its government? What are its abilities and inclinations to fulfill its international obligations? Are its present political institutions compatible with rapid economic growth? Is its present political regime capable of making effective use of large-scale financial or military aid from abroad? Can it make effective use of technological information under some technical-assistance program? All these, and many similar questions, have been asked, and are being asked currently, by many agencies of government as well as by nongovernmental organizations.

None of these questions can be answered by merely saying that each country is "unique," and political events in it "ineffable" or "unpredictable." Rather, political scientists have made what comparisons they could, in order to point out with the help of such comparisons the particular prospects of each situation. In so doing, they have drawn on many social sciences. Many of them steeped themselves in the study of particular geographic or cultural areas; and all had to use more or less explicit conceptual schemes, that is, symbolic models, in order to give order and context to their questions.

With the present trend in the social sciences, political scientists have thus found it increasingly hard to rest content with partial models of isolated traits or situations. Increasingly, they have found themselves in need of models capable of representing the behavior of whole decision systems. This need, in turn, has made acute the problem of choosing the most suitable models from all those that could be constructed.

THE CHOICE OF MODELS

Since there may be many models that match a given empirical situation to the required extent, we may have to choose among them. The first criteria that come to mind are two: relevance and economy of representation. In order to be *relevant* (or "realistic") the model must resemble the empirical system in those aspects with which we shall have to deal in order to do the things we are interested in doing. In order to be *economical*, the model must be in some respect "simpler" than the situation modeled; that is, its construction and operation must require less of those factors (such as material resources, physical or intellectual labor, calculating steps, and so on) that happen to be in short supply at the time and place of our work.[18] "Simplicity" or economy is thus often relative: something is being economized, usually at the cost of spending a little more of something else. Sometimes there are models that are significantly simpler in every relevant dimension than are their closest competitors, but more often a great gain in simplicity in one particularly important direction may have to be paid for by a loss of economy in another, less important one.[19]

In addition to considerations of economy and relevance, models are also chosen to suggest new predictions and new lines of investigation. The *predictive* performance of a model involves the three properties of rigor, combinatorial richness, and extended relevance or organizing power. The *rigor* of a model (as well as of any game, calculus, or logical or mathematical system) consists in its ability to give unique answers at each step of the calculation, or more broadly speaking, at each step of applying the operating rules. The *combinatorial richness* of a model is measured by the range of combinations or patterns that can be generated from it. The extended relevance or *organizing power* of a model consists in the degree of its correspondence to other empirical processes beyond the range of those in respect to which its relevance was first established.[20] A physicist's model of an "ideal liquid" usually has little relevance for the behavior of water above 100 degrees centigrade, but it may nevertheless be applicable to many other liquids and temperatures in addition to the ones for which it was first tested. Similarly, such social science concepts as "the family," "the economic multiplier," or "the state" may be evaluated in terms of their relevance for different epochs and cultures. Organizing power in this sense is indicated by the range of additional situations for which the model would be relevant, and by the precision and specificity of each relevance in each class of such cases.

The different models that are applicable to a given situation usually are not equally probable; that is, they are not equally likely to be produced by combinations of their elements, and thus not equally likely to be found or invented within a limited time. Models or symbolic schemes that are highly probable are called in everyday language "trite" or "obvious." The *originality* of a model could therefore be measured by its improbability within the ensemble of possible models at a given time and place. If models or symbolic schemes have a high degree of originality, simplicity, relevance, and organizing power, they often are said to be works of genius, and yield esthetic satisfaction.

It may be noted that all these dimensions can be measured to some extent, but also that each of them may vary with time, place, culture and personality, since the set of memories to be organized or empirical processes to be matched will vary with each of these. Discussions about the "beauty," "elegance," "interest," and "time-lessness" of a mathematical theorem, a work of art, or a conceptual scheme in the social sciences is likely to show in each case a characteristic mixture of impersonal and measurable criteria with relative historical, cultural, and personal standards. It is thus not surprising that people can never quite agree about matters of elegance, interest, and beauty, and yet can never quite stop arguing about them.

Despite this irremovable element of relativity, there is a strong objective element in judgments of this kind. At any given time or place, and even across many times and places, there are certain sets of models that are highly probable and others that are not. There are certain costs, such as the effort of changing familiar habits, or of carrying out repetitive steps of tedious intellectual labor, which most men at most places will want to minimize; and there may be common areas of past memories and present interest from which common standards of relevance and organizing power can be derived.

Conceptual schemes or models can thus be compared and evaluated to some extent on an objective basis, as long as the historical and cultural facts underlying that basis are not forgotten. Political scientists need not content themselves, therefore, with using a different model for each special purpose, to be discarded for another with every shift in the particular topic of their questions. Rather, they may seek models of more general usefulness for the study of politics in different countries and cultures.

THE UNITY OF HUMAN KNOWLEDGE

We have talked thus far about knowledge in the social sciences, and we shall continue to focus our interest on the social sciences throughout this book. But it is worth remembering that the process of knowledge applies to our understanding of the physical universe as well as to our understanding of human actions. The viewpoint of this book is that of the essential unity of the process of knowing— not by making human beings look overly simple but by bringing out the richness and the sense of wonder in all knowledge everywhere.

We have seen that men think in terms of models. Their sense organs abstract the events that touch them; their memories store traces of these events as coded symbols; and they may recall them according to patterns they learned earlier, or recombine them in patterns that are new. In all this, we may think of our thought as consisting of symbols that are put in relations or sequences according to operating rules. Both symbols and operating rules are acquired, in part directly from interaction with the outside world, and in part from elaboration of this material through internal recombination. Together, a set of symbols and a set of rules may constitute what we may call a calculus, a logic, a game, or a model. Whatever we call it, it will have some structure, that is, some pattern of distribution of relative discontinuities, and some "laws" of operation.

MODELS, KNOWLEDGE, AND STRUCTURE

If this pattern and these laws resemble, to any relevant extent, any particular situation or class of situations in the outside world, then to that extent these outside situations can be "understood," that is, predicted—and perhaps even controlled—with the aid of the model. Whether any such resemblance exists cannot be discovered from the model, but only from a physical process of *verification*, that is, physical operations for matching some of the structure of the outside situation—this we might call "taking information off" the outside situation—followed by some *critical process*, that is, further physical operations that depend in their outcome on the degree of correspondence between the structure proposed from the model and the structure derived from the outside facts.

Models of this kind may unify the thinking of their users. If clearly retained, they make mental operations repeatable: they confer on them the property of *retraceability* that is essential for reason. If used by several persons with identical results they add another characteristic of reason: *cogency*. They will do this whether their actual correspondence to events in nature is close or not.

In one sense, all these models are physical. They consist of symbols that are states of physical objects, and traces of physical processes, whether in brain cells, ink marks, magnetic dots, electric charges, or whatnot. Similarly, the operating rules, according to which these symbols are to be permutated or combined, and new symbols derived from them, are constraints on physical processes.

In this sense, knowledge is a physical process, or rather a particular configuration of physical processes. It is the process in which at least three other physical processes are incompletely matched: one, the "outside" process, which undergoes relatively little change in the matching (such as a stone we look at); a second, the "inside" process, which undergoes a great deal of change during the matching (such as the rods and cones in our retina, and the nerve cells in our brain that retain the image, or like the film in a camera); and a third, in which this stored "information" is recalled in more or less modified form, and reapplied to a new interaction with some outside process, more or less loosely related to the first; and the results of all these different processes of reapplication again are noted and compared for even more comprehensive verification.

Knowledge in general depends, therefore, on physical structure. If anything is to be knowable by *any* physical process, there must be in it some unevenness of distribution. What we call "evenness," as well as "randomness," can be treated as special cases of such distributions. If anything is to be knowable by *a particular process*, however, it must have not merely structure, but a particular structure corresponding to that of the "observing" process, at least to a relevant degree.

Unevenness, structure, and distribution are fundamental physical properties of everything—all matter, all energy, all processes—in the universe we know, and even in any universe we can imagine. Indeed, this unevenness is the physical condition of all knowledge, all observation, and all representation by symbols, of all imagination and all understanding. Yet this argument is not wholly circular nor perhaps wholly trivial. For it suggests that whatever can be at all experienced or observed, indeed whatever can at all interact with anything in the universe we know, must therefore have itself some relative discontinuities, and hence some structure. It must therefore be capable of being known. What interacts has structure. And what has structure can be known.

"The most incomprehensible thing about the world is that it is comprehensible," Albert Einstein has been quoted as saying.[21] Perhaps we may now venture to differ from this suggestion of incomprehensibility. Any universe uneven enough to be observed by us—or to sustain life in it—is uneven enough to be known, potentially though incompletely, by some processes and by some knowing agent. Any universe uneven enough to sustain the life of a flatworm should perhaps be uneven enough to be eventually known by man.

There is still reason, however, for a sense of wonder and surprise, as the physicist Victor F. Weisskopf pointed out to this writer: that the universe should be known in so many of its aspects so readily, in terms of patterns of such simplicity and generality as modern physics has discovered.

That the universe is knowable in general, at some time, by some processes, is then perhaps not surprising. That so much of it has become known to us so soon is a significant aspect of human history. And the particular models that men have used in their thinking in the course of their history may have had something to do with the outcome.

2

Some Classic Models
in the History
of Thought

Throughout history, men have thought in images—rich, imprecise, but suggestive. Some scientists, and some scientific traditions, have excelled in the creation of images that could be imagined visually, that is, in patterns closely related to those familiar from previous visual experience. Such images had many advantages. They were clear, vivid, in part familiar, emotionally relevant, and well suited to simultaneous inspection, so that different parts or aspects could be surveyed at the same time, or so nearly so that they immediately compared and correlated in memory, thus permitting many such correlations, or previously hidden aspects, to become suddenly "visible," or visualizable, to men's imaginations. The classic natural science of the Greeks, in particular, was carried on in large part in terms of such clarifying visual images.[1]

Another type of scientific imagery tends to be verbal, or else numerical and computational. Often it involves the precise knowledge of highly abstract symbols that have no close or obvious visual counterparts, and it may further involve their prolonged manipulation in sequences of steps of abstract reasoning or computation without the aid of visual imagery, perhaps somewhat similar to the unerring pursuit of Ariadne's thread through the darkness of the

Labyrinth.[2] This type of scientific competence and relatively non-visual imagination, together with extreme competence in computing, seems to have characterized some modern mathematicians, such as the Indian, Ramanujan, and in earlier times, the scientific tradition of the ancient Babylonians. Western science, and its offshoot, modern science, it has been persuasively argued, have derived from the marriage, in Hellenistic times, of the visual imagination of classic Greek science with the computational skills of the Babylonians; and the ever-renewed union of new feats of visualization with computations that ever since has accompanied the development of mathematics, and of all the sciences.[3]

In the course of this joint development of science, involving both the powers of visualization and of calculation, men's images became increasingly refined. As these images became more abstract and consistent, they turned into models.

Images and models thus form two ends of one spectrum. Formal or "idealized" models shade off by successive steps of abstraction from the images of the rich material situations from which they were borrowed or derived.

THE USE OF MATERIAL MODELS AS
RESOURCES OF THOUGHT

The models referred to so far have been *formal* models, sets of symbols and operating rules, carried largely in people's heads. Arturo Rosenblueth and Norbert Wiener have discussed the concept of the *material* model; they have defined it as "the representation of a complex system by a system which is assumed simpler and which is also assumed to have some properties similar to those selected for study in the original complex system," pointing out, at the same time, that this "presumes that there are reasonable grounds for supposing a similarity between the two situations; it thus presupposes the possession of an adequate formal model, with a structure similar to that of the two material systems."[4]

In this view every material model implies a formal model behind

23

it, or perhaps we might say that to compare two material situations and to use one of them as a model for the other is, at least, to abstract some more generalized formal model from the two.

What may count in intellectual history, then, is not only the actual properties of a physical or social process that people accept at some time as a material model for some other process, but rather the idealized or implied properties they ascribe to the implied formal model behind it. Not exactly what clocks actually were, nor even only what Newton's mechanics necessarily implied, but also what they seemed to imply to the classic "Age of Reason" (c. A.D. 1650–1790) made up that classic concept of "mechanism" that looms so large in the history of thought.

SOME MODELS IN EARLIER THOUGHT

Since early times, men have tended to order their thoughts in terms of pictorial models. The model itself was usually drawn from something in their immediate experience, available from their technology, and acceptable to their society and culture. Once adopted, it served, more or less efficiently, to order and correlate men's acquired habits and experiences, and perhaps to suggest a selection of new guesses and behavior patterns for unfamiliar situations.

Thus men used the image of their own society (where men influence one another's behavior by talking to each other) as a model for physical nature that was pictured as a society of animated objects that could be magically influenced by talking to them through the right kind of incantations. Later models were derived by men from the work of their hands, which they themselves could put together and take to pieces and which they therefore could analyze and elaborate more adequately in terms of parts and interrelations.

There is the simple model of the potter who shapes clay. It is assumed, in this model, that things have neither will nor mind but are simply inert products made by an invisible craftsman. Speech seems useless when directed to things, but promising when directed to the craftsman.

More complex models become available as men learn to produce more complex contrivances, and when the fruits of their labor can be piled up into houses, towns, and pyramids, which dwarf the individuals beholding them. The impersonal plan or law of the city may then come to serve as a model for an assumed impersonal plan or law of nature, and the structure of this impersonal law or architecture appears to remain effective regardless of the subsequent activities of any invisible architect or lawgiver who might have originated it. These new models permit a clear and more specific correlation of experience. They imply rigid and often immovable arrangements in space, which lend themselves readily to pictorial representation. In this manner, the Egyptian pyramid, with its rigorous order of a very few stones at its apex and the many stones bearing all the burden at the bottom, has served as a model for the conception of a "social pyramid," or, more generally, of a "hierarchy," whether of priests or army officers, or of ideas, values, and purposes, such as in Aristotelian philosophy.

Two other simple models involve at least some movement, and therefore some implication of time. The first of these is the *wheel*. In its simple rotary motion, elevating and casting down each part of its circumference in regular succession, it has been conceived of as a model of human affairs and human history. Whether as "wheel of fortune," "wheel of fate," or Fortune standing on a ball, in each case the model suggests the instability of the parts with a stability of over-all performance; and this model was projected to the skies in the spheres, cycles, and epicycles of Ptolemaic astronomy.

The second of these models is the *balance*, the pair of scales that yields the concept of stable equilibrium, with its implication that the adverse reactions must be the greater, the more the true position of balance has been disturbed. The notion of *diké*, of "nothing too much," of the golden mean, and the statue holding the scales of justice in front of many Western lawcourts all testify to its suggestive power. Both wheel and balance suggest movement that

25

eventually returns to the original position. "The more it changes, the more it stays the same."

Other simple technological operations began to yield models that implied notions of process, progress, and history in the simplest, most elementary form. An outstanding model here is the *thread* taken from spinning, whether as the thread of fate or the thread of an argument or the thread of a human life. A *web* woven from these threads is an obvious extension of this model, implying now, however, the notion of interaction. The German word for reality, *Wirklichkeit*, is related to the word denoting such a textile operation. Goethe has embodied this picture in the words of the Earth Spirit in *Faust:*

> So steh' ich am sausenden Webstuhl der Zeit
> Und wirke der Gottheit lebendiges Kleid.[5]

However, the partial continuity of thread and skein and warp and woof makes these textile models unsuitable for analysis.

THE CLASSIC MODEL OF MECHANISM

Only with the development of far more complex mechanical operations toward the end of the Middle Ages did there emerge mechanical models of greater complexity, and thus slightly less inadequate for describing the world around us. *Mechanisms* can be taken apart and reassembled. This is crucial for the new models. The growing knowledge of mechanical pumps finally enabled Harvey to write his scientific classic on the motion of the heart, *De Motu Cordis,* using the analogy of valves and pumps for the first adequate description of the circulation of the blood.[6]

The development of clockwork, under progress ever since the thirteenth century, yielded the classic model of a "mechanism"— a model applied to a description of the stars in the system of Newton; to government in the writings of Machiavelli and Hobbes; to theories of the "balance of power" and "checks and balances" by Locke, Montesquieu, and the founding fathers of the American

Constitution; and to the human body by such eighteenth-century writers as La Mettrie, author of the book *Man a Machine*. It was extended to joy in Schiller's lyric "Ode to Joy" as the "watchspring of the universe," and to God as the "first mechanic" by Thomas Paine.

The classic concept of mechanism differed from the actual mechanisms that inspired it. It was to have in theoretical perfection those properties for which the designers of admittedly imperfect machinery were striving in practice. This assumption of a perfect mechanism was made more plausible by the success of gravitational astronomy, where the movements of the planets, isolated from each other by vast distances, proved well suited to mechanical interpretations—though they have turned out to be quite unrepresentative of much of the rest of nature.[7]

Classic mechanism implied the notion of a whole that was completely equal to the sum of its parts, that could be run in reverse, and that would behave in exactly identical fashion no matter how often those parts were disassembled and put together again, and irrespective of the sequence in which the disassembling or reassembling would take place. It thus implied the notion that the parts were never significantly modified by each other, nor by their own past, and that each part once placed into its appropriate position, with its appropriate momentum, would remain in place and continue to fulfill its completely and uniquely determined function.

As this model implied certain assumptions, so it excluded others. The notions of irreversible change, of growth, of evolution, of novelty, and of purpose all had no place in it.

The classic notion of mechanism was a metaphysical concept. Nothing strictly fulfilling these conditions has ever been found anywhere. The more complicated a modern mechanical device becomes in practice, the more important become the mutual interaction of its parts through wear and friction, and the interdependence of all those parts with their environment, in regard to temperature, moisture, magnetic, electrical, and other influences. The more exacting we make the standards for the performance of a real "mechanism," the less "mechanical" in the classic sense does it

27

become. Even an automobile engine must be "broken in," and a highly accurate timing device depends so much on its environment that it must be assembled in carefully air-conditioned workrooms by workers with dry fingertips.

To be sure, highly idealized clockwork was not the only model that could have been developed from the facts available to scientists and philosophers during those centuries. It was, however, the model that they did develop, and that fitted well into their notions of perfection carried over into philosophy from technological and social practices.

To this model corresponded a characteristic analytic method: to seek a set of simple, unchanging elements acting by simple, unchanging laws. Scientists and philosophers discovered such simple elements as atoms, corpuscles, or waves in physics; as molecules and elements in chemistry; as "economic men" in economics; and as "increments of pain or pleasure" in the ethics and philosophy of Jeremy Bentham, and these last perhaps in turn have left some lingering echoes in the far more refined formulations of "indulgences" and "deprivations" by Harold Lasswell and Abraham Kaplan.[8]

Professor Philipp Frank has suggested that Newtonian mechanics and the later classic electrodynamics could have been used to describe considerably more sophisticated mechanisms than the idealized clockwork that predominated during that epoch. "There is nowhere in La Mettrie and contemporary materialists the idea," says Professor Frank, "that a 'mechanism' *has to be* of the simple character of a clockwork and that the parts of a mechanism *cannot* be rearranged by the operation of the mechanism."[9]

This situation is different, Frank suggests, from the "breakdown of the mechanism as a model in the twentieth century . . . due to the impossibility of constructing a mechanism for the phenomena within the atom" which required "the new physical theories like relativity and the quantum theory."[10]

If I understand this correctly, Professor Frank suggests that Newtonian physics did not, in itself, force upon scientists and philosophers the narrow mechanical model they adopted. The point seems, however, that this was the model they did adopt. To the extent that actual machinery resembled such idealized clockwork, isolated from its environment, unmodified by time and interaction, to that extent it was considered to be nearer perfection; for that age saw perfection in that classic mechanism we described above.

It is that kind of mechanism, too, that we find in the social sciences of the period. It is still an age preoccupied with discovery of lands, of laws of nature, and of laws of conduct. Nature is to be conquered by being obeyed, in Francis Bacon's view, but nature herself is not expected to change in the process. Similarly, for Machiavelli, the nature of princes and the laws governing their prudent conduct do not change; rather, to the author of *The Prince,* they seem as permanent as the political apathy of the masses of the people, which is so fundamental among Machiavelli's assumptions. Thomas Hobbes, a century and a revolution later, drops this assumption of apathy. In the world of the *Leviathan* all men are intensely and deplorably active, being like wolves unto each other. It is this frantic activity that is now held to be unchanging; whenever the restraints of government break, the "war of all against all" will be the state of nature. Hobbes and Machiavelli hold almost exactly opposite views about the political behavior of the large majority of the populations about whom they write; yet each asserts his view as an objective description of unchanging human nature.

The hallmark of the age of classic mechanism in social science was, perhaps, this attempt to discover a set of simple, unchanging elements that act according to simple, unchanging laws. From these, then, the simple, unchanging rules of prudent conduct in politics, economics, psychology, morality, religion—or indeed even in writing poetry—can be deduced by reasoning and verified by observation. The elements of the system may be the foxy princes of Machiavelli or the wolfish commoners of Hobbes; the prudent businessmen of Adam Smith; the abstract and "inalienable rights" of Thomas Jefferson—but whatever they are, they are as unchanging as the heavenly bodies in Newton's solar system before Kant's introduction of historical evolution into the latter.

This introduction of evolution by Kant, and later by Laplace,

29

through their account of the origin of the planets, is relevant to our point. For it shows the directions in which men might have struck out from the Newtonian framework if they had seen the opportunity, or had wanted to see it. Kant saw it well. His famous sketch of 1787 for a "Universal History" began with interaction and mutual modification between men and their institutions, and arrived at a succession of historical periods, each characterized by different patterns of behavior and leading by necessary steps to a future world government by scientists—a government strikingly different from the institutions Kant accepted as existing in his own time.[11]

Perhaps the reasons that kept most of Kant's contemporaries from continuing successfully his analytic approach to evolution were social at least as much as technical or scientific. Yet if the classic notion of mechanism had dominated much of the epoch's thinking up to his time, the classic notion of organism was to challenge it for the next few generations.

THE CLASSIC CONCEPT OF ORGANISM

Conspicuous breakdowns of the concept of mechanism became most obvious in the social sciences and in biology. Attacks on the inadequacy of mechanistic thinking form a major part of the political writings of Edmund Burke. The emphasis on wholeness, interrelations, growth and evolution—proclaimed in literature and education by Rousseau, and in politics by Burke—was then powerfully reinforced in the nineteenth century through the growth of the biological sciences, resulting in the wide popularity of the concept of "organism" in its classic nineteenth century form as the proper model for reality.

An organism, according to this classic view, cannot be analyzed, at least in some of its essential parts. It cannot be taken apart and put together again without damage. Each part of a classic organism, insofar as it can be identified at all, embodies in its structure the particular function to which it has been assigned. As a rule, these parts cannot be put to any other functions without destroying the organism.[12] The classic organism's behavior is irreversible. It has a significant past and a history—two things the classic mechanism lacks—but it is only partly historical, because it was believed to follow its own peculiar "organic law" that governs its birth, maturity, and death and that cannot be analyzed in terms of clearly identifiable mechanical "causes." It did have something like "purpose": a state of maturity or a function of reproduction, toward which earlier phases seemed to lead, and the attainment of which was followed usually first by continuation or repetition, and sooner or later by decomposition.

The similarity between this "mature phase" and Aristotle's *telos* was obvious, but neither Aristotle nor the nineteenth-century "organicists" or "vitalists" could analyze successfully the process by which this "mature" state (and no other) was achieved; nor could they analyze the process that after maturity seemed to turn all further change into repetition or degeneration; nor, even less, could they suggest any detailed process by which any such cycle with its supposedly inherent goals could undergo some fundamental change.

Here, again, the modern biologists' approach to the study of actual organisms has been far less restrictive than the classic organismic model. A modern discussion of the organism speaks of its "table of organization," "decision points," "feedback loops," "flow paths," and the like, as well as of "innovative behavior," "goals," and an "information model"—in short, it is finding a common language with the modern models of communication and control processes discussed later in this book.[13] It was not, however, the increasingly sophisticated redefinition of the organismic concept by working scientists that was adopted in the thinking of most historians, philosophers, and humanistically oriented writers on politics or economics. Rather, if such men thought of any organismic model, they accepted the classic model of organism with all its crippling restrictions.

"Organism" seemed a more subtle concept than "mechanism." It seemed subtle because it made two justified assumptions: that there was vastly more intricate structural detail, and that there were many more different kinds of structure, than could be found in the crude mechanics and the undeveloped sciences of the age.

Yet the classic organism was in many ways a mechanism with restrictions. It implied restrictions on the possibility of analysis into separate parts, and of reassembly from them; and restrictions on the extent of possible changes in structure or function of either the parts or the whole. Perhaps the most severe restriction was the postulate that certain parts of the organism could never be known: the imponderables," routed from physics and chemistry during the eighteenth century, reappeared as "vital force" or "vital spirit"[14] in later "organismic" thinking. The implied sharp separation between these mysterious "miracle parts" and the ordinary knowable elements of the system, and usually, also, the presumed static characteristics of both the knowable and the "imponderable" elements, then led to the classic picture of an "organism" with certain parts eternally mysterious, and with no chance of fundamental rearrangement of its elements.

Organismic models served a useful purpose in biology, in educational psychology, and even in economics, by directing men's attention to problems of interdependence and growth. But their successes were narrowly limited. While "organismic" models might sometimes help to balance the one-sidedness of a "mechanical" approach, biologists have failed to derive significant predictions or experiments from the supposed "life force" of nineteenth-century "vitalists." Most biologists by now have given up assertions about "imponderables," and have replaced them by sustained efforts at structural analysis and quantitative measurement, with impressive and fruitful results.

The inadequacies of organismic theories of society or history have been even more conspicuous. In one aspect organismic notions could be used to draw attention to processes of growth: organisms, after all, were supposed to grow before they reached maturity, though not afterward. In educational psychology and in the "infant industry" argument of economics, organismic notions perhaps facilitated contributions to social science.[15] But if they suggested respect for the child's innate ability to grow in mind and body, they also encouraged some men to assert innate inequalities between races. In economics the analogy between a steel mill behind a tariff wall and a baby in a crib led to bewildered questions as to why heavy industries so rarely if ever grew up, instead of leading to nonbiological investigations of economic growth.

Neither mechanism nor organism, in their classic forms, could explain well the peculiar social cohesion found in many societies, cultures, or peoples. Organismic views took this cohesion for granted or ascribed it to some "common blood," at the price of increasing difficulties with the facts. Mechanistic explanations in terms of "habits" found it hard to explain why sojourn under one crown or government should implant habits of political cohesion between Englishmen and Scotsmen, but not between Englishmen and Irishmen, nor between Czechs and Germans in Bohemia, nor between Frenchmen and Arabs in Algiers.

In political thought, classic models of *organism* appear in the writings of Edmund Burke, Adam Müller, Friedrich List, Oswald Spengler, and many later writers. These organismic models stressed the interdependence of all parts of a system in their structures and functions, but they excluded all possibilities of major internal reorganization, and of any evolution beyond a final goal of "maturity," prefigured from the outset of each type of organism by its peculiar "organic law."[16]

Even though organismic models are now obsolete in economics, poetic images of "mature" and "immature" political systems sometimes still persist in political science. Their cognitive value has been small. Few correlations have been found between the number of centuries a state has existed and its political processes at any given time. "Maturity" is not a helpful concept in distinguishing among the political institutions of France in the 1760's, the 1860's, and the 1960's, or between the politics of Germany in any two major periods of her history from Charlemagne to Konrad Adenauer. Neither has there been much confirmation for the prediction implied in the "maturity" concept that each political system must either stagnate

33

or else develop through a specific sequence of stages to a particular state of "maturity," which can only be followed by repetition or by overripeness and decay.

The same doubts apply to the second implication of "maturity" —that it is an all-round stage, enabling a people or government to be equally "mature" in dealing with, let us say, constitutional problems, domestic race relations, and foreign policy. Of more relevance here is the level of experience and competence available for each of these subjects in particular, since a government may easily appear "naïve" in dealing with one problem, while appearing "mature" in dealing with another. Although the word "immature" has been plausibly applied to political situations in which the participants seemed to be conspicuously lacking in experience and tradition, such terms as "poor in relevant tradition" or "unconsolidated by relevant experience" could describe the facts without misleading organismic connotations.

Neither of these classic concepts of mechanism and organism could easily be used to deal with the process of learning. Nor are they easy to apply to the problem of knowledge; nor to the way qualitative judgments are made; nor to predictions in many social situations, or for longer trends in history; nor to the problems dealt with by esthetics, ethics, or religion.

To be sure, no mere invention of suitable concepts, schemes of investigation, or testing operations can be a substitute for the actual work of investigation in finding answers to these problems, or in producing coherence among such answers as are found. But perhaps we may yet come to recognize that the deep cleavage between the "natural" and the "social" sciences; between "reason" and "intuition," or "reason" and "wisdom"; between the search for the truth and the search for goodness—perhaps we may come to recognize how much these cleavages were amplified and exaggerated in the thought of many good men between the times of Galileo and those of Einstein, by particular historical and social conditions in the Western world, and perhaps by the rather unwieldy intellectual equipment available during that period.

34

CONCEPTS DRAWN FROM HISTORY

A third group of models was developed out of the experiences of the dialogue, of struggle, and of historical process. All these suggested, in varying degree, a connection between conflict and communication. From these were then developed various notions of *process:* an interplay of changes that might be irreversible—"You cannot step twice into the same river" (Heraclitus)—yet analyzable into unchanging or more slowly changing discrete elements (which might themselves be complex subprocesses or patterns of action) arranged in a specific *structure*—though it, too, might be changing —and with discoverable laws governing their interplay. "This world . . . is an ever-living Fire, *with measures* kindling and *measures* going out."[17] This implied notion of structure is as essential to the models of processes as is their well-known emphasis on change.

In particular, the social sciences themselves produced an approach that was analytical to some degree, and emphasized development and growth. It was the approach of history, particularly after history became thought of not as a mere cycle of events, but as a succession of steps in a pattern leading in a discoverable direction. This view of history, as R. G. Collingwood has shown,[18] was introduced by Christianity, though it may already have had certain roots in Judaism. The notion of a distinction between "genuine" and "false" progress in this sense is explicitly stated in the writings of Vincent of Lerinum about A.D. 434.[19] In the eighteenth and nineteenth centuries the notions of the historical process were developed by Kant, Hegel, and Marx, and by a whole series of "historical schools" that used history as the central notion for interpreting anything from law to economics. Contemporary writers such as A. J. Toynbee and Eugen Rosenstock-Huessy testify to the continuing vigor and diversity of the tradition.[20]

Some of these historical views contained notions of irreversible change, of evolution through conflicts, and of some underlying relations between conflict and harmony. From Heraclitus' vision of war as "the father of all things," to Kant's *Idea of a Universal History* of 1787, and Burke's idealized vision of the continuous growth of civilization, on to Hegel's notion of "dialectical" progress from opposite to opposite, and further to the directed time of Bergson, the "instability forward" which J. C. Smuts saw in racehorses and civilizations, and the "challenge and response" of A. J. Toynbee, men have searched in history for models for the processes of growth, of evolution, of the emergence of novelty, and of creation.

Yet the striking parallels and suggestive insights that they offered remained empty of inner structure. Heraclitus said, "That which opposes, fits." He did not say *how* it fits. His *logos* meant "word" or "language," and so in a sense "structure": the world to him was "an ever-living Fire, with measures kindling and measures going out." But neither this *logos* nor these "measures" could he measure or describe. Both Kant's "unsocial sociality of man" and Hegel's "dialectics" are qualitative notions that disclose little detailed structure behind them. Carlyle's "great men," as well as Toynbee's "creative minorities," are unanalyzed vessels of a creativity that itself has no intrinsic details that could be described and understood.[21]

Nor did an appeal to biology help matters. Creativity as a process remained just as blank and structureless when it was enclosed in a human body labeled "genius," or in groups of such bodies labeled "superior race." Ununderstood patterns of organization found little aid from the ununderstood chemistry of proteins.

As with biology, so with economics. The notions of economic "creativeness" and "innovation" were emphasized by Joseph Schumpeter as central in the process of economic growth, but for a long time little could be said about the inner structure of these processes. They represented labels, as it were, on bottles that remained opaque. Even when their qualitative importance was conceded, as it was by such an authority on national income measurement as Simon Kuznets,[22] their relationship to the rest of the process of economic growth seemed to defy measurement.

When they tried to be more specific, proponents of theories of process often fell back into mechanical analogies. They spoke of evolution as an "unfolding," that is, as of a bringing to light of pre-existing patterns. Others, following a philosophical tradition from Aristotle to Kant, spoke of the "fulfilling of potentialities," that is to say, the presumably exhaustive working out of an already existing, small combinatorial ensemble made up of unchanging elements and laws, disregarding the infinitesimally small probabilities that many of these "potential" combinations might have in any larger universe of elements.

It should have been possible to imagine a process of genuine growth or evolution, involving fundamental rearrangements of the elements, and even of the laws and probabilities of the ensemble. Such changes could also have included explicitly changes in kinds of the interactions of the system with its environment, so as to transform the original system into a new one, with long-run properties not predictable from its previous states. Genuine evolution in this sense involves the possibility of sudden change and genuine novelty, including both internal change within the system and its interaction with the environment. The recent formulation of a distinguished Catholic anthropologist seems instructive here:

> Everything, in some extremely attenuated extension of itself, has existed from the very first. . . . But to have realized . . . that each new being has . . . a *cosmic embryogenesis* in no way invalidates the reality of its *historic birth.*
>
> In every domain, when anything exceeds a certain measurement, it suddenly changes its aspect, condition or nature. . . . Critical points have been reached, rungs on the ladder, involving a change of state—jumps of all sorts *in the course* of development.[23]

In the view of many scientists such evolution does not necessarily lead to one fixed goal, nor does it have to approximate any such single goal ever more closely. Rather, it is an open-ended process, containing the possibility of self-disruption or self-destruction, as well as of a change of goals. Such a possibility seemed at least hinted at in the words of the New Testament, "Now are we the sons of God, and it doth not yet appear what we shall be."[24] Yet if this had been a hint of growth with no definite end, most theories of organization persisted in not taking it.

What all these notions were trying to describe were processes of organization: self-sustaining or self-controlling or self-enlarging or self-transforming processes, as the case might be. Yet the only model they used to describe these processes was human society itself, changing throughout history, of infinite complexity, and baffling to those who tried to understand it while participating in its conflicts. Few of the aids of the natural sciences were available to the social scientists: neither the simplified and yet analogous model,[1] offering the powerful aid of relevant and reproducible patterns; nor the controlled experiment; nor any relative ease of analysis of the interplay between observer and object; nor concepts permitting mathematical treatment; nor the mathematical techniques fitting much of the material. Against the background of these difficulties it appears an even greater accomplishment that the greatest of the social scientists achieved what they did.

In their interplay, all three models contributed to scientific growth. Models of classic mechanism contributed, within their limits, the possibility of rigorous and quantitative treatment. Models of classic organisms permitted greater complexity and some very limited development, but they left no room for consciousness or will, which were assumed powerless to change the organism's inner laws.[25] All qualitative changes in a classic organism were assumed preformed from the start, with no room for problems of choice or decision. Models of historical process left room for direction, for qualitative changes, for influences by consciousness, for genuine novelty. Yet they remained essentially qualitative; they aided in the recognition of certain patterns, but furnished little aid in measuring or counting, and no quantitative predictions over space or time. What was needed were models applicable to problems involving both quantity and quality; and facilitating the recognition of patterns, together with measurement and verifiable predictions.

3

Some Recent Models in the Social Sciences

Some contemporary mathematical models in the social sciences appear to be the intellectual offspring of the classic mechanistic style of thinking. In these models it is not so much the rigid limitations of the classic image of mechanism that have been preserved, but rather the propensity to make extremely simple assumptions about the basic elements of the models—assumptions that are then subjected to more or less sophisticated mathematical techniques.

Such mathematical models in the social sciences may lose much of their usefulness through their overly naïve assumptions, or through the introduction of pseudoconstants, that is, magnitudes represented as constants in the mathematical equations but incapable of being checked by independent and impersonal operations.

SOME APPROACHES BY RASHEVSKY, ZIPF, SIMON, AND RICHARDSON

An example of sophisticated mathematical techniques whose usefulness is limited by regrettably naïve assumptions is found in Professor Nicholas Rashevsky's discussion of changing levels of activity in social groups and of the "interaction of nations," in his *Mathematical Theory of Human Relations*.[1] Professor Rashevsky assumes that members of the politically and economically "active population" differ from the "passive population" by hereditary constitution and that the relative proportions of "active" and "passive" population change according to certain patterns of genetics and natural selection, depending largely on the numbers and density of total population.

It seems possible, however, that Professor Rashevsky's mathematical techniques could be applied to more realistic social and economic assumptions, and particularly to processes of social learning, in contrast to mere heredity. In Rashevsky's model, the initial proportions of "active" and "passive" individuals change in the course of time in accordance with the assumed rates and conditions of reproduction and inheritance that have been put into the model. In more realistic models at least three stages—of "active," "partially active," and "passive population"—might be used, corresponding perhaps to the more useful three-level distinction between a relatively small "elite," usually of less than 5 per cent of the population; a broader set of "politically relevant strata" or "mobilized population" that, in addition to the elite, may often include anywhere between 10 and 90 per cent of the population, depending on the political conditions, the currently salient issues, and the general level of social and economic development of a country; and a "passive" or "underlying" population that takes little or no part in politics, nor perhaps in any extended form of impersonal social communication.[2] More important, the proportions between these groups could be assumed, in an improved model, to change in accordance with mathematical assumptions relevant for the description of more complex processes, such as processes of learning, or of positive or negative conversion (formally analogous to infection and immunization), or some combination of these.[3] To what extent such possibilities will materialize, of course, only the future can show.

Many of Professor Rashevsky's findings have nonetheless proved extremely interesting and suggestive. His demonstration, for example, that a high degree of conformity may tend to reduce the stability of a political system should have fascinating implications for any student of politics.[4]

Some of the more recent work of Professor Rashevsky has dealt to a much larger extent with learning processes, and thus with systems in which at least some of the parts may undergo significant changes in their characteristics.[5] To the extent that this has been the case, such mathematical models transcend the limitations of the classic mechanistic approach and approximate the modern communication and learning models that will be discussed in a later chapter.

A far more striking combination of relatively sophisticated mathematics with utter naïveté in social science can be found in the work of the late George Kingsley Zipf.[6] According to Zipf, the size of communities in each country, ranked in decreasing order of their number of inhabitants, should approximate a harmonic series. In its simplest form, this approach leads to the so-called "rank-order rule," that is, to the prediction that for any city in a "normal" country the product of its population and its rank order by size should remain very roughly constant, so that the second-ranking city should have roughly one-half the population of the first, the third-ranking city roughly one-third, and so forth. Similar rank-order rules have been proposed by several writers, and have found some limited empirical confirmation, even though by no means for all countries.[7] Such a rule, where it does hold approximately, might help to estimate—for example, for poorly surveyed countries, or for past centuries—the size of cities of which we know the approximate rank order but not the population; and it might alert us to look for the possible reasons that make some countries deviate more from this pattern than others.

Zipf, however, went much further. He took the closeness of the actual distribution to the theoretical harmonic series quite naïvely as an indicator of social stability. Thus, Zipf found that Austria between the two world wars had too large a capital city and too few cities of middle size and that the aggregate series of cities in Germany and Austria after Austria's annexation by the Nazis approximated a harmonic series more closely than before. From this he concluded that the German annexations of Austria and the Sudetenland in 1938 had increased the stability of Germany and the social and economic balance of her *Lebensraum*.[8] This "mathematical" conclusion completely overlooked the fact that already before 1938 Germany had been a food-deficit area, dependent on exports for part of her living, and that Austria as well as the Sudetenland had similarly been areas of food deficits, export dependence, and unemployment. What the Nazi annexations of 1938 had produced was a merger of three deficits. The "greater Germany" of 1939 was more dependent on food imports and on export drives to pay for them than its component parts. The pooled threats of unemployment in all three territories were met by an armament drive, and food supplies and exports were sought by imperial expansion. What Professor Zipf has described on paper as a harmonic series was in reality a situation of extreme unbalance and disharmony, which led within a year to a violent explosion in the German invasion of Poland and the unfolding of the Second World War.

Incomparably more sophisticated and fruitful models of social behavior, including models of learning behavior and of different kinds of "rationality," have been developed by Herbert A. Simon. He has distinguished between, on the one hand, "models of optimization" that require a very large amount of information about the alternatives from which the "optimum" is to be chosen, and, on the other hand, the more modest but perhaps more realistic "models of adaptive behavior" that describe choices under conditions of far less perfect information so that the decision-maker has only to choose at each step the relatively more attractive of two perceived alternatives.[9]

Unfortunately, Simon has not applied his powerful and suggestive models to large-scale political and social processes,[10] although he has applied his style of thinking with excellent effect to problems of private and public administration, the business firm, and the study of organizations.[11]

It is perhaps too much to expect at this stage that individuals should undergo the highly specialized training of the advanced professional mathematician and, at the same time, the equally intense training of the experienced social scientist. The difference in the intellectual techniques of these two fields should not obscure the fact that both approaches represent full-time intellectual jobs.

A major task of the mathematician is to concentrate on the single-minded pursuit of long trains of symbolic operations. He may start with any set of given initial conditions, without caring over-much, as a rule, why these particular conditions or assumptions rather than others were selected.

Much of the training of the historian or social scientist is just the opposite. He must become familiar with a very wide range of social and economic situations at different places and times. The outcome of this part of his training is at best a sense of relevance, an experience in judging which factors in a situation must be taken into account and which ones may be neglected without much risk of error.

To be sure, the social scientist can benefit greatly from analytic training. He does and should study economic, political, and psychological theory, and to an increasing extent mathematics and symbolic logic. Yet all analytic work in the social sciences is primarily tied to judgments of relevance, to evaluating the realism of assumptions and the appropriateness of models. This ability is not easily acquired by mathematicians in their periods of rest between or after their more arduous professional labors. And the advice to younger social scientists to study more mathematics should be tempered with the insistence that they will have to judge the relevance of their models against their fund of factual knowledge *as social scientists.* No amount of mathematical knowledge or advice can take this task from their shoulders.

The most hopeful answer to this problem at the present time lies perhaps in the development of teamwork between men who are primarily social scientists but who have had enough analytical training to put their problems into a form where mathematicians can go to work on them, and mathematicians who have had a solid-enough training in the social sciences to understand what the social scientists need from them, and how to select lines of mathematical treatment that will lead toward reality rather than away from it.

Another source of trouble with mathematical models in the social sciences stems from the tendency to put arbitrary constants or coefficients into equations so as to make their results fit a known series of numbers or their extrapolations. Thus, Lewis F. Richardson's "Generalized Foreign Politics" attempts to predict the armaments expenditures of two rival countries by equations that contain numerical coefficients for the "grievances" and the "submissiveness" of each country vis-à-vis the other.[12]

It is well known that any finite series of numbers can be fitted by more than one equation, and, on the other hand, that any result can be attained in an equation by introducing a sufficiently large number of arbitrary constants or coefficients. There is all the difference in the world between such arbitrary coefficients and a constant in physics, such as Planck's quantum constant h. Genuine constants in physics can be verified by impersonal physical operations of measurement, or by impersonally verifiable inferences from measurement. Such constants are the same for all physicists, regardless of their sympathies or political beliefs, and they would be confirmed, in principle, by impersonal recording and measuring devices. The use of such operationally independent and verifiable concepts in models, such as in Bohr's model of the atom, is therefore quite legitimate. Only to the extent that social scientists can specify an impersonal set of operations for producing a numerical measure of "grievance" or "submissiveness" will they succeed in freeing themselves from the grave suspicion that their coefficients are based on arbitrary estimates somewhat akin to the "variable constants" familiar from the folklore of undergraduate humor.

Independent operations, determining such constants in an adequate manner, could be of two kinds. They could be repeatable physical operations of measurement or counting, performed on some part of the outside world that the model is to resemble; or else they could be mathematical operations, which would verify certain assumed values for such constants by means of tests of consistency over a large set of computations and many empirical examples, or which would at least establish acceptable orders of magnitude for such constants, or else critical proportions or thresholds, beyond which the value of such a constant would make a major difference to the outcome predicted by the model.[13]

To be sure, there may be cases where incomplete mathematical models, or even pseudomodels, may describe, however inadequately, some genuine intuitive insight of their author. It would be folly to suggest that only that is real that is measurable by present-day methods. The perception of *Gestalt*, or the vision of a previously unrecognized configuration of phenomena, all have their places among our sources of knowledge. The more incomplete such models are, however, the more it is the qualitative insights that are relevant, and the less the mathematical disguises that they may have prematurely donned.

On balance, even highly imperfect mathematical models often have made valuable contributions to our thinking, particularly when they were allied with a sound knowledge of the substance of the problems to which they were applied. The experience of the last decade strongly indicates to me a positive judgment of the work of such men as L. F. Richardson, even though this represents a modification of the less favorable view that I took ten years ago.[14]

THE "IDEAL TYPES" OF MAX WEBER

None of the models touched upon thus far gives a clear picture of either goal-seeking or homeostasis—the automatic maintenance of certain states or functions—at least among their explicit assumptions. Max Weber tried to analyze social processes and institutions in terms of *ideal types*.

According to Talcott Parsons, Weber meant two different things by an "ideal type." Sometimes he meant a selected and one-sidedly exaggerated pattern abstracted from actual social institutions and practices that had recurred throughout some geographic region and historical epoch, such as "modern rational capitalism" or the "Indian caste system." In other instances, Parsons points out, Weber meant by an "ideal type" a selected and heightened pattern abstracted from a set of recurrent *ideas*, such as the "Calvinistic theology" or the "Brahmanic philosophy of karma and transmigration."[15]

An "ideal type" of either kind was essentially a model that could be used to highlight particular aspects of structures found among the empirical data; to predict the recurrence of certain regularities, where and as long as the similarity of a real situation to a particular "ideal type" continues to apply; and to separate the "subjectively rational," that is, consciously goal-seeking aspects of behavior from the "objectively rational" ones, that is, from those objectively likely to lead closer to the goal; and finally to separate both kinds of goal-oriented or "rational" behavior from "irrational" expressions of inner tensions or emotions. In this last aspect it could be used to measure at least roughly the extent to which any particular action or behavior departed from the "ideal type" of rationality.[16]

The analysis in terms of "ideal types" was not well suited, however, to show the way in which a particular social pattern came into existence, or how it passed away. It could not even specify very well just how much change in how short a time it could withstand. The "ideal type" of analysis could thus point out structures, but it could not measure them beyond noting their greater or lesser departure from the model of purposive rationality. Nor, on the same grounds, could it measure their rate of change in other dimensions, or their limits of tolerance, or give a consistent structural and quantitative picture of the processes of social learning, novelty, initiative, and innovation.

Max Weber did, of course, describe processes of change when he dealt empirically with particular social systems. Thus he pointed out certain self-destructive characteristics in the Roman system of landholding and agriculture during the first two centuries of the Christian Era—characteristics that in his view resulted in the destruction of the foundations of Italian agriculture through soil erosion.[17] It might not have been inherently impossible to go on from there to construct dynamic "ideal types" of social institutions, making them so specific in structure and detail that they could yield predictions of the rate of change and of the probable thresholds of breakdown of the systems studied. If this had been done, however, it would have meant transforming Weber's highly simplified "ideal types" into relatively full-fledged models of communication and control. No such models existed in Max Weber's time, and sociologists, unaided by other sciences, were unlikely to invent them.

At bottom, Max Weber's "ideal types" describe particular ways in which men pursue particular individual or social goals. They imply, therefore, the setting of such goals, but they rest for the most part only on vague and empirical knowledge of the processes by which goals were set and pursued, and of the general conditions underlying the behavior of goal-seeking systems.

STRUCTURAL-FUNCTIONAL ANALYSIS

The second broad group of models that implied goal-seeking, without at first clearly analyzing its process, was the structure-function analysis recently developed by such sociologists as Talcott Parsons and Robert K. Merton.[18] By a "social structure" this school of thought understands a set of social groups marked off from each other by relatively permanent or slow-changing, and more or less clearly observable, differences or discontinuities. Landowners, peasants, industrial wage earners, or rural versus urban populations might possibly form elements of such social structures. By "function" this type of analysis understands either the pursuit of some value or goal, or, more frequently, the contribution made by the unit or process studied to the maintenance of the organism or to the maintenance of the structural continuity of the society.[19] Following the methods used by physiologists in studying organisms, this approach involves fundamentally an interrelated sequence of similar steps:

> First of all, certain functional requirements of the organisms are established, requirements which must be satisfied if the organism is to survive, or to operate with some degree of effectiveness. Second, there is a concrete and detailed description of the arrangements (structures and processes) through which these requirements are typically met in "normal" cases. Third, if some of the typical mechanisms for meeting these requirements are destroyed, or are found to be functioning inadequately, the observer is sensitized to the need for detecting compensating mechanisms (if any) which fulfill the necessary function. Fourth, and implicit in all that precedes, there is

47

a detailed account of the structure *for which* the functional requirements hold, as well as a detailed account of the arrangements *through which* the function is fulfilled.[20]

Although the method of structure-function analysis was borrowed originally from the fields of biological and medical research, its subsequent development in the social sciences has followed a pattern of its own. In biology and medicine, every qualitative statement about the function of this or that structure or process implies from the outset also a quantitative statement. To say that, in an organism, structure *x* fulfills the function *y* is to raise three obvious quantitative questions. *How much* does this structure—for example, a gland—have to contribute of what kind of output in order to perform what kind of function at the minimum level required for the continuation of the organism? Second, how much does it in fact contribute? And third, precisely what happens when the kind of its contribution remains the same but the quantity is varied to just what extent?

Modern medical research seeks answers to all these questions. Behind the original collection of qualitative statements, correlating particular kinds of structures with particular kinds of functions, there has grown up a large and growing body of quantitative medical information supplementing our still growing knowledge of "where" and "what" with a no less vigorously growing body of data on "how much," "how fast," and "how soon."[21] In respect to this transition to quantitative knowledge, the "structural-functional" analysis in political and social science until now has lagged far behind its medical counterpart.

In another respect, however, structural-functional analysis in the social sciences has done a good deal better. Unlike most of its original medical and biological models, it has not remained limited by the relatively narrow and rigid functional specializations of classic organismic models, and of many actual biological systems, but rather has remained open to the much greater richness of combinatorial possibilities inherent in most social systems. In general, the structural-functional analysis in social science pays more attention to the fact that in the service of such a "function" several elements of the social structure could cooperate in several possible patterns. In some ways, this structural-functional approach permits greater freedom than do the "ideal types" of Max Weber. The structure-function approach obviously allows for *functional equivalence:* the same social function may be fulfilled by different combinations of different structural units.[22]

In one sense it could be said that, where Max Weber's "ideal types" stressed those structural-functional patterns that seemed conspicuously more "rational," or perhaps "conceptually pure" (though not necessarily more important, more interesting, or more probable) than others, the structure-function approach of Parsons and Merton stresses by implication the richness of combinatorial possibilities and the large ensemble of possible rearrangements in most social systems.[23]

This suggests two difficulties. Using the "ideal type" analysis, we are in danger of taking too narrow a view: we might overlook in the social situation that we study some probable alternative possibilities for which our "ideal type" does not allow. Using the structure-function analysis, our outlook is in danger of becoming too broad: we might drown in an ocean of apparently equally possible combinations of structures and purposes, with few except crudely empirical tests for choosing among them. In the hands of empirical masters of the field, both methods can give good results. Such results, however, are due less to the excellence of the method used than to the competence of the men who use it—a competence that itself is neither clearly specified nor analyzed in terms of the method.

The two weaknesses of the original structure-function analysis thus seem to be that it presupposes social goals and purposes, but cannot clearly describe how they are set; and that it requires its practitioners to choose among the ensemble of possible combinations without giving them clear criteria for either search or choice, except the criteria of intuitive interest and empirical judgment. Even within the limits of any particular structural-functional combination selected, this method offers no sharp definition of the most important structural elements and goal-seeking functions, which must be accepted on empirical grounds. If these grounds are not obvious, or quickly found by intuition, the structure-function method can give valuable aid in suggesting a combinatorial list or matrix of all the possibilities that might occur, and thus help us to make sure that none of them is overlooked. If the number of possible combinations is large—as it is almost sure to be—we may find little help from basic analysis itself in deciding which possibilities would seem worth investigating first.

For that purpose, *search criteria* must be added to the theory, and it is perhaps part of the strength of the structure-function approach that it permits the adding of such criteria. Such criteria are always present, one may suggest, when a large number of possible structure-function combinations is envisaged. Although these criteria may be hidden, and some of them may be crude or obsolete, there is room in structure-function theory, it would seem, for the recognition of particular patterns of goal-seeking and goal-setting, self-steering and feedback, memory and information flow, novelty and learning.

If this is so, structure-function analysis may well prove able to absorb and use the contributions of more specific kinds of models. Unsupplemented by more specific models, however, the structure-function analysis in its full generality might force upon us in concrete cases a certain arbitrariness in selecting the most important of a large number of possible individual situations of conflict or decision. This arbitrariness may become cumulative when an attempt is made to picture the probable performance of particular decision sequences or decision systems. Here again the structure-function method seems potentially helpful in promoting the qualitative recognition of sets of possibilities, but thus far, in itself, it promises little help in a search for quantities, boundaries, and measurement.

It is important to note, however, that the structure-function analysis has been developing in the latter direction by accepting and incorporating some of the results of somewhat more specific approaches to the study of goal-seeking, communication, and control. In certain fields of sociology, where a number of partial problems could be dealt with successfully without them, such refinements were at first not needed, but they are likely to prove increasingly important for the comparative study of social and political decision systems.

4

The Theory of Games of von Neumann and Morgenstern

The *Theory of Games and Economic Behavior* by John von Neumann and Oskar Morgenstern represents a new approach to the study of political and social decisions, and to the study of strategies or decisions about classes of decisions.

Empirically the approach of the theory of games is based on the existence of far-reaching similarities between certain conventionally standardized games and certain recurrent social situations. Where such similarities exist, it is held to be more profitable to analyze first the games rather than the far less sharply defined social situations.

THE POTENTIAL RELEVANCE OF GAME MODELS

The similarity of certain games and certain social situations is of course not accidental. A considerable body of psychological research deals with the transfer of patterns of social behavior into the play activity of children and back from the play of children into social life. It seems plausible that adults as well as children may tend to find those types of games more interesting that permit them to adopt patterns of behavior they can also apply to some social situation, or that permit them to act out, as games, those patterns of behavior initiated in some experience of social life that can be carried to completion only in the innocuous form of games. Though we cannot wage private war and kill our opponent, we can play chess and checkmate the opponent's king; and the art of deceiving others profitably is more safely practiced in the game of poker than in politics or economic life.

Games resemble real-life situations particularly in three respects. First, they deal with the conditions of "payoffs" or "interests" for the different players, who are rewarded or penalized in terms of what seems valuable to them or else in terms of what will permit them to stay in the game. This leads to sharper definitions and clearer understanding of the concepts of utility and interest, and hence also of certain aspects of rationality in decision-making. Second, the players' rewards or penalties depend on the joint outcomes of their own moves and of the moves made by other players; this permits a clearer analysis of the interdependence of decisions among different actors in a situation of conflict or of cooperation or of mixtures of these two. Finally, in many of the more interesting games the players must act under conditions of uncertainty and incomplete information; this makes the analysis of such games relevant for problems of decision-making under conditions of uncertainty. All these problems—how to recognize one's interest and to act in its pursuit; how to take account of the probable actions of possible allies and adversaries; and how to act prudently under conditions of uncertainty and partial ignorance—are basic in political theory and practice.

Granting the potential relevance of games to the analysis of political behavior, the approach of the theory consists first of all in analyzing simplified prototypes of games such as chess and poker; then, in calculating as accurately as possible the winning chances for each player and each hand; and in determining the conditions under which advantageous coalitions can be made or alternative strategies can be evaluated for their chances of success.

Most of the decisions in games of this kind must be made under conditions of incomplete information. In a card game we may be ignorant of our opponent's hand or of the cards he or we may draw from the pile. In chess we know the position of the piece of our opponent, and have theoretically "perfect information," at least so far as classic game theory is concerned; but even here we do not know his strategy, even though we do know that our decisions must depend on his, and his on ours in turn. In sum, in each game we know the limits and characteristics of a smaller or larger ensemble of possibilities. The theory assumes that they can be treated by a sophisticated application of the mathematics of probability and of decision sequences.

Within certain limits, which will be discussed later, this assumption seems to be justified; and the relevance of this approach to certain problems of politics seems clear. In international as well as in domestic politics, coalitions are made and broken by decisions based on estimates of strength under conditions of incomplete information about the present and uncertainties about the future. If the concept of the balance of power, as developed by Machiavelli and his successors, has its place in the field of political science, then the theory of games cannot be denied a similar standing. To assess the probabilities of success of a political or military venture and to select a strategy most likely to ensure it have long been major preoccupations of statesmen. Even more often, perhaps, statesmen have attempted to assess the strength of a political position or institution and the chances for its change or overthrow in order to be able to select the safest course of action. In one form or another all these problems appear in the theory of games, and the eventual impact of this theory on political and social science should be considerable.

Already some traces of this impact can be noticed. Interest in the theory of games has promoted a new style of thinking, in much the same manner as has the development of social science concepts amenable to mathematical treatment. As a result, political and social theories are more frequently formulated in terms that are at least "conceptually quantifiable" and that are expected to lend themselves eventually to accurate mathematical representation. This has forced social scientists to seek a sharpness in the definition of their terms to which they had rarely been accustomed; it has forced them to ask in the case of each concept whether there existed any practicable operations by which it could in fact be tested or measured. Some of this emphasis on mathematical representability and operational definitions, in turn, may induce political scientists to realize more clearly the implications of familiar notions they previously had taken for granted.

THE CONCEPTS OF TRANSITIVITY AND LOCATION OF SOVEREIGNTY

The theory of games points out that the assumption of "transitivity" must be explicitly made for a game or a decision system. If in a card game a queen has a higher value than a jack and a king a higher value than a queen, we must stipulate that the king must also have a higher value than the jack. At first glance this seems logical, but it is quite possible to have games where this rule does not apply and where A takes B, B takes C, but C takes A. Such nontransitive or loop patterns of dominance have been observed by biologists in the peck order of chickens, and they may have their counterpart in the relationship of the British Parliament to the Prime Minister, where the House of Commons can overthrow the Premier, but the Premier can dissolve the House, or in the relationship of the British voters to their Parliament, where the voters at election time can turn out the old Parliament but where the Parliament can postpone the period of elections and, at least in theory, could postpone such elections on the ground of war or emergency for an indefinite period.

In contrast, the simple notion of sixteenth- and seventeenth-century lawyers that there must always be a single supreme lawgiver or sovereign in a country contains the hidden assumption that the political decision system of each country must be transitive. The notion that in every political system there ought to be one sharply defined place of ultimate decision is based on an assumption that may correspond to the facts in some instances but not in others. In point of fact, it might be worth investigating whether any decision system that has autonomy, that is, self-steering and self-control, can be completely transitive.

THE LIMITED PLURALITY OF STABLE SOLUTIONS

Much of our thinking about politics, economics, and social life is based on the tacit assumption that there is one "best" solution for any set of given conditions and desires. This leads often to heated argument about the presumed all-round "superiority" of this or that political or economic system or the counterassertion that almost any system of solutions should be workable. The authors of *Theory of Games and Economic Behavior* deal explicitly with this problem of multiple solutions, going well beyond the classic emphasis of Montesquieu in suggesting that in general solutions are not unique. Indeed in most cases we shall observe a multiplicity of solutions. "Considering . . . solutions as stable 'standards of behavior' this . . . [means] that given the same physical background, different 'established orders of society' or 'accepted standards of behavior' can be built, all possessing . . . characteristics of inner stability. . . ."[1]

At the same time, the plurality of stable solutions is strictly limited, if it occurs at all in any game that is not trivial. In any such game there are many strategies for the players, individually and jointly, that would clearly not be winning or rewarding—or would be clearly less so than other strategies—and thus would not be stable. There may be more than one way to win, or to do best, in many games, but there are vastly more ways to lose or to do poorly. Game theory thus suggests that we reject indifferentism: as a rule, one strategy is by no means as good as any other. Rejecting indifferentism, however, and remembering that the number of winning strategies, or of stable solutions, is likely to be small, game theory none-theless suggests some open-mindedness and tolerance, for it reminds us that the small number of "best" solutions may yet be more than one.

OBJECTIVE AND SUBJECTIVE STRATEGIES

In addition to emphasizing specificity of definitions, explicitness of assumptions, and limited ensembles of possible solutions, the approach of the theory of games tends to make explicit the contrast between strategies that are "objectively" promising or successful, that is, that have a high probability of being rewarded by the workings of the game that are not controlled by the player, and strategies that are "subjectively" convenient, that is, strategies expressive of some learned habits or felt needs and desires of the player, regardless of their likelihood of being rewarded or penalized by the impersonal biases and rules of the game. Explicitly, game theory deals only with objective strategies that it evaluates as good or bad, better or worse, regardless of the personality structure of the player or the cultural characteristics of the group of players who are to use them. Implicitly, however, it is precisely this identification of objectively good strategies that—as far as it is successful—makes it possible to disentangle impersonal probabilities from personal preferences and to determine the extent and direction of the mistakes of any player, that is, his deviations from the theoretically best strategy. (Some limits upon this possibility of identifying "best" strategies will be discussed below.)

Despite these instances of potential usefulness to political science, most of the implications of game theory to politics lie in the future. If its potentialities are to be fulfilled, game theory must obtain from political scientists concepts and data that are sufficiently well defined and measured to be amenable to its treatment. On the other hand, however, political scientists may feel that many of the present restrictions of game theory reduce its ability to deal with political problems.

A STATIC THEORY: ASSUMPTIONS OF
UNCHANGING RULES AND PERFORMANCE

Generally, present-day game theory assumes no change in the performance characteristics of the game's elements during the time that the game is in progress. If kings are higher than jacks, they usually retain their higher value from the beginning to the end. Changes—even limited changes—in the behavior of the parts of the game are held to be exceptions, not the rule. In society and politics, however, limited changes of behavior may be the rule and exact repetition the exception. This possibility has perhaps found its classic expression in Lewis Carroll's image of the croquet game in *Alice in Wonderland*. In that game, as we all remember, the balls were live hedgehogs, the goals were doubled-up soldiers, and the mallets were live flamingos. The hedgehogs would crawl, the soldiers would stretch, and the flamingos would squirm at every stage of the game. It was a very difficult game indeed, and it would perhaps have been no less difficult for the present theory of games, but it looks in some ways very much like the kind of game that political scientists are trying to describe.

Just as game theory ordinarily does not allow for changes in the performance characteristics of particular elements, so it does not provide ordinarily for changes in the rules of the game. Taken together these two restrictions seem to cut it off from the description of much of the process of learning.

In most conventional social games, moreover, all resources of the players are treated as given from the outside, either in their hands or in some pool of cards or the like, with limited probabilities of combinations given in advance. A typical question of present-day policy —whether to convert a thousand tons of steel into an end product, such as guns, or into capital goods, such as machine tools or mining equipment that will eventually increase the supply of steel—has found few close counterparts among the problems originally treated by the theory of games. The few comparable problems that do appear in conventional games, such as the queening of a pawn in chess, occupy a minor position in the total ensemble of possible strategies of the games in which they are found and which are dominated primarily by quite different considerations.

More generally put, conventional games as well as much of game theory thus far have been more apt to picture problems in the distribution of existing resources and to neglect relatively the problems of the growth of new resources from limited beginnings. In doing so, game theory has not been able to cope with the problems of growth, novelty, and innovation.

This is not to say, however, that game theory as such ignores these problems. On the contrary, by stating its assumptions in an explicit and precise manner it highlights them and prepares the way for their solution. Thus the problem of the change in performance—though not the problem of learning—is being considered in some of the current work on linear programming and in Morgenstern's unpublished work on the "compressibility" of an economy, that is, its ability to provide substitutes for destroyed or otherwise eliminated products or services.

Von Neumann and Morgenstern are candid in admitting the limitations of the theory. They say:

> We repeat most emphatically that our theory is thoroughly static. . . . A static theory deals with equilibria. The essential characteristic of an equilibrium is that it has no tendency to change. . . .[2]

They add that such a static theory is a prerequisite for the later development of any sound dynamic theory. Physical theory advanced in this manner from statics to dynamics, and social science, the two authors suggest, might likewise find a usable dynamic theory of games and social behavior at some time in the future.

An interesting development of game theory toward the analysis of dynamic processes is being carried forward by developing sequences of games, such that the outcome of the first game might determine the nature of the next game to be played. A change of rules following a certain outcome of the first play of a game would have the same effect, since any significant rule change similarly could be considered to turn the subsequent play into a new game. Certain learning processes could thus be pictured as sequences of games in which one or several players would learn to change their utility functions, that is, the values they put on each of the various possible outcomes of the game, and they thus would change the corresponding portions of the payoff matrix where the values of all outcomes for all players are recorded. Alternatively, certain moves in a game might be taken as leading to changes in those rules of the game that limit the capabilities of the players; thus by the transition to successor games in which one or more of the players were less closely limited in their range of choices, the acquisition of new resources or the learning of new skills could be simulated. The so-called "stochastic games," which include a statement of the probabilities of the transitions from one subgame to another, could perhaps be developed in this direction.[3] Another application of the use of sequences of games would be in simulating the effects of credible threats or advance commitments: by renouncing some of their choices in advance, the parties could be thought of as having created a new game with drastically restricted choices.[4]

In the meantime, however, only the static theory of games has been strongly developed. It is this theory that is applied to military strategy and to the subject matter of popular books with such titles as *Strategy in Poker, Business and War*.[5] Since the present theory is static it seems likely to bias many decisions against giving proper weight to changing dynamic factors. Its premature and uncritical acceptance might do little harm in the field of poker, but it might do grave damage in domestic politics or international relations. The risk of such damage would be the greater the larger the time span over which a policy or strategy recommended by it would have to be applied.

VALUES IN GAMES AND IN POLITICS

Another major difficulty in applying game theory to broader political or military problems consists in the inevitable intermingling in them of considerations of value and of consequences. Game theory assumes that values are defined from the outside, that they do not change, and that they are independent from the results of the game.

Statesmen and generals, however, who may have to decide whether to risk more soldiers' lives in order to gain an earlier decision, or fewer soldiers' lives at the price of greater delay, are expected at one and the same time to act in accordance with the value scheme of their society and culture, and to make the decision that will be objectively most conducive to its survival. In making major political decisions, we are always playing at least two games at once, or rather, we are playing much more than a game. On the one hand, we are trying to act out our values—for example, to value white men more highly than colored, or women and children more highly than men, or vice versa. On the other hand, we are trying to survive, at least as a group. Almost every culture or political system assumes tacitly that its values are compatible with its continued survival, but history records that in the past such assumptions proved sometimes mistaken.

To put the matter more broadly, game theory values the pieces in each game in terms of the rules of that particular game only. Human lives, on the contrary, do not derive their value from any one set of their activities—political, economic, military, or whatnot; or even perhaps from any one set of philosophic or cultural values; or still less from any one doctrine. Human beings are not "single-game" or "single-purpose" units. They are at the very least "multipurpose" units, and any single-purpose calculation is likely to underestimate seriously their over-all value.

In the calculation of political and military problems, game theory is thus subject to a serious limitation. Since its probable errors seem large, perhaps its doubts should be regularly resolved in favor of solutions offering the gaining of more time and the saving of more lives, in accordance with Edmund Burke's rule that the statesmen should be in nothing so economical as in the production of evil.

A CRUCIAL POINT: CAPACITIES AND
COSTS OF THINKING

Finally, as game theory cannot deal with major changes over time, so it cannot deal with the problem of finding relevant solutions quickly enough to be of use. It cannot do so, it would seem, because thus far game theory has made no explicit and effective allowance for the time and cost needed for acquiring information. On the assumption that everybody can study quickly and easily all the probabilities relevant for any particular game situation, it has tended to favor the so-called "minimax" type of strategy, that is, the strategy that seeks to incur the least risk of loss, even at the price of accepting the smallest chance of gain. Using this strategy, a poker player will bluff from time to time, not in the expectation of deceiving his opponent, but merely in order to prevent him from relying on not being bluffed. Von Neumann and Morgenstern are careful to point out that

> . . . while our good strategies are perfect from the defensive point of view, they will (in general) not get the maximum out of the opponent's (possible) mistakes, i.e., they are not calculated for the offensive. . . . [A] theory of the offensive, in this sense, is not possible without essentially new ideas.[6]

The assumption underlying the minimax strategy, that one may always be found out, is another form of the assumption that all relevant information about the game is freely and instantly available to all players. Von Neumann and Morgenstern say:

> [We] cannot avoid the assumption that all subjects of the economy under consideration are completely informed about the physical characteristics of the situation in which they operate and *are able to perform all statistical, mathematical, etc., operations which this knowledge makes possible.* . . . Our investigations . . . assume "complete information" without any further discussion. . . .[7]

The theory—as theory—assumes, in short, that thinking or calculating can be carried on without any limitation of time or cost.

This assumption seems unrealistic in politics. It seems even unrealistic in such cases as chess. According to an unpublished study by Dr. L. C. Haimson, Russian handbooks of championship chess have advised promising players since the 1930's not to follow a "strongest position" strategy, but rather to force their opponent to make some definite commitment on the board, even at the cost of some loss in position to themselves. Once the Russian player has induced his adversary to commit his pieces to a particular position on the board, and to commit his mind to working out the possibilities of a particular kind of strategy, he is then advised, according to this theory of chess, to make a radical switch in strategy and to confront his opponent with a new set of problems for which his pieces are not effectively disposed and for which his mind is not prepared.[8] A possible political parallel to these tactics might be seen in the way in which the Soviet-initiated Berlin blockade in 1948 engaged United States attention at a time when the Chinese Communists were winning the civil war in mainland China; and again the way in which the Korean War of 1950 forced United States attention to the Far East, with a corresponding lag in the consolidation of Western positions in other areas.

In such situations the main attack may well be directed at first not so much against the principal material resources but rather against the decision-making capacity of the player. Through confronting his mind with a burden of decisions greater than he can manage within the limits of available time and intellectual resources, the efficiency of his decisions, and only subsequently his physical position, is to be impaired or disrupted.

Since the number of possible combinations in chess is very large, and becomes astronomical if the possible combinations for more than two moves ahead are to be considered, it is impossible for any chess player to consider all potentially relevant possibilities within any practical limit of time. In tournament chess, the time allowed each player for considering his next move is of the order of one hour. During that period he must consider all possible moves for, let us say, two moves ahead; then, on the basis of this preliminary scanning, to select the seemingly most promising strategies; and then to investigate each of these selected strategies intensively, by considering all or some of their possible consequences for another four or six moves ahead. Without the superficial scanning of all possibilities, the player could not be sure that he was not overlooking important strategic opportunities. Without adequate criteria of selection (where adequacy would have to be defined in terms of some probability considerations), he could not be sure that he had recognized the promising possibilities among the vast number of possible moves he had surveyed. And without the intensive investigation of all the possibilities selected as interesting, he could not know whether his tentative selections had in fact been good, or whether any one of the strategies selected as promising was better than the others.

The player would thus have to perform four major operations: (1) broad provisional scanning; (2) highly restrictive selection of a few promising possibilities; (3) intensive development of the possible strategies selected; and (4) a decision as to which of the intensively investigated strategies to put into operation. In order to be completely effective, he would have to make sure that he had scanned superficially *all* relevant possibilities; recognized every single promising strategy among them; developed *each* of these strategies, together with *all* possible countermoves of his adversary, far enough ahead to establish a *clear* probability for the outcome; and chosen the strategy with the *greatest* probability of success. No human player, or any existing or realistically imaginable electronic calculator, could carry out completely these four operations in the time of an hour, of a day, or of a year.

The decisive weakness is in the second stage. There is no sure way of recognizing which of all the combinatorial possibilities studied in the first stage could be developed into winning strategies, just as there is no sure way to teach a million monkeys writing on a million typewriters how to select out of all the possible combinations of letters those sequences that will parallel the merit of the plays of Shakespeare. All that can be done in this selection stage is to fish with a very small net of criteria of interest in a very large ocean of superficially scanned possibilities. In any finite time, this search for interesting possibilities must be superficial rather than exhaustive. A combination of suitable criteria of interest with a broad process of statistical sampling could perhaps improve the efficiency of the process, but could not remove the basic uncertainty about its outcome.

It should now be clear that chess played with ordinary time limitations is not and cannot be a completely determinate game, at least for as long a period of the development of human brains and electronic calculators as we can now foresee. It should also be clear why similar considerations of uncertainty will apply to political or economic decisions that must be selected from large ensembles of possible decisions under definite limitations of time. And it should be clear what the Russian theory of chess playing, as described by Dr. Haimson, hopes to accomplish. It is aimed at overloading the second or selection stage in the strategic thinking of its opponent. Once this opponent has been forced into making a commitment that seems advantageous to him when considered by itself, then his material and intellectual capacity for responding to radically new changes may have been overburdened. From this point on, the player has two enemies against him: the radically changing strategies of his opponent and the ticking of the clock.

The fact that the Russian players have prominently figured among recent chess champions may or may not be germane to this discussion. In any case, there is reason to expect that at some future time the world championship in chess, like so many other championships, will not remain the monopoly of any one country. What seems more likely to remain, however, regardless of the changing fortunes of chess competitions, is the introduction of *time* as an explicit variable in the planning of strategy, and the allowing for a specific time and *cost* element in the making of strategic decisions.

Since the original theory of von Neumann and Morgenstern assumed that all information was available to players who were under no limitation of time or cost in making up their minds, the explicit introduction of these limitations seems now to be leading into a "post-Neumannian" stage of the theory of games—a stage in which some of the pioneers of game theory themselves may well play a leading part.

One major development in this respect has been the interest in games with low content of information. This has led to attempts to combine game theory with learning theory and to provide models for "games against nature."

A particularly intriguing approach in this direction has been taken by Jacob Marschak in regard to organization theory, with obvious implications for the type of game models we have been discussing. Marschak considers an organization whose managers must find a profitable strategy for allocating their costly productive resources between two distant markets, with independently fluctuating prices in each. He assumes that the managers can improve their strategy by spending some money or resources on acquiring more information, and he shows how the cost of this additional information must be weighed against the cash value of the net improvement in the allocation strategy devised with its aid. Marschak proposes to describe each organization in terms of three variables: (1) the "pay-off function," that is, the formula that shows how profit—or some other reward to the organization—depends on its own decisions and on the different states of environment, including the possible actions of one or more competitors; (2) the "probability function" that states the probabilities with which the various possible external states are likely to occur; and (3) the organization cost function that attaches a cost to each of the organizational forms under consideration.[9]

The possible applications of this approach seem very broad. In dealing with a game and various possible strategies, rather than with an organization and various possible communication patterns within it, it would still be possible to assume or estimate a cost of computation for each strategy, and to compare this cost not only with the expected improvement in payoff, as against alternative strategies, but also to compare it with the known or estimated computing time and resources available to the player. Players could then be "rational" in von Neumann and Morgenstern's sense almost up to the limits of their currently available computing capabilities, but they might have to follow a second-order strategy of severely restricted intellectual effort beyond this point. Or they might try to minimize their expenditure of thought or computing effort, even if the evaluation of certain complex or subtle strategies were still well within their capabilities. Such a general preference for strategies that seem easy to compute—a kind of "law of least mental effort"— might not be a wholly unrealistic model for certain types of national or international politics.

Another line of attack could be developed from the concept of "psi-stability" proposed by Duncan Luce and Howard Raiffa. Psi here symbolizes a function stating which coalitions among several players are prohibited, and hence which others are permitted. It is thus held to represent something like a "social function" or social structure, expressed as a constraint on the free forming of coalitions.[10]

It is possible to consider the problem of computing or thinking as one of forming dissociations and associations of subassemblies of information, analogous to the coalitions among players; and to conceive of a set of constraints or prejudices preventing certain associations or strategies from being considered, or at least making their timely consideration improbable. Introducing such terms into game theory, a closer approach to the actual performance in some cases of political "players" or decision-makers could be attempted. As this new stage in the theory of games develops, it should become increasingly applicable to problems of politics, international as well as domestic.[11]

GAMES OF DETERRENCE AND THE BREAKDOWN OF CLASSIC GAME THEORY

Classic game theory lends itself very well to the analysis of "zero-sum games" where any gain by one or more players must be equal to the loss of one or more rivals. Such a game recalls Machiavelli's observation: "The Prince who promotes another's power diminishes his own." This concept is particularly convenient for the analysis of situations of merciless interest antagonism in two-person games, such as duels; and several early applications of game theory have dealt with calculations of the best time at which each of two mutually approaching duelists—or of two mutually approaching fighter planes—should open fire, in order to use his limited ammunition to best effect. Such analyses of duels are useful not only for improving certain tactics of aerial combat. In a world whose international politics seem characterized at least temporarily by a "bipolar power system,"[12] it seems plausible to apply the same style of thinking to duels between individuals and to power conflicts between rival blocs, or between the two nuclear-armed superpowers who appear to lead them.

A more refined approach, then, consists in treating the two-person game as a mixed-interest game, in which both countries have not only antagonistic interests but also significant interests in common. This area of mixed-interest-games has been explored by a number of writers, and most notably by Thomas C. Schelling.[13]

Schelling uses game theory not so much in a technical sense, as a professional practitioner of this subject might do, but as a source of ideas and suggestions that he develops in his own way, perhaps with fruitful effects for the discussion among game theorists themselves. His book *The Strategy of Conflict* represents an unfinished but important intellectual contribution. At times it reads like the notebook of a creative social scientist, communicating the excitement of new insights and discoveries.

In eminently lucid and often charming language, Schelling's work opens to rational analysis the international politics of threat or deterrence. In this field, his analysis goes well beyond what has been done by earlier writers. At the time of its appearance it was the best, most incisive, and most stimulating work on the subject, and will rank among the top contributions for a long time to come.

Threats, Schelling suggests, are meaningful only among persons or countries that simultaneously have important interests in common. A fruitful mathematical model for such situations is offered by "mixed-interest games," rather than by the "zero-sum games" of pure hostility and completely opposite interests—on which too much attention of the popular writers on game theory has been concentrated.

The logical opposite of these zero-sum games are the pure coordination games that occur between players whose interests coincide completely but who must coordinate their moves in the face of incomplete information, the pressure of time, or other handicaps. Thus, even if the United States and Russia had none but common interests in preventing third countries from acquiring nuclear weapons, they would be faced with a difficult game problem in coordinating their policies in the face of mutual ignorance, and before other countries—such as, say, China, Japan, or Germany—would enter the ranks of the atomic powers. Since the United States and Soviet Russia also have important interests that clash, their mutual foreign policy problem resembles a "mixed-motive game"; and it provides, according to Schelling, a suitable field for the use of both promises and threats as instruments of policy.

Threats are effective, according to Schelling, in proportion to their intensity and credibility. Since nuclear weapons have made it easy to increase greatly the intensity of war among great powers, the crucial problem that emerges is that of making such threats credible—since their execution normally would involve also some serious damage to the threatening party.

The credibility of threats in international politics is treated as a crucial variable. Schelling stresses repeatedly that rationality and perceptiveness may reduce the credibility of threats, since they make the threatener more aware of the heavy price he would have to pay in carrying out his threat, and since the threatened party will know that the threatener knows this price and may not really want to pay it. Obtuseness, recklessness, a poor capacity for communication, an inability to foresee even suicidal damage to oneself, a blithe willingness to accept such damage, or a reputation for such obtuseness or recklessness, Schelling insists through much of his book, may thus be genuine bargaining assets. He suggests that it also may be useful to create deliberately situations in which one is no longer master of one's own decisions, wholly or in part. A motorist who wants to have the right of way at an intersection might get it best by speeding up so that he could not slow down for cross traffic, even if he wanted to. If he speeds up in this manner, all other drivers will concede to him the right of way, if they are rational and do not act from "mere spite." Similarly, a ruler might publicly delegate to sadists the power to punish,[14] or a great power might put effective pressure on another by deliberately placing over the other's territory some nuclear-armed ballistic satellites, whose imperfectly controlled triggering devices have significant probabilities of going off, or by giving nuclear weapons to a smaller and more reckless ally whom it cannot entirely control. This might be a possible rationale for supplying nuclear weapons to the Chiang Kai-shek government on Formosa or to our allies in Europe.[15] Other examples of the successful use of weakness, ignorance, or irrationality as bargaining assets are seen in certain patterns of behavior of children, criminals, and the inmates of lunatic asylums.[16] All these, and certain techniques of kidnapers and blackmailers,[17] offer potentially valuable lessons, it is plainly suggested, for the conduct of foreign policy.

These pages in Professor Schelling's book offer fascinating intellectual experiments in a half-finished and half-understood new field of knowledge. Experience shows, however, that the techniques mentioned with such zest by the author do not work in practice for any prolonged sequence of repeated encounters.

Most reckless drivers who speed habitually across intersections do not live very long; even the most obstreperous small children do not control their families; and even the most intractable mental patients do not wind up as directors of their institutions. The uncritical application of Professor Schelling's imaginary experiments in "brinkmanship" and "threatmanship" to the future conduct of the foreign policy of the United States might well be wholly disastrous; and one is left to hope that his book will not be translated too quickly into Russian.

Any premature application of these ideas would be an irresponsible use of a brilliant and responsible book. Theorists must be free to make certain experiments in their minds, precisely in order to save us all the disastrous costs of making them in reality. The crucial point is that Professor Schelling's intellectual experiments, as well as his analysis of them, are quite unfinished. The "credibility" of a threat and the "rationality" of a response to it both involve assumptions about psychological facts, and yet little or no empirical evidence from the relevant research of psychologists has been used in the book.

Game theory usually assumes that most games have an end, but international politics resembles rather an unending game in which no great power can pick up its marbles and go home. Any gain by reckless threats in one encounter may have to be paid for by mounting odds against the chances of repeating this success in the encounters that follow. Professor Schelling deals in his sixth chapter also with sequences of repetitive encounters, and with the problem of learning from experience how to improve one's strategy,[18] but many of the strategies and situations treated in the earlier chapters seem to rest upon a tacit "end of the world" assumption.

An even more decisive factor in the effectiveness of threats is not mentioned. This is the *autonomous probability* of the behavior that the threat is supposed to inhibit. Even the most intense and credible threats may not stop people from sneezing; nor might they stop social revolutions in Asia or Africa. Related factors are those of the need and the motivation for the behavior that the threat intended to prevent. No threat can stop men from breathing. The strength of autonomous motivation may influence perceptions as well as acts. The more strongly people are motivated to act in a certain way, the more they are apt to disbelieve the most "credible" threats designed to stop them. The credibility of a threat, in short, is again a psychological problem, on which most serious research has yet to be done. Until then, credible threats may merely trigger off "preventive" violence by the threatened party.

Schelling's distinction between "rationality" and "spite" as governing motives of behavior, and his almost complete dismissal of the latter, also rest on untested assumptions about psychology. Here some knowledge is available. It is known that repeated frustrations increase the probability of an "irrational" or "spiteful" response, and frightened or overstrained men may react aggressively. The theory of deterrence, however, first proposes that we should frustrate our opponents by frightening them very badly and that we should then rely on their cool-headed rationality for our survival.

Clearly, Professor Schelling could not have dealt with all these problems in his first book in this new field. He deserves our gratitude for having opened so much of the subject so brilliantly, and he has made it easier to assess the intellectual work that remains to be done in examining the intellectual foundations of deterrence theory in general.

SOME GENERAL ASSUMPTIONS OF DETERRENCE THEORY

A quick review of some of the assumptions underlying much of deterrence theory reveals a mixture of restrictions inherited from classic game theory and conventional nationalistic folklore. Like classic game theory, the theory of the "balance of terror" usually treats the capabilities of the players as fixed for the relevant time span; therefore it treats weapons systems normally as stable, and it tends to neglect the quick or slow accumulation of technological change or economic growth.

In the second place, the theory usually treats the losses or penalties from partial accommodation or poor bargaining as much larger than the risks of thermonuclear conflict growing out of accidental or catalytic war, or from war set off by human failure or insubordination. [19]

Furthermore, the theory tends to treat as negligible the autonomous probability of the behavior to be deterred, and thus also to slight consideration of autonomous motivation and "vital national interest" of the governments of the contending great powers.

In the fourth place, the theory counts on the continued rational behavior of the recipient of intense and credible threats; that is to say, it simply assumes that his thinking, calculating and decision-making capabilities will be adequate to the burdens put upon them and that they will remain unimpaired by the emotions of fear, anger, and frustration such threats may produce, as well as unimpaired by the pressures of aroused elite and mass opinion stirred up in our age of mass politics by the governments and mass media of each great power.

In the fifth place, much of the writing about deterrence assumes a hidden asymmetry in the basic morale and motivations of Americans and foreigners, such as Russians or Chinese, to the effect that extremely irritating or humiliating threats—posed, for example, by Schelling's nuclear-armed and loose-triggered allies, or missiles in orbit—would intimidate Russians, while similar tactics would only provoke Americans.

Finally, all five kinds of assumptions just reviewed would be expected to hold good not only for a single encounter, or for one brief "showdown" crisis, but for a long sequence of repeated encounters extending over many years.

To list these six assumptions is to recall their extreme dubiousness, and thus the very great weakness of the intellectual foundations on which much of the theory of deterrence in the early 1960's seemed to rest.

Despite its dubious foundations, the theory perhaps answered a psychological need, since it embraced a relatively comforting picture of a static world, and of largely unchanging political habits, with a tacit reassurance as to the substantially superior stamina and courage of one's own government, ethnic group, and national culture, in comparison to those of the governments and peoples of the West's adversaries. The theory thus has some characteristics of a palliative, useful to ease the shock of adjustment to the full impact of a less comfortable reality. It is a makeshift device that permits some thought to be carried on, and some policies to be formulated and put into effect, which may work passably for another few years, and with unusual luck perhaps for as long as a decade. Even at its best, however, present-day deterrence theory does not seem good enough for the long run. It may take much improvement in the basic models of game theory, its intellectual parent, to give us something less inadequate.

Even with such improvements, however—which may be a long time in coming—game-theory models will remain partial. They gain their power by focusing attention on the "payoff" situation, but must take the goals of all players as simple, and the inner structure of each player as given. Game models are hard to imagine visually, or as a flow of processes. They are likely, therefore, to supplement other models rather than to replace them; and the search for more adequate basic models must go on.

PART II

Cybernetics: New Models
in Communication
and Control

CHAPTER

5

A Simple Cybernetic Model

Mechanic, organismic, and historical models were based, substantially, on experiences and operations known before 1850, even though many of their implications were worked out more fully only later. A major change in this situation began in the 1940's. Its basis was in the new development in communications engineering, with its extensive use of self-monitoring, self-controlling, and self-steering automatic processes. By making equipment that fulfills the functions of communication, organization, and control, significant opportunities were gained for a clearer understanding of the functions themselves.

These new developments in science and engineering were the beneficiaries of long-standing developments in social organization. Communication was social before it became elaborately technological. There were established routes for messages before the first telegraph lines. In the nineteenth century, factories and railroads required accurate coordination of complex sequences of human actions—a requirement that became central in the assembly-line methods and flow charts of modern mass production. The same age saw the rise of general staffs, and of intelligence organizations for diplomatic as well as for military purposes. These staffs and organizations, just as the modern large-scale industrial research laboratory itself, represent in a very real sense assembly lines of information, assembly lines of thoughts. Just as the division of manual labor between human hands preceded the division of labor between human hands and power-driven mechanisms, so the increasing division of intellectual labor between different human minds preceded today's divisions of labor between human minds and an ever-growing array of electronic or other communications, calculating, and control equipment.

What have the new machines of communication and control to offer for a further understanding of historical and social processes? For thousands of years, the operations of communication and control were largely carried on inside the nerve systems of human bodies. They were inaccessible to direct observation or analysis. They could be neither taken apart nor reassembled. In the new electronic machines of communication and control, messages or control operations can be taken apart, studied step by step, and recombined into more efficient patterns.

THE VIEWPOINT OF CYBERNETICS

The science of communication and control, ~~which has been derived from this technology and~~ which Norbert Wiener has called "cybernetics," is therefore a new science about an old subject. In investigating the old subject of communication and control, it uses the facilities of modern technology to map out step by step the sequence of actual events involved.[1]

Cybernetics, the systematic study of communication and control in organizations of all kinds, is a conceptual scheme on the "grand scale," in J. B. Conant's sense of the term.[2] Essentially, it represents a shift in the center of interest from drives to steering, and from instincts to systems of decisions, regulation, and control, including the noncyclical aspects of such systems. In its scope, it is comparable to Lavoisier's stress on quantitative chemistry, or to Darwin's concept of evolution. As to its performance and success, the future will have to tell, but it is perhaps safe to say that social science is already being influenced by the interests implicit in cybernetics at this time.

The fundamental viewpoint of cybernetics and its relevance to social science have been well expressed by Norbert Wiener:

> The existence of Social Science is based on the ability to treat a social group as an organization and not as an agglomeration. Communication is the cement that makes *organisations*. Communication alone enables a group to think together, to see together, and to act together. All sociology requires the understanding of communication.
>
> What is true for the unity of a group of people, is equally true for the individual integrity of each person. The various elements which make up each personality are in continual communication with each other and affect each other through control mechanisms which themselves have the nature of communication.
>
> Certain aspects of the theory of communication have been considered by the engineer. While human and social communication are extremely complicated in comparison to the existing patterns of machine communication, they are subject to the same grammar; and this grammar has received its highest technical development when applied to the simpler content of the machine.[3]

In other words, the viewpoint of cybernetics suggests that all organizations are alike in certain fundamental characteristics and that every organization is held together by communication. Communication is a process different from transportation on the one hand and from power engineering on the other. Transportation transmits physical objects such as liquids in pipelines, or boxes or passengers in trains or on escalators. Power engineering transmits quantities of electric energy. Communication engineering, by contrast, transmits neither tons of freight nor kilowatts of power. It transmits messages that contain quantities of information, and I shall say more about this concept of information later in this chapter. It is communication, that is, the ability to transmit messages and to react to them, that makes organizations; and it seems that this is true of organizations of living cells in the human body as well as of organizations of pieces of machinery in an electronic calculator, as well as of organizations of thinking human beings in social groups.[4] Finally, cybernetics suggests that steering or governing is one of the most interesting and significant processes in the world, and that a study of steering in self-steering machines, in biological organisms, in human minds, and in societies will increase our understanding of problems in all these fields.

ANALOGIES AND CONVERGENT DEVELOPMENTS

Why should anyone think that this viewpoint represents a conceptual scheme and not a mere analogy? Actually, the meaning of the term *analogy* is often poorly understood. Analogy means limited structural correspondence. All mathematics is based on analogies, and so is a large part of every science. Darwin himself tells us that it was his perception of the analogy between Malthus' theory of human population and certain processes in the animal kingdom that led him to his theory of evolution. When scientists speak disparagingly of "mere analogies," they mean, more accurately, "false analogies" or "poor analogies." The test by which we discriminate between a false analogy and a good analogy consists in the extent of actual structural correspondence between the two systems from which the analogy is drawn.[5] How many and how significant are the instances in which the analogy holds good, and how numerous and how important are the instances in which it fails to work? These are the questions by which we test analogies and which serve to unmask the many false analogies which look plausible at first glance but fail completely after the early stages of the application. The test of a good analogy, conversely, is that it continues to be confirmed after we have penetrated more deeply into the subjects it purports to connect and that it becomes more fruitful of new ideas and of new investigations as we continue to apply it. Darwin's analogy with the work of Malthus was a good analogy in this sense, and so was Torricelli's analogy between the atmosphere and a "sea of air." It is suggested that cybernetics is currently proving itself a good analogy or conceptual scheme in a similar manner.

The rise of the viewpoint of communications in the present period has not been fortuitous. Rather, it has been the result of convergent developments in a whole series of different sciences. Among these trends is the development of mathematical and statistical methods for the study of randomness and order, and thus of probability, leading to the mathematical theory of communication as developed by Norbert Wiener, Claude Shannon, and others. During the same decades the concept of homeostasis was developed by Claude Bernard, and later by Walter B. Cannon and Arturo Rosenblueth in physiology. This medical work found its parallel in the mathematical and empirical studies of control mechanisms, from Clark Maxwell's early paper on the governor in steam engines to the highly developed automatic control engineering of today. Problems of flow in various organizations were studied in production engineering, traffic engineering, city planning, and the design of telephone systems. Advances in the design of automatic switchboards eventually merged with the long-standing efforts to design effective calculating machines, from the early days of Leibniz and later of Charles Babbage to the analogue computor constructed by Vannevar Bush and the big digital computors of today. These advances in mathematics and the study of physical systems were paralleled by Ivan Pavlov's emphasis on the material nature of psychological processes, and on the discrete structure of the conditioned reflexes on which many of them were based. This emphasis was balanced by the rise of the school of *Gestalt* psychology led by Kurt Koffka and Wolfgang Köhler, emphasizing the importance of pattern and order, and the rise of the depth psychology of Sigmund Freud and his followers.

It is the experience of this new group of sciences that finds its reflection in some of the major ideas of cybernetics, such as the notion of the physical reality of patterns and of information and of the statistical nature of the latter, as well as the related notions of the physical nature of control processes, memory, and learning.

Taken together, the new experiences and notions promise to replace the classic analogues or models of mechanism, organism, and process, which so long have dominated so much of scientific thinking. All three of these models have long been felt to be inadequate. Mechanism and the equilibrium concept cannot represent growth and evolution. Organisms are incapable of both accurate analysis and internal rearrangement; and models of historical processes lacked inner structure and quantitative predictability.

79

In the place of these obsolescent models, we now have an array of self-controlling machines that react to their environment, as well as to the results of their own behavior; that store, process, and apply information; and that have, in some cases, a limited capacity to learn.

None of this is *thought* in the human sense of the word, as we find it in the behavior of individuals or groups, but it has significant parallels to it. Above all, the storage and treatment of information in machines, and its application to the control of the machines themselves, are taking place under conditions where every step can be traced distinctly and where every system can be taken apart for study and reassembled again. This is a research advantage that it would be neither easy nor entirely desirable to parallel in the case of human beings.

The test of the usefulness of this new science, as that of any science, must be its results. In the field of scentific theory it must offer new concepts rather than mere explanations. The analogies cybernetics may suggest between communication channels or control processes in machines, nerve systems, and human societies must in turn suggest new observations, experiments, or predictions that can be confirmed or refuted by the facts. They must be meaningful, that is, capable of being tested by practicable operations, and they should be fruitful, that is, lead to new operations and new concepts.

THE GENERAL CONCEPT OF
A SELF-CONTROLLING SYSTEM

To the extent that we can demonstrate that such analogies exist, and that they are fruitful in research, we may derive from them a generalized concept of a *self-modifying communications network* or *"learning net."* Such a "learning net" would be any system characterized by a relevant degree of organization, communication, and control, regardless of the particular processes by which its messages are transmitted and its functions carried out—whether by words between individuals in a social organization, or by nerve cells and hormones in a living body, or by electric signals in an electronic device.[6]

How does a modern communications mechanism look and what concepts can be derived from it?

Let me refer here to a brief sketch I gave elsewhere:

> A modern radar tracking and computing device can "sense" an object in the air, interacting with its beam; it can "interpret" it as an airplane (and may be subject to error in this "perception"); it can apply records of past experience, which are stored within its network, and with the aid of these data from "memory" it can predict the probable location of the plane several seconds ahead in the future (being again potentially subject to error in its "recollections" as well as in its "guess," and to "disappointment," if its calculation of probability was correct, but if the airplane should take a less probable course); it can turn a battery of antiaircraft guns on the calculated spot and shoot down the airplane; and it can then "perceive," predict, and shoot down the next. If it should spot more than one airplane at the same time, it must become "infirm of purpose," or else decide ("make up its mind") which one to shoot down first. . . .
>
> Man made machines actually operating or designable today have devices which function as "sense organs," furnish "interpretations" of stimuli, perform acts of recognition, have "memory," "learn" from experience, carry out motor actions, are subject to conflicts and jamming, make decisions between conflicting alternatives, and follow operating rules of preference or "value" in distributing their "attention," giving preferred treatment to some messages over others, and making other decisions, or even conceivably overriding previous operating rules in the light of newly "learned" and "remembered" information.
>
> None of these devices approach the overall complexity of the human mind. While some of them excel it in specific fields (such as the mechanical or electronic calculators), they are not likely to approach its general range for a long time to come. But, as simplified models, they can aid our understanding of more complex mental and social processes, much as sixteenth century pumps were still far simpler than the human heart, but had become elaborate enough to aid Harvey in his understanding of the circulation of the blood.[7]

What are some of the notions and concepts that can be derived from this technology? Perhaps the most important is the notion of information.

THE CONCEPTS OF INFORMATION,
MESSAGE, AND COMPLEMENTARITY

Power engineering transfers amounts of electric energy; *communications engineering transfers information*. It does not transfer events; it transfers *a patterned relationship between events*. When a spoken message is transferred through a sequence of mechanical vibrations of the air and of a membrane; thence through electric impulses in a wire; thence through electric processes in a broadcasting station and through radio waves; thence through electric and mechanical processes in a receiver and recorder to a set of grooves on the surface of a disk; and finally played and made audible to a listener—what has been transferred through this chain of processes, or channel of communication, is not matter, nor any one of the particular processes, nor any significant amount of energy, since relays and electronic tubes make the qualities of the signal independent from a considerable range of energy inputs. Rather it is *something* that has remained unchanged, invariant, over this whole sequence of processes.

The same principle applies to the sequence of processes from the distribution of light reflected from a rock to the distribution of black or white dots on a printing surface, or the distribution of electric "yes" or "no" impulses in picture telegraphy or television. What is transmitted here are neither light rays nor shadows, but information, the pattern of relationships between them.

In the second group of examples, we could describe the state of the rock in terms of the distribution of light and dark points on its surface. This would be a *state description* of the rock at a particular time. If we then take a picture of the rock, we could describe the state of the film after exposure in terms of the distribution of the dark grains of silver deposited on it and of the remaining clear spaces, that is, we should get another state description. Each of the two state descriptions would have been taken from a quite different object—a rock and a film—but a large part of these two state descriptions would be identical whether we compared them point by point or in mathematical terms. There would again be a great deal of identity between these two descriptions and several others; such as the description of the distribution of black and white dots on the printing surface, or of the electric "yes" or "no" impulses in the television circuits, or the light and dark points on the television screen. The extent of the physical possibility to transfer and reproduce these patterns corresponds to the extent that there is "*something*" unchanging in all the relevant state descriptions of the physical processes by which this transmission is carried on. That "something" is *information—those aspects of the state descriptions of each physical process that all these processes had in common.*[8]

To the extent that the last state description in such a sequence differs from the first, information has been lost or distorted during its passage through the channel. From the amount of information transmitted as against the information lost, we may derive a measure of the *efficiency* of a channel, as well as of the relative efficiency or *complementarity* of any parts or states of the channel in relation to the others.

These patterns of information can be measured in quantitative terms, described in mathematical language, analyzed by science, and transmitted or processed on a practical industrial scale.

This development is significant for wide fields of natural and social sciences. Information is indeed "such stuff as dreams are made on." Yet it can be transmitted, recorded, analyzed, and measured. Whatever we may call it, information, pattern, form, *Gestalt*, state description, distribution function, or negative entropy, it has become accessible to the treatment of science. It differs from the "matter" and "energy" of nineteenth-century mechanical materialism in that it cannot be described adequately by their conservation laws.

But it also differs, if not more so, from the "idea" of "idealistic" or metaphysical philosophies, in that it is based on physical processes during every single moment of its existence, and in that it can and must be dealt with by physical methods. It has material reality. It exists and interacts with other processes in the world, regardless of the whims of any particular human observer; so much so that its reception, transmission, reproduction and in certain cases its recognition, can be and sometimes has been mechanized.

These, then, were the main developments that came to a head after 1940. Cybernetics as the science of communication and control arose in response to a technological and social opportunity. It was made possible by advanced and parallel developments in neuro-physiology and psychology, in mathematics, and in electrical engineering, and by the growing need for cooperation among these and other sciences.[9] The result of these developments was a new body of experience, going beyond classic organism in its rationality, that is, in its ability to be retraced step by step in its workings.

The concept of information grew out of this new body of experience, and particularly out of the separation of communications engineering from power engineering. Information is what is transferred in telephony or television: it is not events as such, but a patterned relationship between events. Information has physical, "material" reality; without exception, it is carried by matter-energy processes. Yet it is not subject to their conservation laws. Information can be created and wiped out—although it cannot be created from nothing or destroyed completely into nothingness.[10] Finally, it differs from the classic notion of "form" in that it can be analyzed into discrete units that can be measured and counted.

Information consists of a transmitted pattern that is received and evaluated against the background of a statistical ensemble of related patterns. The classic example for this is the standardized birthday telegram transmitted by telegraphing a single two-digit number indicating the message to be selected from the limited set of prefabricated messages held ready by the company. All information at bottom involves the indication of some pattern out of a larger statistical ensemble, that is, an ensemble that is already stored at the point of reception.

From this it follows that recognition can be treated as a physical process and can, in fact, be mechanized in many instances. Current mechanical devices embodying operations of matching and recognition range all the way from the lowly fruit-grading and candling machines to the Moving Target Indicator and the Friend and Foe Identification device of the Armed Forces.[11] Similar standardized recognition processes are embodied in processes that have been only partly mechanized thus far and that still embody standardized human operations at some stages. Examples of such semimechanized recognition processes include qualitative analysis in chemistry and the Crocker-Henderson odor classification scheme and its successor, the flavor profile, according to which each of five hundred well-known smells can be identified by a four-digit number.[12] These recognition devices have grown up empirically, but the application of the theory of information forms part of the current development work on more complex devices of recognition—devices that are to be used to permit the deaf to understand spoken messages and the blind to read printed books, as well as for work on machines that will transcribe dictation or translate printed matter from one language into another.[13] Work on all these problems has been under way since the 1950's at several institutions of research.

MEMORY AND RECOGNITION

Since information has physical reality, its storage, that is to say, *memory*, is also a physical process. Most processes of thought can be represented in terms of a seven-stage process:

First, abstraction or coding of incoming information into appropriate symbols;

Second, storage of these symbols by means of quasi-permanent changes in the state of some appropriate physical facilities, such as the patterns of electric charges in certain electronic devices, the activity patterns of cells in nervous tissue, or the distribution of written marks on paper;

Third, dissociation of some of this information from the rest;

Fourth, recall of some of the dissociated items, as well as of some of the larger assemblies;

Fifth, recombinations of some of the recalled items into new patterns that had not been present among the input into the system;

Sixth, new abstraction from the recombined items preserving their new pattern, but obliterating its combinatorial origin. Steps five and six together make up the operation of creating *novelty;* and

85

Seventh, transmission of the new item to storage or to applications to action. This application of novelty to behavior we may call *initiative*.

A similar multistep sequence could consist of matching an incoming pattern of information against another pattern recalled from storage or memory. Both patterns are exposed to a *critical process*, that is to say, a physical process the outcome of which depends critically on the degree of correspondence between the two patterns to which it is applied. If the difference between the two patterns is smaller than a certain threshold given by the process, the critical process will have one result; if the difference is larger, the process will have another outcome. The process of recognition is completed by applying the outcome of the critical process to the behavior of the system.

AN OPERATIONAL APPROACH TO QUANTITY AND QUALITY

In a much more general aspect the notions of information and complementarity might be used to clarify the notion of quality that has sometimes baffled social scientists. From Plato and Aristotle to Oswald Spengler, Otto Strasser, and Ernst Jünger, authoritarian philosophers and political theorists have invoked qualitative judgments, the "all or nothing" reactions of taste or esthetic appreciation, as weapons against rationality or democracy. Only the coarse and simple things of social life can be counted and measured, so the argument has run, while all truly subtle and important things defy quantification and step-by-step analysis. Their imponderable and incommensurable peculiarities make them a law unto themselves, and a proper analogue to the superiority of mankind's privileged individuals, classes, or races. By contrast, if those social scientists who favored privilege have invoked quality in its defense, some of those who attacked privilege have tried to ignore problems of quality altogether.

Perhaps definitions of quantity and quality might be developed in terms of the operations from which they are derived, that is, from the operations involved in the processes of recognition and of measurement. At Massachusetts Institute of Technology a preliminary survey has been made of six processes involving *recognition*. These six systems are in actual use. Two of them are mechanical: the Yale lock and the automatic sorting of punched cards. Two are electronic: the equipment for the Identification of Friend or Foe (I.F.F.) and the Moving Target Indicator (M.T.I.). The last two involve biological or chemical processes within a systematized sequence of steps of human labor: the Crocker-Henderson odor classification scheme, and the scheme of qualitative analysis in chemistry.

In all cases it was found that the critical step in the recognition of quality was the establishment of a structural correspondence between a part of the recognizing system and the system that was recognized, and the testing of that correspondence by a *critical process*, that is, a physical process the outcome of which depends critically on the extent of that correspondence.[14] Quality is recognized, therefore, by the matching of two structures. The decisive step is to establish whether or not such matching has occurred.

Quantity in this view would appear to be really a more complicated notion than quality. It can be measured only *after* some qualitative matching has occurred or has been established; and it consists, then, in the matching of these matchings, that is, in comparing these operations of matching with each other, so as to derive a result of "more" or "less" from this comparison, or in comparing them with some counting structure, so as to record the number of complete matchings.

Quality in this view is derived from simple matching; quantity is derived from second-order matching. Despite this fact, quality has appeared to some writers as the more complex of the two notions, since quantitative measurement occurred only in those relatively well-understood situations where qualitative recognition had already taken place and where the latter could, therefore, already be taken for granted. The situations where qualitative problems were conspicuous were precisely those more difficult cases where structural matching had not yet been accomplished well enough to permit quantitative comparisons. There is reason to suspect that many of the qualitative problems in social and political science may turn out to be problems of matching and complementarity in social communication.[15]

FEEDBACK AND EQUILIBRIUM

Another significant concept elaborated since the 1940's is that of the "feedback." The feedback pattern is common to self-modifying communications networks, whether they are electronic control devices, nerve systems, or social organizations. "In a broad sense [feedback] may denote that some of the output energy of an apparatus or machine is returned as input. . . . [If] the behavior of an object is controlled by the margin of error at which the object stands at a given time with reference to a relatively specific goal . . . [the] feedback is . . . negative, that is, the signals from the goal are used to restrict outputs which would otherwise go beyond the goal. It is this . . . meaning of the term feedback that is used here."[16] "By output is meant any change produced in the surroundings by the object. By input, conversely, is meant any event external to the object that modifies this object in any manner."[17]

In other words, by feedback—or, as it is often called, a servomechanism—is meant a communications network that produces action in response to an input of information, and *includes the results of its own action in the new information by which it modifies its subsequent behavior*. A simple feedback network contains arrangements to react to an outside event (for example, a target) in a specified manner (such as by directing guns at it) until a specified state of affairs has been brought about (the guns cover the target perfectly, or the automatic push-button tuning adjustment on a radio has been accurately set on the wavelength approached). If the action of the network has fallen short of reaching fully the sought adjustment, it is continued; if it has overshot the mark, it is reversed. Both continuation and reversal may take place in proportion to the extent to which the goal has not yet been reached. If the feedback is well designed, the result will be a series of diminishing mistakes—a dwindling series of under- and over-corrections converging on the goal. If the functioning of the feedback or servomechanism is not adequate to its task (if it is inadequately "dampened"), the mistakes may become greater. The network may be "hunting" over a cyclical or widening range of tentative and "incorrect" responses, ending in a breakdown of the mechanism. These failures of feedback networks have specific parallels in the pathology of the human nervous system ("purpose tremor") and perhaps even, in a looser sense, in the behavior of animals, men, and whole communities.[18]

This notion of feedback—and its application in practice—is at the heart of much of modern control engineering. It is a more sophisticated concept than the simple mechanical notion of equilibrium, and it promises to become a more powerful tool in the social sciences than the traditional equilibrium analysis.

If we say that a system is in *equilibrium*, we make a number of rather specific suggestions. We suggest that it will return to a particular state when "disturbed"; that we imagine the disturbance is coming from outside the system; that the system will return with greater force to its original state the greater has been the disturbance; that the high or low speed with which the system reacts or with which its parts act on each other is somehow irrelevant (and we term this quality "friction" to denote that it is a sort of imperfection or blemish that has no proper place in the "ideal" equilibrium); and finally we suggest that no catastrophes can happen within the limits of the system, but that, once an equilibrium breaks down, next to nothing can be said about the future of the system from then on.

Such equilibrium theories are based on a very restricted field of science, called "steady state dynamics." They are not well suited to deal with so-called *transients;* that is, they cannot predict the consequences of *sudden* changes within the system or in its environment, such as the sudden starting or stopping of a process. Altogether, in the world of equilibrium theory there is no growth, no evolution;

there are no sudden changes; and there is no efficient prediction of the consequences of "friction" over time.

On all these points the feedback concept promises improvements. Instead of pushing the effect of "friction" into the background, feedback theory is based on the measurement of *lag* and *gain*. *Lag* is the time that elapses between the moment a negative feedback system reaches a certain distance from its goal and the moment it completes corrective action corresponding to that distance. *Gain* means the extent of the corrective action taken. An inexperienced automobile driver tends to have slow reflexes: he responds tardily to the information of his eyes that his car is heading for the right-hand ditch. His lag, in feedback terms, is high. Yet when he acts, he may turn his steering wheel sharply—with a high gain—and head for the left-hand ditch until he notices the overcorrection and corrects his course again. If we know three quantities—the speed of his car and extent of his lags and of his gains—we can try to predict the wobbliness of his resulting course.

Lag and *gain*, in the feedback approach, are the most important variables to work on. Of the two, *lag* is the more important. It can be reduced by improving the system, as when our novice driver learns to react faster; or lag can be compensated for by a lead—a prediction of a future distance from the goal—as when an experienced driver compensates for an anticipated skid at the first sign of its onset. What *lag* still remains will permit control engineers to calculate just how much gain—how drastic a self-correction at each step—the system can afford under known conditions without endangering its stability.

To sum up, equilibrium analysis is based on a restricted part of dynamics; it is restricted to the description of steady states. Cybernetics is based on full dynamics including changes of state; and it combines these full dynamics with statistics. Cybernetics is the study of the full dynamics of a system under a statistically varying input. The potential usefulness of this approach to such economic problems as, for example, the so-called "cobweb theorem" has been stressed by some economists.[19]

From a historical point of view, the rise of equilibrium analysis meant the neglect of problems of purpose. Cybernetics offers not only a gain in technical competence but also a possibility of restoring to problems of purpose their full share of our attention.

LEARNING AND PURPOSE

Even the simple feedback network shows the basic characteristics of the "learning process" described by John Dollard in animals and men. According to Dollard, "there must be (1) drive, (2) cue, (3) response, and (4) reward." In a man-made feedback network, "drive" might be represented by "internal tension," or better, by mechanical, chemical, or electric "disequilibrium"; input and output would function as "cue" and "response"; and the "reward" could be defined analogously for both organisms and man-made nets as a "reduction in intensity" (or extent) of the initial "drive" or internal disequilibrium.[20]

A simple feedback mechanism implies a measure of "purpose" or "goal." In this view a goal not only exists within the mind of a human observer; it also has relative objective reality within the context of a particular feedback net, once that net has physically come into existence. Thus a *goal* may be defined as "a final condition in which the behaving object reaches a definite correlation in time or in space with respect to another object or event."[21]

This definition of a goal, or purpose, may need further development. There is usually at least one such external goal (that is, one relation of the net as a whole to some external object) that is associated with one state encompassing the relatively lowest amount of internal disequilibrium within the net. Very often, however, an almost equivalent reduction of internal disequilibrium can be reached through an internal rearrangement of the relations between some of the constituent parts of the net, which would then provide a more or less effective substitute for the actual attainment of the goal relation in the world external to the net. There are many cases of such surrogate goals or *ersatz* satisfactions, as a short circuit in an electronic calculator, intoxication in certain insects, drug addiction or suicide in a man, or outbursts against scapegoat members of a "tense" community. They suggest the need for a distinction between merely internal readjustments and those that are sought through pathways that include as an essential part the reaching of a goal relationship with some part of the outside world.

This brings us to a more complex kind of learning. Simple learning is goal-seeking feedback, as in a homing torpedo. It consists in adjusting responses, so as to reach a goal situation of a type that is given once for all by certain internal arrangements of the net; these arrangements remain fixed throughout its life. A more complex type of learning is the self-modifying or *goal-changing* feedback. It allows for feedback readjustments of those internal arrangements that implied its original goal, so that the net will change its goal, or set for itself new goals that it will now have to reach if its internal disequilibrium is to be lessened. Goal-changing feedback contrasts, therefore, with Aristotelian teleology, in which each thing was supposed to be characterized by its unchanging *telos*, but it has parallels in Darwinian evolution.[22]

We can now restate our earlier distinction as one between two kinds of goal-changing by internal rearrangement. Internal rearrangements that are still relevant to goal-seeking in the outside world we may call "learning." Internal rearrangements that reduce the net's goal-seeking effectiveness belong to the pathology of learning. Their eventual results are self-frustration and self-destruction. Pathological learning resembles what some moralists call "sin."

Perhaps the distinction could be carried further by thinking of several orders of purposes.

A first-order purpose in a feedback net would be the seeking of *immediate satisfaction*, that is, of an internal state in which internal disequilibrium would be less than in any alternative state, within the range of operations of the net. This first-order purpose would correspond to the concepts of "adjustment" and "reward" in studies of the learning process. Self-destructive purposes or rewards would be included in this class.

By a second-order purpose would be meant that internal and external state of the net that would seem to offer to the net the largest probability (or predictive value derived from past experience) for the net's continued ability to seek first-order purposes. This would imply *self-preservation* as a second-order purpose of the net, overriding the first-order purposes. It would require a far more complex net.[23]

A third-order purpose might then mean a state of high probability for the continuation of the process of search for first- and second-order purposes by a group of nets beyond the "lifetime" of an individual net. This would include such purposes as the *preservation of the group* or "preservation of the species." Third-order purposes require several complex nets in interaction. Such interaction between several nets, sufficiently similar to make their experiences relevant test cases for one another, sufficiently different to permit division of labor, and sufficiently complex and readjustable to permit reliable communication between them—in short, such a *society*—is in turn essential for the higher levels of the learning process that could lead beyond third-order purposes.

Among fourth-order purposes we might include states offering high probabilities of the *preservation of a process* of purpose-seeking, even beyond the preservation of any particular group or species of nets. Such purposes as the preservation or growth of "life," "mind," "order in the universe," and all the other purposes envisaged in science, philosophy, or religion, could be included here.

The four orders overlap; their boundaries blur; and there seems to be no limit to the number of orders or purposes we may set up as aids to our thinking. Yet it may be worthwhile to order purposes in some such fashion, and to retain, as far as possible, the model of the feedback net that permits us to compare these purposes to some degree with physical arrangements and operations. The purpose of this procedure would not be to reduce intellectual and spiritual purposes to the level of neurophysiology or mechanics. Rather it would be to show that consistent elaboration of the simpler processes can elevate their results to higher levels.

93

VALUES AND THE CAPACITY TO LEARN

The movements of messages through complex feedback networks may involve the problem of "value" or the "switchboard problem," that is, the problem of choice between different possibilities of routing different incoming messages through different channels or "associative trails"[24] within the network. If many alternative channels are available for few messages, the functioning of the network may be hampered by indecision; if many messages have to compete for few channels, it may be hampered by "jamming."

The efficient functioning of any complex switchboard requires, therefore, some relatively stable operating rules, explicit or implied in the arrangements of the channels. These rules must decide the relative preferences and priorities in the reception, screening, and routing of all signals entering the network from outside or originating within it.

There are many examples of such rules in practice: the priority given fire alarms in many telephone systems; or the rules determining the channels through which transcontinental telephone calls are routed at different loads of traffic; these last include even the "hunting" of an automatic switchboard for a free circuit when the routing channels are fully loaded. They illustrate the general need of any complex network to decide in some way on how to distribute its "attention" and its priorities in expediting competing messages, and how to choose between its large number of different possibilities for combination, association, and recombination for each message.

What operating rules accomplish in switchboards and calculating machines is accomplished to some extent by "emotional preference" in the nervous systems of animals and men, and by cultural or institutional preferences, obstacles, and "values" in groups or societies. Nowhere have investigators found any mind of that type that John Locke supposed "to be, as we say, white paper." Everywhere they have found structure and relative function.

In much of the communications machinery currently used, the operating rules are rigid in relation to the content of the information dealt with by the network. However, *these operating rules them-selves may be made subject to some feedback process.* Just as human directors of a telephone company may react to a traffic count by changing some of their network's operating rules, we might imagine an automatic telephone exchange carrying out its own traffic counts and analyses, and modifying its operating rules accordingly. It might even modify the physical structure of some of its channels, perhaps adding or dropping additional microwave beams (which fulfill the function of telephone cables) in the light of the traffic or financial data "experienced" by the network.[25]

What seems a possibility in the case of man-made machinery seems to be a fact in living nerve systems, minds, and societies. The establishment and abolition of "conditioned reflexes" have long been studied in animals and men, and so have the results of individual and group learning. Such processes often include changes in the "operating rules" that determine how the organism treats subsequent items of information reaching it.

Any network whose operating rules can be modified by feedback processes is subject to *internal conflict* between its established working preferences and the impact of new information. The simpler the network, the more readily internal conflicts can be resolved by automatically assigning a clear preponderance to one or another of two competing "channels" or "reflexes" at any particular moment, swinging from one trend of behavior to another with least delay. The more complex, relatively, the switchboards and networks involved, the richer the possibilities of choice, the more prolonged may be the periods of indecision or internal conflict. Since the net acquires its preferences through a process of history, its "values" need not all be consistent with each other. They may form circular configurations of preference, which later may trap some of the impulses of the net in circular pathways of frustration. Since the human nervous network is complex, it remains subject to the possibilities of conflicts, indecision, jamming, and circular frustration. Whatever pattern or preferences or operating rules govern its behavior at any particular time can only reduce this affliction, but cannot abolish it.[26]

Since the network of the human mind behaves with some degree of plasticity, it can change many of its operating rules under the impact of experience. It can learn, not only superficially but fundamentally: with the aid of experience the human mind can change its own structure of preference, rejections, and associations. And what seems true of the general plasticity of the individual human mind applies even more to the plasticity of the channels that make up human cultures and social institutions and those particular individual habit patterns that go with them. Indeed, this cultural learning capacity seems to occur in some proportion to the ability of those cultures to survive and to spread.

Since all learning including changes in goals or values consists in physical internal rearrangements, it depends significantly on material resources. The *learning capacity* of any system or organization, that is, the range of its effective internal rearrangements, can thus be measured to some extent by the number and kinds of its *uncommitted resources*. Such resources need not be idle; but they must be reassignable from their current functions. There is a qualitative element in learning capacity, since it depends not only on the amount of uncommitted resources but also on their configurations. Yet, since learning capacity consists in an over-all performance, a particular configuration of internal elements can be replaced, in many cases, by some functionally equivalent configuration of others. This is the more probable, the richer the range of available rearrangements, and thus, again, the greater the amount of uncommitted resources, and of facilities for their quick and varied recommitment.

Learning capacity can be tested by two independent sets of operations: first, by outside tests of a system's over-all performance in a given situation, much as the learning capacity of rats is tested in a maze and that of armies is tested in battle; and second, by analysis of its inner structure. Thus the greater learning capacity of rats compared to frogs can be predicted from the greater size and complexity of the rat's central nervous system, and the greater learning capacity or adaptability of one army relative to another can be predicted if, other things being equal, it has greater facilities of communication and transport and a greater "operational reserve" of uncommitted man power and equipment. Since over-all performance tests are cheap in rats, but expensive in armies, or in the defense of cities against atom bombs, the prediction of probable learning capacity from structural analysis and the suggestions for probable improvements by the same method may have considerable practical importance.

So far we have described two kinds of feedback: "goal-seeking," the feedback of new external data into a net whose operating channels remain unchanged; and "learning," the feedback of external data for the changing of these operating channels themselves. A third important type of possible feedback is the feedback and simultaneous scanning of highly selected internal data, analogous to the problem of what usually is called "consciousness."

6

Consciousness and Will
as Patterns of
Communication Flow

Consciousness may be defined, as a first approximation and for the purposes of this discussion, as a collection of internal feedbacks of secondary messages. *Secondary messages* are messages about changes in the state of parts of the system, that is, about primary messages. *Primary messages* are those that move through the system in consequence of its interaction with the outside world. Any secondary message or combination of messages, however, may in turn serve as a primary message, in that a further secondary message may be attached to any combination of primary messages or to other secondary messages or their combinations, up to any level of regress.

In all these cases, secondary messages function as symbols or internal labels for changes of state within the net itself. They are fed back into it as additional information, and they influence, together with all other feedback data, the net's subsequent behavior. "Consciousness" does not consist merely in these labels, but in the processes by which they are derived from the net and fed back into it, and in the processes by which two or more such secondary messages are brought to interact with each other.

CONSCIOUSNESS IN SOCIAL ORGANIZATIONS

Feedback messages about some of the net's internal states occur in simple form in electronic calculators where they serve important functions in recall. They may occur, in extremely complex patterns, in the human nervous system, where they are not easy to isolate for study. But they also occur, and can be studied with relative ease, in the division of labor of large human teams that process information and collectively fulfill certain functions of thought. We find such teams in industrial research laboratories, and in political or military intelligence organizations.

We can observe how guide cards and index tabs are added to the information moving through, or stored within, the filing systems, libraries, card catalogues, or "document control centers" of intelligence organizations (such as the State Department or, during World War II, the Office of Strategic Services), and how these secondary symbols influence the further treatment of the information. The heads, policy boards, or project committees of such organizations cannot deal with all the vast information in the original documents. They deal mostly with titles, description sheets, summaries, project requests, routing slips, and other secondary symbols, while a great deal of the material continues to be processed "below the level of the consciousness" of the guiding and policy-making parts of the organization. Only those feedback circuits and decisions that are "picked up" through the attachment and feedback of secondary symbols become directly "conscious" for the organization.

To be sure, the selective function of any network is by no means limited to this "conscious" zone of secondary symbols. On the contrary, what reaches that zone for separately labeled and recorded processing depends in turn on what has been selected or rejected, associated or disassociated, routed or blocked, recorded or misfiled or erased within the rest of the system. There is some automatic screening carried out by the reporter on the beat, and by the desk analyst in the intelligence organization; and we may suspect similar screening processes in the "nonconscious" remembering and forgetting, the "aversions" and "hunches" of the individual mind, as well as in many of the "unverbalized" conventions and assumptions, preferences or taboos of human societies and cultures.[1]

The powers of the "nonconscious," internally unlabeled processes within a network, can be positive as well. An experience may be built up into a perception and recorded in memory, two and two may be put together, new associations, discoveries and insights may be put together "nonconsciously" without the intervention of secondary symbols, until secondary symbols are attached to the new combination, and suddenly the image of the new synthesis breaks through into the realm of consciousness, seeming all ready and armored, like Pallas Athene springing forth from the head of Zeus in the Greek legend.[2]

By attaching secondary symbols to some of our steps in a calculation or sequence of behavior we may change its outcome. For these secondary symbols are fed back into the net, and the message of which the net has become "conscious" may then appear in the net with greater frequency than its unlabeled alternatives, and it may remain more readily available for preferred treatment. This treatment may be preferred association, recording, transmission, blocking, or suppression, according to the current operating rules of the system.

If secondary symbols become attached to parts or connections in the net that embody these operating rules, then these rules themselves become "conscious" for the net. By being fed back into it, they become statistically reinforced for more effective application; and they may be changed more easily if this possibility is included in the net. The effects of such internal labeling may be thought of as to some extent comparable to the effect of dramatic symbols or publicity devices in a society. Once attached to particular ideas, practices, or laws, they may lift them from their previous obscure existence into the crossfire of public attention.[3]

The ensemble of secondary symbols may easily misrepresent the net's actual content. Some primary symbols may be "overrepresented" by ample feedback, while others may not be made "conscious" at all. Consciousness, therefore, may be false consciousness, much as the actual personality of a man may be quite different from what he thinks it is. Similarly, by attaching suitable symbols and feedbacks to selected aspects of their behavior, groups or nations can be given highly misleading ideas about their own character.

CONFRONTATION FOR SIMULTANEOUS INSPECTION

Consciousness, however, involves not one operation but at least two. It requires first of all a high degree of selection and abstraction from the stream of primary or lower-order messages, and their highly condensed and abridged mapping into a much smaller number of higher-order messages. But it also implies, as a rule, the more or less simultaneous scanning or inspection of as much of this abridged second-order information as can be encompassed in the "focus of consciousness"—or the "span of attention" or "span of control"—of a person, or in the effective range of surveillance or control of an organization.

Physical examples of such condensed and concentrated arrangements of secondary symbols for their simultaneous—or nearly simultaneous—inspection are abundant. They include the nineteenth century military staff maps on which colored pins and other movable symbols represented troops; the underground plotting center in the Battle of Britain in 1940 where, on a large simplified map of southern England and the Channel, wooden counters were moved with rakes by army personnel, so as to represent the strength, position, direction, and speed of attacking and defending aircraft and to permit quick decisions about the best use of still disposable British fighter defenses; and the transparent plastic screen in the antiaircraft control center of post-World War II vessels in the premissile age, when the quickly changing reported numbers and movements of attacking enemy aircraft were chalked in color on one side of the plastic, so as to permit the officer on the other side to encompass at one glance the rapidly mounting attacks from many directions against his ship, and to decide on the best allocation of his own antiaircraft batteries, and perhaps fighter planes, for his defense; and the "situation room" of the early 1950's, where the President of the United States was reportedly briefed almost daily by his subordinates on the changing conditions and crises around the world, was similarly designed to facilitate simultaneous inspection. A current offspring of all these simpler devices could perhaps be seen in the vast warning and computing systems of the late 1950's and early 1960's—such as the SAGE system—that are designed to collect and compare a large number of highly abbreviated data, radar readings, and the like, so as to make or keep their operators aware of all actual or apparent movements of aircraft or missiles toward the territory of the United States.

The last stage in this approximation to certain aspects of consciousness would be reached when these early-warning and computing systems were made fully automatic. In this stage, not only would the collection, abridgment, and collation of the primary messages be carried out by electronic equipment, but so would their confrontation with selected data automatically recalled from the memory banks of appropriate computers, and, further, the interpretation of data and memories, as confronted with each other, for purposes of defensive or retaliatory action. Here the automatic simultaneous inspection of abridged symbols may lead to highly fallible decisions about war and peace, and thus about the life and death of nations and perhaps of all mankind, much as the quick, simultaneous inspection of the few matters of which an individual is aware may lead him to some highly fallible decision about his own fate. Here our man-made machinery of quasi-consciousness shows once again its close relation to problems of command and government. The subject of a recent thoughtful paper in communication engineering and command problems in national defense, entitled "Emergency Simulation of the Duties of the President of the United States," indicates some of the more remote perspectives that might possibly follow someday from trends now under way.[4]

The dangers from a premature and poorly understood extension of these techniques to the making of high-speed and almost inevitably shallow decisions about the life and death of millions are appalling. No one has warned more emphatically and cogently against this overextension of engineering in advance of broader and more fundamental knowledge than one of the intellectual fathers of much of this technology, Norbert Wiener.[5] The realism of his warnings was illustrated by the news that, on November 24, 1961, at a tense moment during the Berlin crisis, bombers of the United States Strategic Air Command had been moved to the runways in response to an erroneous signal.[6]

There is no reasonable way in which we can transfer tasks of individual and social thinking, decision-making and consciousness to some aggregation of electronic machinery, unless we first have taken good care to understand this particular task or aspect of thought and consciousness in its social and individual setting. Before we hand any task of consciousness to a machine, we should understand at least to some extent what consciousness is; what the processes are that it describes; what the differences are that it makes in a set of probable outcomes; and what the facilities are that it requires. The answers to these questions are not at all complete; but the notion of consciousness, derived here from the viewpoint of communications, may help us to get more and better answers in the course of time.

How does this feedback notion of consciousness compare with other approaches? In the behaviorist school of psychology, we are told that "consciousness" and conscious processes "are excluded as not subject to scientific investigation, or . . . reinterpreted as covert language responses."[7] In social science writings, consciousness is often stressed, and ascribed to groups, but usually this is done without definition or description in any but intuitive terms.[8] Two recent writers describe individual consciousness as follows:

[The] integrative (regnant) process in the brain . . . according to the findings and speculations of neurophysiologists . . . are capable of self-awareness (as if they had a mirror in which to see themselves). During the passage of one event many, but not all, of the regnant processes have the property of consciousness, at the moment of their occurrence or soon afterwards if recalled by retrospection. Thus the stream of consciousness is nothing more than the subjective (inner) awareness of some of the momentary forces operating at the regnant level of integration in the brain field.[9]

This is a suggestive description in the language of everyday life in which processes behave like small individuals who "reign," "see themselves as if they had a mirror," and "have the property of consciousness" that "is nothing more than . . . subjective (inner) awareness." But it is not very helpful as a concept from which we might derive new observations and experiments.

In contrast to this, what are the operational implications of our feedback model? First of all, if consciousness is a feedback process, then it requires material facilities and is carried on at some material cost in terms of facilities and time. Some of the facilities that are tied up, and some of the delay imposed on primary processes, should be capable of measurement.

Second, feedback processes have structures, circuits, channels, switching relationships, incompatibilities, and discontinuities that might be susceptible of mapping.

In the third place, if we cannot isolate the physical facilities involved, we might devise functional tests for possible patterns, limits, and discontinuities in the performance of the process of consciousness. If these tests should yield a map of discontinuities in performance, we might derive a basis for further inferences about the structure of the underlying facilities and processes themselves.[10]

Similar considerations might apply to the processes of "consciousness" in nations, classes, or other social groups. If there are such processes, how are they organized and patterned? What are the manpower, facilities, symbols, learning processes, and teamwork relations by which they are carried on? If consciousness resembles a feedback, does it also resemble the feedback's peculiar kinds of instability? A small change in a feedback circuit can bring about a large change in its over-all performance. Are there analogies for this in social life?

The feedback model of consciousness is more than a verbal explanation. It is a concept. For it suggests many questions that sooner or later should be answered, one way or another, by observation and experiment.

WILL AND THE CLOSURE OF DECISION SYSTEMS

Consciousness seems related to "will"—or to that sense of conation, or making autonomous decisions, which we mean when asserting that "our will is free." This notion of will includes not only decisions with internal labels attached to the very moment of action, or to several steps within an action. It also includes mere decisions to start an action, now or on a later signal, with the actual parts of the action following automatically without any "conscious" labels attached to them.[11] *Will* in all these cases may be tentatively defined, in any sufficiently complex net, nervous system, or social group, as the set of internal labels attached to various stages of certain channels within the net, which are represented by these labels as relatively unchanging, so that "we merely trip the purpose and the reaction follows automatically."[12]

In other words, *will* may be called the set of *internally labeled decisions and anticipated results, proposed by the application of data from the system's past and by the blocking of incompatible impulses or data from the system's present or future.* Since the net cannot foretell with certainty either the outcome of the subsequent trains of its own internal messages and switching orders, or the outcome of its own efforts to inhibit information incompatible with the "willed" result, it knows only what it "will do," not what it "shall do." It may "know its mind," but it cannot know with certainty whether or when it will change it.[13]

A fundamental problem of "will" in any self-steering network seems to be that of carrying forward and translating into action various data from the net's past, up to the instant that the "will" is formed (the determination becomes "set" or the decision "hardens"), while blocking all subsequent information that might modify the "willed" decision. Will resembles the "deadline" in a newspaper: it could be called the *internally labeled preference for predecision*

105

messages over postdecision ones. The "moment of decision" might then be seen as that threshold where the cumulative outcome of a combination of past information begins to inhibit effectively the transmission of contradictory data.

This general problem of "will" seems to apply, at least to some extent, to man-made devices whose operations can be accurately specified. Automatic pilots or steering mechanisms exclude or compensate for subsequent "experiences," such as gusts of storm, which might deflect them from their course. Guided missiles, homing torpedoes, proximity fuses, and similar weapons involve in their design problems of this kind.

A primitive once-for-all process of a somewhat comparable type seems to be involved in the process of "learning by imprinting" that has been observed in goslings and certain other young birds:

> Lorenz first made known the curious fact that whatever a gosling . . . first sees in the hours after hatching, be it bird, beast or man, the gosling will follow as it normally would follow its mother. The fixation is demonstrated as . . . essentially . . . on any first moving object perceived. . . . How persistent is the fixation was shown in another experiment in which the first thing presented to the eyes of a budgereegah remained forever its only object of attachment and its days of courtship were spent in trying to make love to a ping-pong ball. . . .
>
> A working model of the mechanism is simple. A feedback trigger circuit provides channels for the reception of a number of possible stimuli, and is so constructed that, when any one of them is activated, it locks on, and a common reflex puts all the other channels out of action—that is, excepting the one already locked.[14]

This process of "learning by imprinting" resembles what we have called "will" only to the extent that a stage of openness of the acting system to different messages is followed by its closure after a threshold period, and/or a threshold message, so that all competing or conflicting messages are thereafter excluded. "Will" differs from imprint learning, however, in that it is usually internally monitored and labeled, and thus appears as a conscious decision to the acting person himself and possibly to other observers. Moreover, will often involves repeated loosening and hardening of decisions, that is, the setting and resetting of goals, purposes, or courses of action that remain fixed only for limited lengths of time. Imprint learning, so far as we can tell, occurs without any awareness on the part of the animal; and it lasts for a lifetime in some of the experiments described. It is thus a kind of extreme caricature of will: a blind slipping into an irrevocable decision about one's own further preferences and desires—an extreme form of learning *not* to learn in the future.

Isolating the pattern of "will" in feedback machines may help us to recognize it in men and communities. Men may shut out the experiences of pain or fear or doubt or pity that might deflect them from their "fell purpose." Cultures or states, ever since the days of the Spartans, have often put taboos or legal prohibitions in the way of all messages that might change their previously determined patterns of behavior. Modern nations, governments, or political parties in war or peace may strive to perpetuate their policies by blocking all incompatible experiences from the life of their community through all means at their disposal—legislation, indoctrination, pressure, censorship, police, or propaganda. It is in that sense, perhaps, that the concept of "will" can be applied meaningfully to the behavior of political movements, peoples, and social organizations. In government and politics, will is a pattern of relatively *consolidated preferences and inhibitions, derived from the past* experiences of a social group, *consciously labeled* for a relevant portion of its members, *and applied* to guide the actions, to restrict the subsequent experiences of that group and its members.[15]

THE NATURE OF "FREE WILL"

In what sense is this "will" free?

First of all, this will is relatively free from the pressures of the outside world at any one moment, since it represents the stored outcome of the net's past now being fed back into the making of present decisions. Without effective feedback of its past, the net's behavior would be determined largely by outside pressures.

It would not steer, but drift, in both its external and internal arrangements.

As long as it has autonomy, the net wills what it is. It wills the behavior patterns (the "personality") that it has acquired in the past and that it is changing and remaking with each decision in the present. Thanks to what it has learned in the past, it is not wholly subject to the present. Thanks to what it still can learn, it is not wholly subject to the past. Its internal rearrangements in response to new challenges are made by the interplay between its present and its past. In this interplay we might see one kind of "inner freedom."

In its external actions, the net does what it can do. Its outward behavior will be the result of the interplay between the orders transmitted to its effectors and the feedback data about their results among the pressures of the outside world. In this type of interplay we may see a kind of external freedom for the net to continue to seek its goal.

Freedom in a feedback network could go further. A chess-playing machine could be constructed that would rapidly compute all admissible moves on both sides for two or three moves ahead, and choose the ones more profitable for its side, according to a schedule of values derived from the rules of the game. It would play mediocre chess. It could be improved, however, by giving it a suitable memory and additional circuits, so that it could learn to modify its play on the basis of experience. The quality of its playing would then depend largely on that of its experience. If all its past opponents were mediocre, the machine might never learn to play brilliantly. It would remain imprisoned by the limitations of its past. But it could be aided to play better by building into it a device to break or sometimes override the patterns learned from its past, giving the machine a chance for initiative and creativity.

This function of autonomous internal habit-breaking could be fulfilled by building into the machine a circuit breaker controlled by some "internal receptor," such as the flipping of a coin, that is, by some element of the network whose state would not altogether be determined by the previous states of other parts of the net.[16] Such a device could be so connected as to break up established connections or patterns of response from time to time, and to permit new combinations within the net to be formed, recorded internally in memory and carried through into external action.

The results might resemble those of a "spontaneous impulse." Like all "spontaneity," they would be subject to limitations. All they could do would be to replace an old or highly probable configuration by a new or less probable one, *provided that the elements for the new configuration were already present in the net* at the critical moment—even though they might have got there only through some input in the immediately preceding instant.[17] The range of possible new combinations would therefore also depend, among other factors, on the range of possible new input information from the outside world and on the effectiveness of the inner "habit breaker" in breaking up blocks against the integration of such new inputs with other data in the net. Apart from facilitating this inflow of new information, "spontaneity" could only bring out a wider flow of the potentialities already contained within the net.

This type of feedback network might provide an analogue for the problem of "free will." Such an analogy might be found in a machine combining a determinate store of memories with a randomly varying inner receptor in the circuits governing recall and combination. The random effects of the inner receptor (or "sudden impulse") are then limited by the statistical weight of alternatives as well as of critical recognition processes or patterns available from the stored past of the machine (its "personality"). Such a machine might act "freely," with initiative, but "in character."[18]

The analogy suggests that moral responsibility is conferred by the determinate, cumulatively learned element in the combination. To treat a man as "responsible" is to treat him on the assumption that his learning process has not been disrupted. Each of us is responsible for what he is now, for the personality he himself has acquired by his past free decisions.[19]

7

Political Power
and Social
Transactions

Will is related to *power*. Hardening a decision—that is, closing the decision-making system against any further messages by which that decision might possibly be modified—is insignificant in practice if there are no facilities to put it into effect against possible external resistance, or in any case, to put it into effect in such a manner as to make some appreciable difference to the ensemble of outcomes in the environment that would have occurred anyway.

THE INTERDEPENDENCE OF POWER AND WILL

Will is thus ineffective without power; but power is only randomly effective without will. Power cannot accomplish more than a succession of random impacts on the environment, unless there is some relatively fixed goal or purpose, some decision or strategic class or sequence of decisions, by which the application of power can be guided and directed. This guidance is indispensable for the sustained effectiveness of any system that applies power to its environments; and any such system must receive this guidance from its memories, its past decisions, its will, or somewhat more generally, from its character.

It is perhaps in connection with will and character—with the more or less stable inner program of a system, a person, an organization, or a government—that the concept of the power of any of these actors must be understood and that our present understanding of the problems can be most promisingly developed.[1]

The point may bear elaboration. In their internal relations, an individual or an organization may give preference to the value or behavior patterns that correspond most closely to the structure of the habits and memories they have acquired in the past. In their dealings with the outside world, individuals and organizations may try to act in "character" but they may not succeed in doing so. By the *power* of an individual or organization, we then mean the extent to which they can continue successfully to act out their character. Differently put, by power we mean the ability of an individual or an organization to impose extrapolations or projections of their inner structure upon their environment. In simple language, to have power means not to have to give in, and to force the environment or the other person to do so. Power in this narrow sense is the priority of output over intake, the ability to talk instead of listen. In a sense, it is the ability to afford not to learn.

Power in this narrow sense is conceived on the analogy of the hardness scale of minerals, of the scratching of glass by a diamond, or of the "pecking order" in a chicken yard.[2] It should not be confused with strength or growth. When carried to extremes, such narrow power becomes blind, and the person or organization becomes insensitive to the present, and is driven, like a bullet or torpedo, wholly by its past. The extolling of power by certain conservative writers, often in preference to its analysis, may not be unrelated to this pattern.

The simple view of power can be restated in probabilistic terms. Gross power can be thought of as the probability of a system acting out its internal program by imposing a given amount of changes upon the environment; and net power can be derived from this as the difference between the probability of these changes imposed on the outside world, and the probability of another critical or relevant amount of changes occurring in the inner structure of the system.

CONFLICT AND ITS MEASUREMENT

From this view of power, a concept of *conflict* can be developed that would, in principle, be susceptible to measurement. Conflict between two acting systems, A and B, could be measured in terms of:

1. the probable extent of *incompatibility* between their respective programs for the future; and

2. the probable *costs of avoiding collision* between them, wholly or in part. Each of these could be measured in terms of expected changes in the structure of the two acting systems; and the sum of these changes—perhaps expressed in measures of information—would measure the scope and intensity of conflict.

Incompatibility between two acting systems can be measured in terms of the sum of the probable changes—that is, the probable changes in inner structure—that would occur in System A, and of the changes in System B, if the inner programs of each of these two systems were carried out. The incompatibility of the proposed courses of two ships, or of two states, would thus be measured by the probable collision damage if both ships or governments stayed on their respective courses.

The costs of avoiding collision could then be measured in terms of the probable changes in the inner structure of System A, if its program, of course, were to be altered sufficiently to avoid collision, even though B's course remained unchanged; or in terms of the corresponding changes in the inner structure, and hence the program, of System B so as to avoid collision, even without any change in A's program; or in terms of the aggregate changes that would have to be distributed between the inner structures and future programs of both A and B if collision were to be avoided. How much change in terms of information patterns, as well as perhaps in terms of energy, strains, or internal organizational arrangements, would be required in either or both of two ships, or of two governments and bodies politic, in order to get them off collision course? Clearly, there may be in each case not one answer to this question, but a series of answers that should be susceptible to ordering.

It should be possible in many cases to state what would be the probable minimum costs of avoiding conflict if the most efficient of the possible patterns were selected.

An impending conflict would then be reckoned to be the more serious the greater the amount of expectable changes that this conflict, if it were joined, would impose upon the structures of one or both of the acting systems; and, also, the greater the changes that would be required in one or both of these systems if this conflict were to be avoided. Ships' captains and automobile drivers usually find it less trouble to change course than to let their vehicles run full tilt into collisions, but there are occasions when the physical or psychic changes required—the costs of effective steering—are prohibitive, and catastrophe results. In the case of governments, the costs of physical, social, or psychological change may appear even higher; and it may seem less "unrealistic" to political decision-makers to let their countries run into war—as they did in 1914, and as the Axis rulers did in 1939 and 1941—rather than to take the risks of the changes in policy, and internal programs and structure, that might still avoid the collision.[3]

None of the measurements or probability estimates proposed here, it should be clear, would exhaust the nature of conflict. Yet they might be useful in illuminating some of its aspects, and perhaps in bringing the entire problem of conflict somewhat nearer to more adequate rational and quantitative analysis in the future.

In fact, the current analysis of conflict and of power has been carried much further. There is a large and growing literature on power in the political and social sciences, to which the approach of cybernetics and the study of the problems of control systems may in the future offer some contributions.[4]

THE ANALYSIS OF POWER BY DAHL AND LASSWELL

Some of this literature offers interesting contrasts, as well as bridges, to the approach suggested here. Robert A. Dahl considers political power as measurable in two respects. The first is the ability to produce a change in the probability distribution of a class of repetitive outcomes; the second is frequency of association of an actor with outcomes that appear "successful" from his presumable viewpoint. Both tests tend to merge: if bills endorsed by Senator X have a markedly greater probability—that is, frequency—of passing, then Senator X may be thought to have caused this higher probability of their passing, or else he may be a political chameleon who seems influential to us only by the prudent timing of his rushes to the assistance of the victors.[5] Dahl's measurement of power would tend to eliminate the manifestly powerless: those unwilling to conform to the expectable majority, yet unwilling to change it. But among the seemingly powerful it becomes unambiguous only when other information is added, such as the timing of the senator's first endorsement of the bill; or each particular bill's autonomous probability of passing on grounds other than his endorsement (which is different from the frequency of passing of the possibly less popular bills he did not choose to endorse); or the senator's reputation among his colleagues and among seasoned observers for being either a political chameleon or else an independent leader.[6]

Lasswell and Kaplan define power as "participation in the making of decisions," with a "decision" defined as "a policy involving severe sanctions."[7] Such effective participation is founded upon an actor's control over any one or several of a range of "base values." These are things, relationships, or situations that are strongly desired by other persons who, in order to avoid sanctions or obtain rewards in terms of some base value, are willing to subordinate their behavior in regard to some less strongly desired "scope value" to the commands, hints, or even the anticipated wishes, of the power-holder.[8] Any value can serve as a base value, or as a scope value, or as both: control over wealth may be used to command respect, or control over respect may be used to win riches, or riches may be employed so as to make their owner still richer.[9]

None of the views given thus far, however, undertakes explicitly to measure the cost of power to the power-holder. They measure at best the narrowed choices of the ruled, but not the narrowed choices of their rulers. What, if anything, must Dahl's senator give up to improve the chances of passage of the bill he favors? What sacrifice, if any, did Lasswell's controller of base values have to make—in terms of matters valuable to himself—in order to obtain a certain amount of control over the scope values depending upon the behavior of another person? How many pecks or scratches did the chicken high in the pecking order have to take, and what was the cumulative wear on the diamond that scratched so many windowpanes?

In the draft of a new work, Dahl discusses the "opportunity cost" of influence to those who wield it. He makes this the basis of his concept of the "influence gap" that prevails ordinarily between the political influence an individual actually exercises and the influence he could exercise if he devoted all his disposable time and resources to this sole purpose. The same reasoning as for influence holds, of course, for power. These gaps between the actual and the potential influence and power of most people in ordinary times account, in Dahl's view, for the great potential instability of politics whenever crises or changed circumstances induce many persons to shift more of their resources to the pursuit of political goals.[10]

Questions of this sort may lead us to a concept of net rather than gross power, and to an appreciation of the power of the powerless. "The only way the white man in the South can keep the Negro in the ditch," Booker T. Washington is reported to have said, "is to stay in the ditch with him." A classic example of a similar process is given by the historian Arnold Toynbee, who reports that the Spartan conquerors of Messene found the continued subjugation of their Messenian Helots a full-time job that turned them into prisoners of their own victory and distorted permanently and fatally their politics and culture.[11] In our own time, the "price of greatness" is frequently mentioned by the governments of all great powers around budget time.

A concept of net power might define it as a difference—the difference between the amounts of changes imposed and changes accepted by the actor. The changes imposed are those imposed by the actor upon his environment, including changes imposed on relevant antagonists. The changes accepted are those accepted in the values and in the communication and action systems of the actor. If the first group of changes is measurable, at least in principle, then so should be the second group. The greater the difference between gross and net power, the greater might be the proportion of national income, and perhaps also the proportion of national attention in the mass media, and the proportion of time of political leaders, that must be allocated in order to maintain some given gross power position—at the expense, of course, of learning capacity and of whatever other adaptations or goals the society might have pursued. In this view there are, for any particular task or conflict, not two states of power for an actor—adequate or inadequate —but three: (1) comfortable, (2) tightly strained and partly overcommitted, and (3) bankrupt. Many nations and governments find themselves in the middle of these three categories, with corresponding sacrifices of their ability to steer their own actions and to remain masters of their fate—the very things the pursuit of power originally seemed to promise.

Dahl has opened the way to the quantitative measurement of power in certain types of situations. Lasswell has put power into the context of a network of other possible base and scope values, and has thus clarified its meaning over a wide range of conditions. Talcott Parsons, in his current work, is taking the next step. He is putting power into the dynamic context of a flow of interchanges between the main functional subsystems of society; and, in so doing, he has perhaps opened a path to a more fundamental reinterpretation of power than has been possible since the days of Hobbes and Locke.

THE GENERAL INTERCHANGE MODEL OF
TALCOTT PARSONS

Parsons distinguishes four functional prerequisites for any social system: (1) the maintenance or reproduction of its own basic patterns; (2) adaptation to the environment and its changes; (3)

the attainment of whatever goals the system has accepted or set for itself; and (4) the integration of all the different functions and subsystems within it into a cohesive and coordinated whole.

Each of these four main functions—pattern maintenance, adaptation, goal attainment, and integration—must be served to some extent by all subsystems of the society, but to each of the four basic functions there corresponds a major subsystem of the society, devoted to a markedly greater extent to activities serving that particular function rather than any of the rest.

The function of pattern maintenance is thus primarily served, in Parsons' view, by the subsystem of families and *households*, which are the child-rearing, labor-force-restoring and kin-group-preserving elements of the society. To the task of adaptation there corresponds in the main the *economy*, including its scientific and technological aspects. Goal attainment is mainly served by the *polity*, the political subsystem of the society, and particularly by the government. Finally, the integrative function is carried on to the largest extent by the subsystems of *culture*, including the social institutions of public and quasi-public education, religion, and mass communications.

Among these four main functional subsystems, which may be conveniently pictured as four corners of a square, there are six possible major flows of interchange, corresponding to the four sides and the two diagonals of the square, and connecting each of the four main subsystems with the three others. Thus, in the most simple case the households may be viewed as delivering labor to the economy, and eventually receiving consumer goods from it, in a flow of barter-type transactions of services for goods.

In a more advanced system, however, transactions are made more flexible and general by a social mechanism that is "narrowly specialized in generality." Such a mechanism we may call a *currency*. In this case, the currency is money, in the form of gold, paper, or checks; and it enhances greatly the flexibility of interchange and the ranges of choice open to the participants. Household members now exchange their labor for money wages; these wages are turned into consumer spending, either at once or after some delay; and for these consumer expenditures, goods are then obtained. There are thus two transaction flows in each direction, one in terms of the physical things and acts concerned, and the other in its generalized and flexible form in terms of the currency employed. The households put first labor, and later consumer spending, into the economy, while the economy furnishes to the households first money wages and then goods.[12]

The physical flows, and even more the flows of currency, lend themselves to quantitative study in terms of equilibrium analysis, familiar to economists, and their dynamic changes might perhaps be traced fruitfully with the aid of feedback models, which could be used to trace the cumulative shift of the system from certain levels and states to others.

Similar flows of transactions can be envisaged among all the other pairs of major subsystems. Those interchanges may also occur in two or more forms, once, directly in terms of the matters, facilities, or information conveyed or allocated, and second, indirectly through the reciprocal flows of symbols in terms of some "currency," analogous to the economy-and-households case.

SOME INTERCHANGES OF THE POLITICAL SYSTEM

As regards the political system, households may be considered in the most simple case as making specific demands upon the political system. They offer specific support to rulers who in turn use this support to make and enforce binding decisions of the kind desired by their supporters. Thus, in effect, specific support appears exchanged for dependable specific decisions, responsive to specific demands, in a political analogy to economic barter.

In a slightly more extended case, however, the government may assume a generalized leadership role—it assumes *responsibility*—far beyond this or that particular decision; and the population may give it general political *loyalty*—that is, generalized political support and trust—to some extent regardless of the greater or lesser popularity of any one of the government's policies. Far beyond the former political logrolling, or trading of favors, generalized support is asked for and given in terms of an only partly quantifiable "currency" of responsibility and loyalty, where the political system bestows formal protection, citizenship, or permission to reside, on countable numbers of persons, and demands loyalty and allegiance from every one of them above the age of infancy. (The currencies of citizenship and loyalty are not immune to disorders resembling those of severe inflation. Examples may be found in the wholesale grant of citizenship by the Roman Emperor Caracalla in A.D. 212, or in the "loyalty oath" campaigns characteristic of both ancient and recent periods of political anxiety.) More accurately, countable currencies, such as votes, may appear in additional interchanges of transactions, where political systems give the franchise to certain groups of citizens, and votes are then put by the citizens back into the working of the system.

In the interchange between the economy and the political system, the economy provides the political system with a stock of disposable resources, skills, and expectable levels of productivity and capabilities (for example, the economic "war potential") while the political system provides the economy with guarantees of certain dependable expectations (for example, the protection of the prevailing patterns of private or collective property). Using once again the monetary currency, the economy furnishes taxes to the political systems, and every householder may have to pay an income tax in his secondary role as a member of the economy. The political system, and particularly the government, in turn, furnishes the economy with the regulation and preservation of contracts and credit, and thus with an important part of the control of interest rates and high or low levels and configurations of investment.

Credit and investment policies thus appear, from the viewpoint of this theory, largely as political inputs into the economy—a relationship illustrated by the close connection between public policy and central banking. To the extent that such central banking functions are carried out by wholly private and unsupervised banks, or other financial organizations—or to the extent that such organizations share in these policies—it might be surmised that banks and

119

their executives have acquired a substantial amount of political power.

There is neither time nor space here to discuss all the remaining interchanges that could be traced among the main elements of the Parsons model. All that can be done here is to indicate the possible significance of this approach for a new and perhaps more adequate understanding of political power. The remarks that follow are based on the interim results of a continuing collaboration between Professor Parsons and the present writer. All weaknesses of this preliminary sketch must be, however, my own.

POWER AS A CURRENCY

From this perspective, power may be seen as the most important currency in the interchanges between political systems and all other major subsystems of the society.

Like other currencies, power can be quantified, although far more imperfectly so. Power cannot be counted exactly, but it can be estimated in proportion to the power resources or capabilities that are visibly available, such as the numbers of countable supporters, voters, or soldiers available or required in a particular political context. Levels of intensity of support, of morale, of skills and resourcefulness, insofar as any or all of these can be estimated, may also be taken into account by appropriate weighting, much as manpower budgets or estimates of military forces can be at least roughly calculated. On the other hand, these estimates of potential force may have to be modified or discounted in terms suggested by the work of Lasswell and of Dahl, that is, in terms of the control over the particular base values and scope values they afford, and in terms of the autonomous probabilities of the class of outcomes that are to be changed by the promised or actual application of power in the given situation.

Let us look at the problem from a slightly different perspective. From this viewpoint, power is the coordinated expectation of significantly probable *sanctions*, that is, of substantial shifts in the allocation of highly salient values. The expected capability to inflict sanctions, however, is closely related to the quantifiable capabilities discussed above. This concept of power, and of sanctions, is much wider than the concept of enforcement. Prestige is then to power as credit is to cash. And physical force—enforcement in the narrow sense—is to power as gold is to paper money or to savings accounts and checks.

These analogies are perhaps neither fanciful nor trivial. Banks often lend out several times as much money as they have received in deposits—since they rely on their customers not all demanding back their deposits at one and the same time. In much the same way, governments can promise to back with sanctions many more of their binding decisions, rules, and laws, and to do so against many more people, than any government could possibly do if all people started disobeying it at one and the same time.

Governments, like banks, thus base their operation on the fact that the popular expectations favorable to them—that one ought to leave one's money in the bank and that one ought to obey the law and the police—are highly coordinated, so that most individuals most of the time can count on everybody else to do as they do; while the opposite expectations—that one should withdraw money, or break the law—are usually quite uncoordinated, so that no individual could count on bringing down a bank or a government by starting a concerted run on the first, or a concerted revolution against the second.

The relations of gold to coins and paper money, of paper cash to all kinds of money, and of money to national income are all well known in quantitative terms. In the United States in early 1962, the national income was roughly $3,000 per inhabitant, while the gold reserve was only about 3 per cent of that amount, or roughly $90 per capita. The per capita amounts of cash (currency), and of all kinds of money, including instruments of credit, were between these two extremes, with about $160 and $810 respectively.[13] In economic life, it appears, a large amount of human cooperation, corresponding in its results to the national income, is generally carried on with the help of a smaller amount of monetary currency, and a relatively very small amount of gold. The last two mechanisms, gold and cash, thus appear as marginal aids or reserves rather than as the essence or substance of the wealth-producing process.

GOLD AND FORCE AS DAMAGE-CONTROL MECHANISMS

The political system, like the economic system, thus depends to a large extent on the fabric of coordinated expectations. Where and when this fabric is injured, particularly under conditions where strains and tensions are already present, coordination may break down in a spreading pattern, unless the damage is controlled. Gold bullion is the simple damage-control mechanism to stop a financial panic. If enough gold is available, all depositors could be paid off in full; and by making this prospect highly visible the timely arrival and public display of gold shipments may stop an incipient panic in its early stages.

Much in the same way, physical force with its instrumentalities—men with tanks and guns—is a damage-control mechanism of society. It can function as such a mechanism in situations where compliance with legal or political commands has broken down and where non-compliance or open resistance might start to spread. If a government, or an occupying army, commands enough physical force to kill or to coerce all persons disobeying its orders, it enjoys the most primitive kind of political solvency; and by displaying its possession of raw power it may forestall or stop in its early stages a possible chain reaction of disobedience or defiance. The tanks that President de Gaulle ordered into the streets of Paris on a critical day in early 1962 were thus analogous to the gold trucks conspicuously arriving at a bank threatened by a panic among its depositors. Each type of vehicle served to display its own kind of liquidity.

In less extreme crises of financial confidence, paper money or checks may suffice to preserve liquidity; and in less extreme political crises, demonstrations of political support through votes, public declarations, or demonstrations may be enough to preserve the fabric of confidence in the political process.

Politics, like economic life, depends on human cooperation, based on coordinated expectations. The essence of economic activity consists in the coordinated, flexible, and dependable division of labor— in the productive combination of human skill and effort with technological machinery and with resources drawn from the environment. It is this fabric of flexible, productive cooperation that produces wealth and the capacity to produce more wealth, rather than any amount of paper money, coins, or gold bars. To mistake gold for wealth was the mistake of a primitive school of economic thinkers in the seventeenth century, the bullionists.[14] A less crude error consisted in mistaking money—such as foreign currencies— for wealth, and caused some financial writers to predict, as they did in 1940, that Hitler's Germany was bound to suffer economic collapse within a few months because its gold and foreign-exchange reserves were close to exhaustion. In fact the history of our century has shown that when a large country lacked gold, other damage-control mechanisms often were used to keep its economy working.

Something similar is true of politics. The coordination of human efforts toward the attainment of some goal or goals, set by the society or by any of its subsystems, can be greatly accelerated or facilitated by the use of power, and at particular times and places to some extent by the use of force. This is particularly true on occasions when some more normal machinery of social control has broken down. Troops or police may have to control riots where communal habits of compliance with the law have broken down, or policemen may have to arrest the driver who has shed the habit of stopping at a red traffic light or the juvenile delinquent who is no longer amenable to the controls of school and family.

Yet in the main it is coordinated habits, rather than threats, that keep things moving. It is the traffic engineers and the drivers' habits, aided by the streets, signals, and cloverleaf crossings, that keep the traffic flowing; and the role of fines and arrests is marginal, though it may be by no means negligible. It is the families and schools that educate our children, and the role of truant officers and

123

policemen, though not negligible, again is marginal. At intersections where there are no traffic policemen, traffic still moves, though sometimes with more difficulty. Where there are no truancy laws, most children still go to school where this is expected in their culture.

A PERSPECTIVE ON POLITICAL THEORY

Power is thus neither the center nor the essence of politics. It is one of the currencies of politics, one of the important mechanisms of acceleration or of damage control where influence, habit, or voluntary coordination may have failed, or where these may have failed to serve adequately the function of goal attainment. Force is another and narrower currency and damage-control mechanism of this kind. Influence and the trading of lightly desired favors—the traditional "playing politics" of American colloquial speech—are still others. All these are important, but each is replaceable by the others, and all are secondary to what now appears from this perspective as the essence of politics: the dependable coordination of human efforts and expectations for the attainment of the goals of the society.

This line of thought might have some implications for the long-standing argument whether the coercive aspects of government may be expected to recede in the long run with the increase in wealth, education, and perhaps in cultural and social integration, so that these aspects of the state might eventually "wither away," as envisaged by Marx and Engels, and more recently and vividly by H. G. Wells; or whether coercive government will have to be with us in all eternity, or as long as mankind lives.[15] The perennial vision of an eventual noncoercive world, so attractive to many early radicals and revolutionists, has become somewhat embarrassing to the bureaucratic rulers of the Communist states.[16] Yet it may not be impractical in principle; and it might be ironic if the most appreciable advances in this direction should come to be taken in the constitutional democracies of the West.

SOME QUANTITATIVE IMPLICATIONS

The interchange model of the political subsystem, and of its relations to the other main subsystems of society, has quantitative implications. The volume of effective demands made on a government can be estimated, and so can the range of matters for which the government assumes overt responsibility, as well as the amount of relevant resources and capabilities at its disposal. For these and similar interchanges, limiting conditions or equilibrium relations may be found to hold as a first approximation. Specific decisions of the government may require a commensurate backing by specific interest groups; and general demands for loyalty may have to be balanced by generalized political support extended by corresponding numbers of the populace.

A more refined analysis might trace the cumulative changes in these reciprocal transaction flows. If households consistently put more labor into the economy than that which corresponds to the consumer goods they take from it, savings and investments may result. If the government assumes responsibility for more matters than are effectively demanded from it, we may have an easily recognizable type of traditional paternalism. If the government on the contrary refuses responsibility for matters that are urgently demanded—such as demands for a tolerable level of living, for health, education, social security, or employment—political alienation may result, with eventual effects on political stability. If most of the specific demands made on a political system are met with specific and adequately rewarding responses, a process of reinforcement learning may increase the number of persons feeling a generalized loyalty to that political community—such as a nation or a federation—or to its form of government, or even to the particular party, group, or person in power.

The rates of many of these processes could be measured or estimated, at least in principle. Savings rates and investment rates are familiar to economists. It might be possible to estimate very roughly the rise in the volume of political demands made upon the govern-

125

ment from the rate of social mobilization, that is, the rate at which people leave the seclusion of subsistence agriculture and village life, their control of tradition, and the isolation of illiteracy and lack of contact with mass communications. The rates at which people leave these conditions and enter the ambit of the money economy, wage labor, urban life, literacy, exposure to mass media, and partial acculturation to modernity have been in part measured, and average estimates for the over-all process have been derived from them.[17] Similarly, the rate at which the responsibilities of the government are expanding might be estimated from the expansion of the share of the gross national product passing through the government sector, as measured perhaps by the ratio of government revenue to gross national product in different years, or between different countries, ranging in non-Communist countries in the mid-1950's from 9 per cent for India to 47 per cent for Western Germany.[18]

More directly, from voting data and perhaps from sample surveys, estimates could be derived for the political integration ratio, that is, the proportion of persons extending generalized political support to the government or to political parties pledged to such support—including "loyal opposition" parties. Similarly, a political ratio could be estimated as the proportion of people denying generalized support to the country and its type of government, or supporting opposition parties repudiating any such generalized allegiance to the state and its regime.

The rates of political integration and alienation are, then, the ones at which the respective ratios change over time; and a rate and ratio of political neutralization for the indifferent, the apathetic, and perhaps for those paralyzed by cross-pressures, might also be estimated in order to complete this part of the picture.

A POSSIBLE PROGRAM

These few examples of ratios, and of their rates of change, must suffice here to indicate the possibility of eventually making the interchange model in its entirety quantitative and in part predictive. A part of this development would be the application of cybernetic concepts to the system, making larger and more explicit use of time variables as well as of probabilistic and statistical considerations. This would mean, among other things, the measurement or estimation of the extent and probable distribution of imbalances in the transaction flows; of the corresponding loads upon the equilibrating or adjusting mechanisms in the subsystems; of the lags, gains, and leads in their responses; and hence of the probable stability and future states of the entire system and its parts.

What has been sketched here implies a very large intellectual program. First of all, it will be necessary to complete the qualitative sketch for all six interchanges among the four major subsystems. This would include the explorations of such matters as legitimacy and its symbols, which may turn out to be currency in some of the interchanges between politics and culture, that is, between the goal-attaining and the integrative subsystems. After this qualitative development of the model, the quantitative steps just sketched would follow. Altogether this adds up to a large enterprise. Parts of it may be carried out soon, while others may take a long time. At this stage, however, even this bare sketch may have some use for purposes of orientation and perspective. It may suggest ways of looking at some problems of political theory here and now; and it may serve to outline at least some of the possibilities of political theory in the future.

Whether the next steps in the evolution of political theory will indeed come from the development of some form of dynamic interchange model no one can know. All we can say is that there is some promise in the prospect and that it seems very much worth trying.

8

Autonomy,
Integrity,
and Meaning

By now we have suggested, perhaps, the main elements of a theory of self-determination. All self-steering networks have three basic elements: receptors, effectors, and feedback controls. What "selfhood," or autonomy, such simple networks have is in their feedback controls. If these are destroyed or impaired, steering ceases and is replaced by drifting with external influences, or by coasting on momentum, or by some combination of these two. On the other hand, considerable damage to receptors or effectors may still permit steering as long as the feedback controls remain unimpaired. Even in simple systems of the type of self-steering automata, then, autonomy and integrity have operational meaning: they refer to their main feedback circuits and to their specific location and vulnerability.

AUTONOMY AND THE LOCATION OF CONTROL

More complex systems can change their goals, or "reset" their feedbacks, by interaction with information from their past, stored in particular memory devices. There, autonomy in the long run depends on memory. Where all memory is lost, where all past information and preferences have ceased to be effective, we are no longer dealing with a self-determining individual or social group, but with a self-steering automaton. The facilities for memory storage, and particularly the circuits of channels for recall, recombination, new storage, and reapplication of memory data are critical here. There is no will, no conation, without some operating memory. The will of individuals or groups can be paralyzed by destroying their stored past information or by disrupting its flow into the system.

Still more complex networks may include processes of "consciousness," of internal monitoring of certain states of the net. Where consciousness exists to a sufficient extent, there it becomes a determining element in the over-all behavior of the system. The critical locations for autonomy are then the monitoring channels and the pools of information fed by them, which together carry the function of consciousness. The autonomy of an individual, a corporation, a social group, a party, or a government can be destroyed, without impairing its memory, by depriving it of consciousness, that is, by cutting the flow of information about the state of its different parts, and disrupting those controls over its own parts that depended on such internal information. Where this has occurred, gross automatic feedback controls may still function, as may the recall and feedback of some remembered data from the past, but the over-all effect might at best resemble that of a man "punch-drunk," or walking in his sleep, or a victim of severe brain injury.

A society or community that is to steer itself must continue to receive a full flow of three kinds of information: first, information about the world outside; second, information from the past, with a wide range of recall and recombination; and third, information about itself and its own parts. Let any one of these three streams be long interrupted, such as by oppression or secrecy, and the society becomes an automaton, a walking corpse. It loses control over its own behavior, not only for some of its parts, but also eventually at its very top.

Or let the monitoring of internal data be unimpaired, let consciousness exist, but inhibit its feedback into the behavior of the system—create a consciousness at once informed and powerless—and you have the pattern of a man who feels himself "possessed," who watches his own behavior in helpless surprise, unable to change it. On the level of a society, this is the experience of Cassandra watching her city rush to its doom. In both cases, the crucial element is not the presence of a new intruder, but the absence or breakdown of an inner channel of control. The patterns of internal feedback channels—the flow charts of information—may be used to evaluate the performance of particular communication systems. They could well be used in the investigation of social groups; of business enterprises; of large research organizations; of parties or governments. In all such cases, they could help to reveal the location of control, the critical connections or configurations of the channels of information and decision that keep the system behaving as it does.[1]

In self-determination, the location of the "self" can be sought at the location of the feedback circuits of the relatively highest hierarchical type. These feedback circuits themselves are never located at a single point; rather they may have a broad topological basis. When the channels of the highest type are lost or disrupted, the self-controlling behavior of the system is lowered to the next lower level, and its more primitive remaining "self" must now be sought at the location of the relatively highest type of feedback circuits that continue to function. Thus, if there is consciousness, selfhood is effectively located at the system of self-monitoring feedback circuits that carry it. If consciousness is lost, selfhood may rest on memory and the feedback of its data into the making of decisions, which we have called "will." If memory is lost, what selfhood remains would have to be sought in the system of feedback channels that connect and control receptors and effectors; and if even this were lost, the last poor remnants of "self-determination" might have to be sought in the reflex arcs. Evidence of what happens in the progressive destruction of the central nervous system would seem to bear out this view.

One test of "functioning" on all these levels would be the capacity to learn, that is, to produce internal rearrangements in the system so as to bring about changes in its behavior. The "self" under this aspect lies in the channels carrying the highest type of learning process of which the system at each stage is capable.

Selfhood, in this view, appears not as a static property but as the functioning of particular sets of channels in a communications system. Self-determination may increase with the increase in the number, effectiveness of organization, and level of type of these sets of channels. This view might well fit in with the suggestion of A. J. Toynbee that growth in organisms and civilizations should be measured by their increase in self-determination rather than by gains in size or complexity.[2]

INTEGRITY AND DIGNITY

Integrity, then, means the unimpaired functioning of the *facilities* that carry the processes of self-determination. The "integrity" of any self-steering system can be impaired either by imposing a non-autonomous change on some of its channels—such as by cutting a channel or disrupting its connections—or by leaving its channels intact, but forcing such traffic loads on some of them as to disrupt their functioning. The familiar case of "overpersuasion" or "high-pressure methods," and the frequent resentment against them, may illustrate the point.

When we defend our "integrity," we are defending our autonomous learning equipment, the structure of the personality we have acquired. When we defend a man's *dignity*, we defend his ability to use his personality: we defend him against the imposition of an intolerably high speed of learning, an intolerable speed of changing his behavior—intolerable, that is, because incompatible with the continuous functioning of his self-determination, his autonomous learning. A man's dignity is impaired, in this view, if he is forced to do something that deprives him of autonomous control over his own behavior, and makes him instead into the

131

object of another process, a "means" instead of an "end," in Kant's terminology. The more sweeping the loss of self-control, the deeper the loss of dignity.

Dignity can be lost or impaired temporarily. It is the suspension of a process of self-determination that later may be resumed again. Integrity when lost or impaired implies a permanent change in inner structure. Autonomy then may be regained, but most likely it will not be quite the same as before.

Concepts of "human dignity," "integrity," and "worth of the human personality" have had an important political and emotional appeal. They have been incorporated in the United Nations Charter and in the United Nations Declaration on Human Rights. They have been criticized sometimes as being vague, but it appears now that they can be given explicit and operational meaning: respect for every man's right to learn at his own speed and with his own inner equipment, in an unbroken sequence of autonomous acts of learning, in which his own unique stored past and his own acquired preferences at every single step have at least some share in the outcome.

Dignity is nondisruptive learning. Integrity is undisrupted or unimpaired inner learning equipment. In catastrophes or catastrophic emergencies these may not always be compatible with survival. Where the power of events forces men to learn at breakneck speed, two types of casualties may result: the proud, stiff-necked men of the "old school" who "nail their colors to the mast" and kill and die; and the spineless opportunists who survive at the price of living for nothing but survival.

Perhaps the solution of the problem rests in an increase of inner facilities for continuous undisrupted adjustment at high speeds. To permit a high speed of learning and wide changes of behavior, without loss of inner structure and of an effective past, is perhaps best accomplished by increasing the inner communication channels in variety, flexibility, and numbers.[3] To ensure continued self-determination, integrity and dignity are not enough. In the language of religion, pride may mean death where a change of heart may mean survival. In less exalted terms, the best way to strengthen a communications system against the impact of large external changes may well consist in enriching its internal structure and its range of possible new configurations.

A CONCEPT OF MIND

Perhaps a concept of mind may be tentatively suggested from this very sketchy survey of patterns of communications. *Mind* might be provisionally defined as any self-sustaining physical process that includes the nine operations of selecting, abstracting, communicating, storing, subdividing, recalling, recombining, critically recognizing, and reapplying items of information.

Discrete items of information moving through a net may be called "messages." Physically, each message is a reproducible pattern of changes of state of parts of the net, regularly followed by determinate processes depending on that pattern.[4] Any message that has acquired a relatively stable association with an event outside the net, or with another message within it, may function as a symbol; and a mind may be considered a self-preserving physical process of communicating and manipulating symbols.

Such a physical process may include the production of novelty and of initiative. If information from events in the outside world is abstracted and stored analytically, that is, if information about some of its different parts or aspects is stored separately (such as remembering not only a whole bird but also separately its wings), then these may be separately recalled and recombined into new patterns that did not exist in the outside world (such as imagining Daedalus, a man with wings, three thousand years before the first airplane). To complete the production of *novelty*, this new combination of old elements must itself be matched or abstracted in the mind: a new image or symbol must be stored, *pertaining to the new pattern as a whole, regardless of its earlier combinatorial origin*.

Creativity is consummated in this second step. Both creativity and eclecticism recombine old elements, but while eclecticism does no more than that, creativity abstracts and reapplies new patterns from the combination. After this secondary abstraction and storage, the

133

new pattern may be applied to new recombinations within the mind, or more directly to new patterns of action by the effectors of the net. This latter result of novelty, the beginning of some new item of behavior, we may call initiative. More important instances of initiative may concern whole sequences of behavior, where novelty would lead to changes in more general patterns of preference and value, and thus change the probabilities of whole classes of future actions.

The combinatorial richness of possibilities for novelty may already be vast within a single mind, vaster still in any mind that is in communication with others, vastest perhaps in a mind that is *open*, that is, that applies *initiative to the widening of its range of intake* of information from what we may still believe to be an infinite universe. The more capable a mind is of such *creative learning*, the more new kinds of information can be reached by its self-steering, abstracting, and combinatorial powers, the more properly it may be considered inexhaustible. Indeed, the only way a mind has to keep itself inexhaustible may well be to keep itself open in this sense.[5]

As a physical process of communication, mind depends on a set of physical facilities, circular communications channels, and the like, which are themselves physical processes of a simpler order. In this sense, there is no mind without "body." Processes constituting mind may occur in the body of a single human individual, or in the communication among several individuals, and their stored records of past information, in a social group, organization, culture, or society. There are mental processes that go beyond the capacity of any single individual, discoveries that may be the result of mental teamwork extending over several generations.

If we are to ascribe tentatively any meaning to such concepts as "group mind," "collective personality," "ideology," or "configuration of culture," then the concept of mind we have outlined so far may suggest observations and experiments to test it. Where and how in such groups is past information stored? How is it recalled, how applied to new decisions? Is there *group* learning, that is, does new information lead to significant changes in the structure of the group? If answers to these and similar questions should confirm

134

the notion of social mind, or group mind, as meaningful, it would follow that there can be plural membership of minds—that one individual or smaller group can participate in several self-steering communications networks that generate and process thoughts.

The process we have called "mind" depends on a particular configuration of physical facilities, but it does not depend on the preservation of any one of these facilities, so long as it is replaced by another without destroying the configuration. In this manner stones are replaced in repairing a cathedral; wires and relays are replaced in a telephone exchange; cells are replaced in a living body; men live and die and are replaced in their functions in a society— all without necessarily destroying the relevant configurations of these structures. If the last two structures named, the individual and the society, are also carriers of processes of mind, then mind may be found to persist over any number of material changes in their parts—including conceivably the replacement of every single part— provided only that the configuration of the whole remains preserved. Mind, in this view, depends among other things on a particular configuration of "body," within which every single part may be replaceable.

If this view is accepted, the greatest practicable speed and scope of safe replacements of the material parts that carry the processes of a mind become a question of empirical fact. Whether more radical transfers of mind are possible from one set of physical facilities to another is not known at this time, but this, too, appears now as a question of fact. As such, it can only be answered by observation and experiment. It may be noted, however, that there seems to be no deductive principle of science or philosophy incompatible with such a possibility. All such transfers would have to occur by physical processes, from one set of physical facilities to another.

Some fairly complex patterns of information are already capable of being transferred from one set of facilities to another. The sound of a symphony may be transferred from the score to the orchestra, to the electric recording device and, finally, to the phonograph record; thus recorded it may "survive" its composer and the musicians of the orchestra. We cannot say whether a similar preservation by an agency in the universe would be possible for the vastly more complex patterns of a higher order, such as the patterns of living tissue or the patterns of mind, but in the light of today's science of communications there seem to be no deductive considerations opposing this possibility, as there would have been in the science of the nineteenth century. It is, of course, quite possible that such fundamental considerations will be discovered, precluding the possibility of preserving or transferring mind, or permitting it only within definite limits. All we can say now is that the question is again open, in a way in which it was not open thirty years ago.

Since mind depends on physical facilities, it necessarily depends on a process by which such facilities are preserved: it thus depends on *life*. Organic or social life can be called, from one point of view, a self-preserving, self-reproducing, and self-modifying autocatalyst, or more generally, a self-preserving, self-reproducing, and self-modifying structure of material processes.

If we imagine a complex machine, or set of machines, capable of self-repair and self-maintenance, capable of seeking out and utilizing sources of energy and materials in its surroundings, and even of producing and storing sufficient supplies of spare parts to build functioning replicas of itself, with lesser or greater modifications, then we should be imagining something close to life. It would be capable of metabolism, reproduction, and even under certain conditions—through chains of variously modified replicas more or less suited to their environments—capable of evolution guided in part by natural selection. Yet it would not have mind. Its incredibly complex processes would be wholly taken up with merely maintaining their own ensemble. It would use information from the outside world only for immediate purposes, to locate needed supplies. It would have no facilities for storing or recombining information, which are essential functions for mind.

No such machines could be built now—although parts of them could be designed, and trees in nature might come close to their performance—but our "experiment in imagination" may have served to clarify a basic relationship: life can occur without thought, because channel maintenance can continue without additional information feedbacks,[6] but mind cannot occur without life, because information feedbacks cannot continue without channel maintenance.[7]

Mind is not the configuration and maintenance of communication channels and storage devices; it is the pattern of information flow within them. Injury to channels may disrupt the information flow, much as bodily injury may damage mental health in people. Even with all physical facilities intact, information flow may be disrupted by the rise of "pathological" traffic patterns, much as traffic jams in a city may disrupt traffic flow without any change in the layout of the streets, or as certain undamaged electronic computers can be deadlocked or thrown into circular sequences of operations by feeding them problems involving paradoxes. In the latter case, traffic overloads may ultimately damage the channels: the disruption originates in the information flow and later spreads to the channels, resembling what has been called "psychosomatic illness" in man. Apart from such eventual "bodily" damage, it would appear that functional mental disturbances may occur in an individual in the course of his history without necessarily being preceded or accompanied by bodily changes.

Certain sets of channels, such as calculating machines, can be cleared of all information flow, and a new run can be started unaffected by anything that went before. Similarly, a city could be evacuated, and a new traffic pattern substituted for the old. Other communication systems, however, such as the human brain, are never wholly cleared; they function like "single-run machines." In fact, Norbert Wiener has suggested that the analogy to man should not be a calculating machine, but rather a single run on one.[8] This point may be put more generally: Mind is not a machine, but a run. It is a single-run pattern of information flow.

The nature of mind thus implies individuality. Two runs on two identical electronic calculators may go through different channels; or two calculators, exact copies of each other when fresh from the factory, may become different in operating characteristics if their memories acquired different data during their run, and remain different until they are cleared. If two minds operate over longer periods in a nonstandardized environment, it would seem almost impossible for them not to become different, even if their "bodily equipment"—their channel facilities—had been exactly identical at the outset. The development of personality differences between identical twins would seem to confirm this view.

What has been said about mind thus far may suggest certain perspectives. If mind can be defined as a particular class of physical processes, then there seems to be no compelling reason for assuming a priori that processes of this type are limited to mankind and to this planet. The more we understand the characteristics of the process we call mind, the more plausible it may appear that processes of mind and thought may exist more widely in the universe, as do such simpler physical processes as crystals, storms, and flames, or as catalysis or cyclical nuclear reactions, and as biological and ecological processes.

We may perhaps infer from the study of entropy that the occurrence of mind will be relatively rare: processes of a high degree of order are statistically less frequent than those involving less order (that is, more entropy). The known facts likewise suggest that nuclear processes are more frequent in the universe than chemical processes, chemical processes more frequent than biological ones, and processes of life more frequent than processes of mind.

Yet by these same considerations, mind, though relatively rare, may be expected to exist widely in the universe. Centuries ago, the work of Copernicus and Giordano Bruno gradually brought home to men's imagination the fact that in astronomy the earth was not unique but was one world among many. Today the thought that man's mind is not alone in the universe, but represents one type of mind among many—a thought long vaguely held in many versions by religious or philosophic intuition—may well be on the verge of entering the fabric of rigorous and scientific thought.

A second perspective follows from the first. If mind is the name of a class of processes, united by significant common characteristics, then there should exist certain regularities or "laws" applying under suitable conditions to all members of the class. We may therefore expect the existence of some "laws of mind," as we expect the existence of laws of gravitation or combustion or biology, and expect them to hold good for any kind of mind regardless of the particular physical processes that make up their internal channels of communication. Any mind, for instance, must have memory, autonomy, and individuality. It must somehow balance present information from the world outside it against stored information from its own past, recalled from memory. It cannot operate without preferences or values. What we have said above about selfhood, integrity, and dignity will apply to it; so will the connection between creative and pathological learning.

It is well known that much in the ethical norms of the world's great philosophies and religions is similar, or even identical. Such norms of ethics may now be compared carefully and critically with what we may call "laws of mind": testable, predictive statements about the probable self-destruction of minds following upon certain patterns of overt or covert behavior, both on the level of the individual and of the community or social group. We have long had concepts of "mental health" and "moral health" and some intuitions about their connection. It should eventually become possible to fill these general concepts with more specific structural detail, testable by operations, and of more general validity.

From the foregoing, it will appear that cybernetics could offer social scientists not merely an approach toward a theory of self-determination but also an approach toward a theory of *growth*, and particularly of the growth of minds—of human personalities and organizations. The two concepts of self-determination and growth are connected, and a recent philosopher of history has considered an increase in self-determination to be the most essential criterion of growth.[9] Nevertheless, it may now be suggested that the concept of growth should go further.

Growth should mean not merely the highest degree of unity and self-determination within the existing limits of a system (which Parsons might call "integration"); nor should growth mean a mere enlargement of the system with no change in its characteristics of performance (that is, growth in terms of Parsons' "pattern maintenance"). Rather, growth also should mean an application of learning

139

capacity toward an increase in openness, that is, an increase in the range, diversity, and effectiveness of an organization's *channels of intake* of information from the outside world (similar to Parsons' "adaptation"). Still further, growth should mean an increase in an organization's ability to make effective responses to its environment and to change this environment in accordance with its needs, that is, to fulfill Parsons' function of "goal attainment." And, finally, growth should mean an increase in the range and diversity of goals the organization is able to follow, including the power to change goals and to add new ones. The third of these tests of growth—openness and adaptation—has long been known by philosophers and religious leaders under the name of humility. The last, the ability of an organization to change its goals and not to remain a prisoner of some temporary goal, has sometimes been spoken of as the ability of man to avoid the "idolization of ephemeral institutions."[10]

SPIRIT AND MEANING

A final note may be added. The concept of "mind" is frequently associated in some vague manner with the concepts of "spirit" and of "meaning." From the point of view of communications, this empirical association may be spelled out in more specific terms. While no mind can operate without values, *spirit* denotes second-order value. It is the set of preferences about sets of preferences. A man, a people, or an epoch are among other things also systems; the *spirit* of a man, or a people, or an epoch is the configuration of rules according to which their value systems are patterned and operated. Spirit is related to values as strategy to tactics or as policy to operations. A change in "spirit" means, therefore, a strategic change in the patterns of behavior. And, under suitable conditions, such a change can be communicated.

As "spirit" deals with the internal patterns of a mind, "meaning" deals with those of its wide context. When we ask for the *meaning* of a series of events, we are trying to abstract some pattern from them that applies both to the continuation of this sequence itself and also to the continuation of another series of a higher logical type, that is, a series abstracted from a sequence of physical events on a larger scale in space or time, so that this second series comprises within itself the continuation of the first. More briefly, meaning is context. To recognize meaning is to recognize similarities in a series of one logical type, and to recognize further its extrapolation in another series at least one logical type higher.

Meaning, in this view, is physical position in a sequence of events. Meaning, therefore, is always relative. There are as many meanings as there are levels of logical type. And there are as many logical types as there are physical contexts, that is, objective sequences of physical events. In this sense "meaning" is real, whether perceived by an observer or not: the stone placed by a small boy on a railroad track may "mean" an accident in the context of the railroad, regardless of whether the boy was aware of this or not; at the same time it may mean a subsequent change in other contexts, such as in the education of the boy, or in his personality development, and these again need not depend on his knowledge, although they may be influenced by it.

Events may be "given meaning," therefore, in two ways: symbolically, by attaching symbols to them and to the context in which they already actually function; and physically, by putting an event physically into a context, that is, into some larger series of events. These two ways, of course, can, and often do, occur together. The first of the two, the imputing of context through symbols, is often useful for purposes of prediction. It is subject to error, and to verification, much as other statements about interactions among events in nature or society. The second—physical participation in a context—seems essential to the continued functioning of any mind: its stored information would become ultimately meaningless if it became closed to all further information from any context larger than itself.

It seems clear from our earlier description of minds that the imputation of meanings to events, and the verification of the imputed

141

meanings, are a major part of their activities; and, in the case of conscious minds, that this search for meaning will include their own position and their own activities in the context of their surroundings and in the even wider contexts of the universe they surmise or discover.

PART III

Communication Models and Political Decision Systems

9

Communication Models and Decision Systems: Some Implications for Research

The recent models of communication and control may make us more sensitive to some aspects of politics that have often been overlooked or slighted in the past. This, as we know, is a major function of models in their early stages. Well before they permit quantitative inferences, they may already aid in adding new criteria of relevance: What kinds of facts are now interesting for us, since we have acquired a new intellectual context for them?

This chapter will deal with such possible areas of relevance. It will survey a few of the concepts, and suggest a few of the questions that could be asked in political research, once we are willing to entertain the proposition that governments and parties—that is, political systems or networks of decision and control—are dependent on processes of communication and that they resemble certain aspects of man-made communication equipment to a sufficient degree to arouse our interest.

The first major point of resemblance is the dependence of all governments, as of all communication systems, upon the processing of information.

THE CONCEPT OF INFORMATION

Let us recall what was said about information in Chapter 5, and let us remember the distinction made by theorists like Norbert Wiener between communication engineering and power engineering. Power engineering, we saw, transfers energy which then may produce gross changes at its place of arrival. In the case of power engineering, these changes are in some sense roughly proportionate to the amount of energy delivered. Communication engineering transfers extremely small amounts of energy in relatively intricate patterns. It can produce sometimes very large changes at the point of arrival, or in the "receiver" of the "message," but these changes need in no way be proportionate to the amount of energy that carried the signal, much as the force of a gun shot need not be proportionate to the amount of pressure needed to set off the trigger.

Power, we might say, produces changes; information triggers them off in a suitable receiver. In the example just given, the most important thing was not the amount of pressure on the trigger, once it had reached the required threshold, but rather the fact that it was delivered at the trigger, that is, at one particular point of the gun. Similarly, the information required for turning the gun to a particular target need not be carried by any amount of energy proportionate to the energy delivered to the target by the gun. The important thing about information is thus not the amount of energy needed to carry the signal, but the *pattern* carried by the signal, and its relationship to the set of patterns stored in the receiver.

Generally, *information* can be defined as a patterned distribution, or a *patterned relationship between events*. Thus the distribution of lights and shadows in a landscape may be matched by the distribution of a set of electric impulses in a television cable, by the distribution of light and dark spots on a photographic plate, or on a television set, or by the distribution of a set of numbers if a mathematician had chosen to assign coordinates to each image point. In the case of photography or television the processes carrying this information are quite different from each other: sunlight, the emulsion on the photographic plate, the electric impulses in the cable, the television waves, the surface of the receiving screen. Yet each of these processes is brought into a state that is similar in significant respects to the state of the other physical processes that carried the image to it.

A sequence of such processes forms a *channel of communication,* and information is that aspect of the state description of each stage of the channel that has remained invariant from one stage to another. That part of the state description of the first stage of the channel that reappears invariant at the last stage is then the information that has been transmitted through the channel as a whole.[1]

THE RECEPTION OF INFORMATION

The effectiveness of information at the receiver depends on two classes of conditions. First of all, *at least some parts of the receiving system must be in highly unstable equilibrium,* so that the very small amount of energy carrying the signal will be sufficient to start off a much larger process of change. Without such disequilibrium already existing in the receiver, information would produce no significant effects.

This obvious technical relationship might have some parallels in politics. The extent of the effect of the introduction of new information into a political or economic system might well be related, among other things, to the extent of the instabilities that already exist there. A crude empirical expression of this problem is found in the perennial debate concerning the relative share of "domestic instabilities" versus "foreign agitators" in strikes or political disturbances. On a somewhat more sophisticated level, the problem reappears as the question of the role of ideas in inducing or prompting social change, and it has relevance for studies of the conditions favoring political reform or technological innovations in different countries. In all such cases a search for "promising instabilities," that is, instabilities relevant for possible innovation, should be rewarding.

RICHNESS OF INFORMATION AND
SELECTIVITY OF RECEPTION

The second class of conditions involves the *selectivity* of the receiver. What patterns are already stored in the receiver, and how specific must be the pattern of the incoming signal in order to produce results? A simple example of this problem is furnished by the relationship of lock and key. How many tumblers and notches have been built, let us say, into a particular Yale lock, and what restrictions do they impose upon the distribution of notches on any key that is to turn it? Clearly, the effectiveness of any key in turning a particular lock depends only slightly on the energy with which it is turned (beyond a minimum threshold), and far more on the correspondence of the configuration of its notches with the configuration of the tumblers in the lock.

This crude example shows that there is a measurable difference between locks that are simple and those that are elaborate. Simple locks may have few tumblers in them, and may be turned by a wide variety of differently patterned keys, as long as each of these keys corresponds to the others and to the lock at the few relevant points determined by the distribution of the tumblers. A more elaborate lock will have more tumblers and thus is likely to impose more restrictions on the patterns of keys able to turn it. The selectivity of receivers, then, is related to, among other things, the richness and specificity of information already stored in them.

Similarly, there is a measurable distinction between the richness of information contained in different images. The amount of detail that a photographic film can record is limited by, among other things, the fineness of the grain. Reproductions of photographs in ordinary newspapers are made with the help of screens with only a few hundred lines to the inch, and are thus much poorer in detail and cruder in appearance than photographs. The same is true of pictures in television, and of details of the human voice in telephoning or recording. In all these processes details can be lost and the amount of lost information can be measured. Altogether a large amount of thought and experience has gone into the measurement of information, of the possible losses of information under certain conditions, and of the carrying capacity of certain communication channels in terms of quantities of information.

THE MEASUREMENT OF INFORMATION AND THE FIDELITY OF CHANNELS

The upshot of all this work has been the emergence of information as a quantitative concept. Information can be measured and counted, and the performance of communication channels in transmitting or distorting information can be evaluated in quantitative terms. Some of these measurements in electrical engineering have reached high levels of mathematical sophistication.[2]

Other methods of measuring information may be simpler. Information could conceivably be measured in an extremely crude way in terms of the percentage of image points transmitted or lost on a line screen of a given fineness, or in terms of the number of outstanding details lost as against the number of outstanding details transmitted; or perhaps in a slightly more refined way, information could be measured by the number of such details lost or transmitted in terms of their probability in the context of the set of details already stored in the receiver.

The fact that social scientists may have to use some of the cruder rather than the more refined methods for measuring the amounts of stored or transmitted information should not obscure the importance of being able to measure it at all. In the investigations of Gordon Allport and L. J. Postman on the psychology of rumor, quantitative measurements of information were used to good effect: a subject was shown a picture for a short time and then told to describe it to a second person who had not seen it. The second person then had to tell a third, and so on through a chain of ten, and the amount of details lost or distorted at each stage was recorded. When each successive stage of retelling was plotted along a horizontal axis, and the number of details retained correctly were plotted vertically, the result was a curve of the loss of details that paralleled strikingly a well-known curve of the forgetting of details by individuals in the course of several weeks. In both cases the details were flattened and sharpened, that is, simplified and exaggerated, and they were assimilated by distortion to the prevailing opinions and cultural biases of the individuals carrying the memories or rumors.[3]

INFORMATION AND SOCIAL COHESION

If we can measure information, no matter how crudely, then we can also measure the cohesion of organizations or societies in terms of their ability to transmit information with smaller or larger losses or distortions in transmission. The smaller the losses or distortions, and the less the admixture of irrelevant information (or "noise"), the more efficient is a given communications channel, or a given chain of command.

If we think of an ethnic or cultural community as a network of communication channels, and of a state or a political system as a network of such channels and of chains of command, we can measure the "integration" of individuals in a people by their ability to receive and transmit information on wide ranges of different topics with relatively little delay or loss of relevant detail.[4]

Similarly, we can measure the speed and accuracy with which political information or commands are transmitted, and the extent to which the patterns contained in the command are still recognizable in the patterns of the action that are supposed to form its execution.

The difference between a cohesive community or a cohesive political system, on the one hand, and a specialized professional group—such as a congress of mathematicians—on the other hand, consists in the multiplicity of topics about which efficient communication is possible. The wider this range of topics, the more broadly integrated, in terms of communications, is the community, or the "body politic." In traditional societies this range of topics may be broad, but limited to topics and problems well within the traditional culture; the ability to communicate widely and effectively on nontraditional topics may be relevant for the cohesion and learning capacity of peoples and political systems in countries undergoing rapid industrialization.

All this is not to say that the measurement of losses in the transmission of information on different ranges of topics is the only way in which the predisposition for political or social cohesion can be measured. Approaches in terms of interlocking roles and expectations might be another way. It is suggested, however, that the information approach offers an independent way of measuring basic cohesion, however crudely, and that it can do so independently from the current political sympathies of the participants. Such sympathies or conflicts might show up sharply in the execution of controversial commands, such as, let us say, between Northerners and Southerners in the United States in the 1850's and again during the Reconstruction period, or between nationalists and Social Democrats in Germany before 1914. Measurements of the accuracy and range of topics of information transmitted in a state or a political or social group would also show the extent and depth of the remaining area of effective mutual communication and understanding among its members. In this manner we might gain important data for estimating the chances for strongly unified behavior of the political system, as well as of the underlying population, in later emergencies.

FACE-TO-FACE COMMUNICATION NETWORKS AND LEGITIMACY SYMBOLS

If many studies of politics have stressed *power,* or enforcement, it should now be added that information precedes compulsion. It is impossible to enforce any command unless the enforcing agency knows against whom the enforcement is to be directed—a truism that has given much delight to readers of detective stories. The problem becomes more serious where enforcement is to be directed against a significant number of personally unknown members of an uncooperative population, as in situations of conspiracy, political "underground activities," resistance to military occupation, or guerrilla warfare.

151

Similarly, information must precede compliance. It is impossible for anyone to comply with a command unless he knows what the command is. In this sense, a "legitimacy myth," discussed by some writers, is an effective set of interrelated memories that identify more or less clearly those classes of commands, and sources of commands, that are to be given preferential attention, compliance, and support, and that are to be so treated on grounds connecting them with some of the general value patterns prevailing in the culture of the society, and with important aspects of the personality structures of its members. Yet, even where such legitimacy beliefs are effectively held in the minds of a large part of the population, its members must have ways of receiving the commands rapidly and accurately if they are to act on them. Governments-in-exile or leaders of underground movements during World War II not only had the task of maintaining their status as legitimate but also the task of maintaining an actual network of communication channels to carry the essential two-way flow of information.

In evaluating the political significance of this fact, two mistakes may easily be made. The first mistake consists in overestimating the importance of impersonal media of communication, such as radio broadcasts and newspapers, and underestimating the incomparably greater significance of face-to-face contacts. The essence of a political party, or of an underground organization, consists in its functioning as a network of such face-to-face contacts. These face-to-face contacts determine to a large degree what in fact will be transmitted most effectively and who will be the "insiders" in the organization, that is, those persons who receive both information and attention on highly preferred terms.

The second mistake might consist in considering legitimacy myths or symbols in isolation from the actual communications networks, and from the human networks—often called "organizations," "machines," "apparatus," or "bureaucracy"—by which they are carried and selectively disseminated. During World War II, several governments-in-exile continued to be considered legitimate by most of the population of their respective Nazi-occupied countries. The decisive failure of Nazi legitimacy beliefs to gain wide acceptance in those countries was followed by the growth of underground resistance organizations staffed to a significant extent by Communists or Communist sympathizers. The initial opportunities for Communist participation in this underground depended in part on the legitimacy beliefs that permitted it; without these beliefs, which transferred some of the prestige of the French or Czechoslovak republic or the royal government of Norway to all participants in the underground, the Communists would have had to carry on separate and weaker underground activities. While the governments-in-exile often retained control of radio broadcasts from London, the political outcome of the underground period depended in considerable degree upon the actual position of Communists in the underground network of face-to-face contacts and decisions. Where that position had been strong, the governments or National Committee in exile had to deal with a far stronger Communist organization and influence than the legitimacy beliefs of the country in themselves would have led one to expect.

Without widespread and favorable legitimacy beliefs, a face-to-face communications network is exceedingly hard to build, as, for example, the failure of the Quisling group in Norway has demonstrated. Without effective control of the bulk of the actual face-to-face communication networks, on the other hand, the nominal holders of the legitimacy symbols may become relatively helpless vis-à-vis those groups that do have this control. The Polish government-in-exile, as well as the group of President Beneš of Czechoslovakia, found themselves with far less power at the end of the war than their symbolic status of legitimacy would have suggested.

Perhaps we may suspect, accordingly, that it is rather in the more or less far-reaching *coincidence* between legitimacy beliefs and social communication channels that political power can be found. Thus, when we speak loosely of the "manipulation of political symbols" we might do well to distinguish sharply between their manipulation in a speech or book, and the manipulation of those human and institutional chains of communication that must carry and disseminate these symbols and all other information and that are crucial for the functioning of political power.

The frequent superiority of networks of face-to-face contacts over either isolated legitimacy symbols or even impersonal media of mass communication can be illustrated by two examples. The Democratic party in the big cities in the United States has shown persistent electoral strength despite the fact that it is notoriously weak in newspaper support; however, it is relatively strong in face-to-face contacts on the ward level. The second example was demonstrated to television viewers in the United States during the presidential campaign of 1952: the discrepancy between the amount of publicity and symbolic reputation attracted by Senator Estes Kefauver in his campaign for the Democratic presidential nomination, and his inability either to overcome the coldness or hostility of the "insiders" and "machines" of the Democratic party or to attract really substantial support without their aid.

As these examples indicate, the discrepancy between the "newspaper strength" of a leader or candidate and his real strength, not at the "grass roots" but *at the decisive middle level of communication and decision,* may be a promising field for comparative political research.

THE "MIDDLE LEVEL" OF COMMUNICATIONS
AND COMMAND

The strategic "middle level" can perhaps be defined somewhat more closely. It is that level of communication and command that is "vertically" close enough to the large mass of consumers, citizens, or common soldiers to forestall any continuing and effective direct communication between them and the "highest echelons"; and it must be far enough above the level of the large numbers of the rank and file to permit effective "horizontal" communication and organization among a sufficiently large portion of the men or units on its own level. From this point of view, there are usually too few generals to receive direct information from, or give direct orders to, the large mass of private soldiers; and there are too many sergeants and lieutenants in most armies to permit their effective organization for political purposes. On both counts, colonels seem to be most favorably placed for political intrigue; and in countries where officers are traditionally permitted or expected to engage in politics, colonels are indeed the most prominent group. By the same consideration, smaller countries would offer chances of promising intrigue to professional officers from the rank of colonel down, usually to the level of captain; and larger countries, let us say above the size of interwar Poland, would offer political opportunities almost exclusively to officers from the rank of colonel up, including generals. Everywhere, however, colonels emerge as the strategic "middle-level" group, provided, of course, that the legitimacy beliefs prevailing in the country permit their political or conspiratorial activity at all.

The "middle-level" concept permits perhaps a relatively simple approach to the short-run analysis of governments, parties, or political decision systems, where time and resources for research are limited. In all such systems we might look for the crucial middle-level group—or rather upper-middle-level group—of between fifty and five hundred persons without whose cooperation or consent (or, of course, replacement) very little can be done in the decision system. In the army these are the colonels; in the government, perhaps the permanent undersecretaries in the ministries, and the heads of personnel departments, such as, for example, Juan D. Perón in the Argentine War Ministry in 1943; in the police force, the police chiefs of the major districts or cities (provided that the police has become at all politicized to the extent, for example, of the German Weimar Republic or of most Latin countries); in mass communications, the managing editors of the largest papers; in party politics, the secretaries or "bosses" of important regions or cities, and the leaders of important pressure groups, and so on. In part, these persons may be expected to reflect the influence of others who put them into their positions. In part, they will themselves be agents shaping the course of events in terms of their desires. Their crucial characteristics are two: (1) Without them, taken all together, little can be done, and particularly, little can be changed. (2) Each of them must count with the group of his peers, with whose support he can win easily but against whom he is nearly powerless. Together, they form a small universe of political possibilities that can be studied intensively or that can perhaps be scanned by listing the "middle-level" jobs and men, and selecting a random sample of one-half or one-fifth or one-tenth for intensive investigation. It might be worthwhile to try this approach for one or two countries, and compare the results of complete "middle-level" inventories with the results of 10 per cent or 20 per cent samples taken from that level, so as to find the smallest sample size that still offers a fair chance of being representative of the system.

It should be noted that the persons on this strategic "upper-middle-level" usually receive very little publicity. They are the "men behind the scenes" in the sense that they are the "men who do the work" of making, permitting, and executing the largest number of strategic decisions. To investigate this group systematically by structure and personnel requires us once again to supplement the study of symbols and publicity, or of general "elites," by the study of samples of an unpublicized but crucial set of persons.[5]

By way of caution it should be added that any study can at best illuminate a political decision system as a currently going concern. It would completely ignore any fundamental malfunctions or long-run changes so long as they had not penetrated the "upper-middle-level" of decisions. A study of "upper-middle-level" personnel might have told us much in 1788 about the probable behavior of the Bourbon regime in France, not merely in terms of what Louis XVI might have liked to do but also in terms of what he could reasonably hope to get done by his important courtiers and officials; but it would have told us little about the government of France only five years later, in 1793. To say anything relevant about the latter problem, an entirely different kind of study would have been needed.[6]

A related set of problems arises in the study of underdeveloped countries that have been passing through a series of less drastic, but still considerable, changes since World War II. In many such countries a political elite of "transitional" personality types has arisen. Their entry into the crucial middle-level positions in the communication and decision networks of their countries has offered fascinating topics of study for political scientists. The rise in many

156

underdeveloped countries of vernacular-speaking politicians, re-cruited from provincial regions rather than from the capital, might be usefully studied under this same aspect.[7]

THE INTERNAL INTELLIGENCE FUNCTION AND CONTINUING LEADERSHIP

If politics requires a machinery of enforcement, and a set of habits of compliance, then politics is impossible without a flow of information to those who are expected to comply with the commands. These two streams of information can be taken for granted in what has been called "normal" politics, that is, in politics in a Western European state during the late nineteenth century, in times of peace, with no immediate danger of war or domestic political upheaval. Under these conditions, common beliefs about legitimacy would be sufficiently widely held to identify clearly most laws and most law-breakers, and to ensure cohesion within the law-enforcing agencies.

A large part of politics during the last fifty years, however, has not occurred in such "normal" situations, but rather under conditions of crisis, emergency, revolution, war, and extreme factional conflict. Under such conditions it has sometimes been very difficult for enforcing agencies to know against whom to direct their force, or to know the consequences of particular commands given, or the consequences of attempts to enforce them.

Indeed, under such conditions it has often been difficult for an enforcing agency to know which members of its staff, or which of its subsidiary organizations, were still reliable. Purges in dictatorships and "loyalty tests" in democracies are attempts to obtain and verify such information when reliability is no longer taken for granted. At this stage the enforcing agencies believe that they can rely on the loyalty of individuals who carry out the investigations essential for the purges or the tests. History is replete with instances, however, where the armies, police forces, totalitarian parties, or secret police organizations have themselves become unreliable. The best known cases of this sort are the revolts of the Praetorian Guard in Imperial

157

Rome; but the cases of the Russian police chief H. G. Yagoda, of the French police chief Jean Chiappe, of the Argentinian police chief General Domingo Martínez, and of the chief of the German Intelligence Service, Admiral W. Canaris, all occurred between 1935 and 1945 alone; and the revolt of the French O.A.S. in Algeria, and its terror action in France itself, demonstrated the recurrence of the pattern in early 1962.

In such situations of unrest, governments face not only a substantive problem of ensuring the retention of desirable loyalties or values by their officials but also a technical problem of obtaining a continuous flow of accurate information about their behavior. Up to a point, the question "Who watches the watchmen?" is answered by "Their peers, and the population at large, as long as both are sufficiently motivated by established legitimacy beliefs." If this problem arises, however, in a society in which most persons are political opportunists who care little about legitimacy, and rather wish to rush to the assistance of the victor, the problem turns into a calculation as to how many men may change their political alignments to what extent within a given time. In a country or period in which legitimacy beliefs are weak, the time element in political realignments, conspiracies, and purges may thus be most important. Even where legitimacy beliefs are well established, potentially insubordinate sub-leaders may have to be demoted slowly and by honorific stages—as has at times been done in the Soviet Union—so as to give their followers time to disassociate themselves from them with the least loss in their own status.

In addition to the failure of the enforcement agency to keep itself informed about the probable behavior of its own officials or subsidiary organizations, political enforcement may fail because of a failure to predict correctly the reaction of the population to it. Under this aspect, the history of revolutions appears to a significant extent as the history of internal intelligence failures in the governments that were overthrown. Thus between 1789 and 1792 the King of France seems to have misjudged or disregarded the probable reaction of almost every major element of the French population. He misjudged the reaction of his creditors who refused to lend him more money;

the reaction of the Paris Parliament that refused to register his new tax decrees; the reaction of the French nobles who refused to pay their share of taxes; the reaction of the representatives of the Third Estate who defied his command by their Tennis Court Oath; the reaction of his troops who proved unreliable against the Parisians; the reaction of the Parisians who stormed the Bastille; and the reaction of the population of the little town of Varennes who stopped his flight and forced him to return to the custody of the Legislative Assembly. Perhaps most fatally of all, he misjudged the reaction of the French people to the defeat of their armies in a foreign war: instead of surrendering to the Duke of Brunswick, many Frenchmen supported the Revolution more strongly, even to the beheading of their monarch.

What occurred dramatically in the French Revolution occurs less spectacularly every day in politics. Everywhere political decisions depend for their effectiveness on the correctness with which the relevant reactions to them have been predicted. Lacking such information, they are apt to produce results quite different from those intended, and all attempts at enforcement are then apt to make the danger of an eventual breakdown worse.

Detailed studies of leadership are indicating the very large extent to which the emergence of a leader and his continuance in that role depend on his ability to anticipate correctly the likes and dislikes of his followers, and hence their probable reactions. The most important single function a leader must perform, according to these studies, is to "maintain his acceptability with the group." This maintenance of acceptability is bound up primarily, at least in most situations, with the ability to anticipate explicitly or intuitively the configuration of their reactions as a group: Will this or that policy unite them, or will it split the group and drive out some of its members?

Leadership in the group, as well as in the state, thus depends to a very significant extent upon something that we may call the "internal intelligence function." Even in warfare the first thing a general must know is not the numbers and capabilities and intentions of the enemy, but the numbers, capabilities, and reliability of his own troops. To misjudge the strength and intentions of an enemy may be very serious, but to order into battle nonexistent armies, or armies in rebellion, is apt to be fatal.

The channels and institutions by means of which a government or a party obtains and uses information concerning its own constituency and personnel, and the efficiency with which such information is collected, applied, and perhaps stored for future use in records, or in the memories of men, are all promising objects of comparative political studies. In democracies, such studies may deal with the comparative effectiveness of hearings, opinion polls, "grass-roots" politics, pressure-group activities, and the like. In dictatorships, or under conditions of war or near war, such studies may throw some light on the ability of particular political regimes or organizations to appraise their own internal resources and obstacles, and to steer their own behavior accordingly.

VOLUNTARY IMITATION AND MORALE: THE CONCEPT OF MIMESIS

A counterpart to the ability of leaders or rulers to get and use information from the populace is the willingness of the population to accept information and suggestions, rather than mere commands, from its rulers. This problem touches upon the general setting of the political process.

In estimating the political capabilities of a government, we often ask: Does the population accept messages and orders from the government? Do they follow such orders with little or no supervision, and do they lend them active support above and beyond mere compliance?

Now, however, we can add a further question, asked by some social scientists: Are the rulers accepted as models or reference groups by the ruled? This question has been applied to the breakdown of empires by A. J. Toynbee: Does the population *imitate voluntarily* the behavior patterns demonstrated or suggested by its rulers? In Toynbee's view, buttressed by a number of historical examples, the failure to imitate occurs long before the failure to obey, and is predictive of the latter. In his terminology, expanding civilizations are characterized by ruling minorities who are able to "charm" the masses of the population into imitating them. With the failure of this voluntary imitation, or "mimesis," the "creative minority" turns into a "dominant minority," the Pied Piper turns into the drill sergeant, and charm is replaced by awe and fear. In Toynbee's view, this change represents an early but major step in the internal breakdown of states and civilizations.[8]

Questions about voluntary imitation and compliance have a clear bearing on politics, and they make it possible to use the very considerable literature on morale studies,[9] both as to methods and results, for studies of the behavior of political systems.

DECISION SYSTEMS AND INFORMATION-CARRYING CAPACITY

Another line of research interest might deal with the ability of decision-makers to predict the kind and intensity of the reactions to their decisions, both by possible opponents and by supposed passive bystanders, or supposed supporters or subordinates. We cannot find out, of course, except after the event, how well a politician or ruler has anticipated such reactions, but we can find out well in advance of the event what efforts were made to collect the relevant information, through what channels it was brought to the point of decision, and what chance the decision-makers had to consider it at all.

In this sense we may be able to identify political decision systems that are equipped with adequate facilities for the collection of external and internal information as well as for its transmission to the points of decision-making, and reasonably well equipped for its screening and evaluation before the decisions are made. Such systems will be no means be infallible, but they will have at least a chance to use the information they need. On the other hand, we may be able to identify decision systems where this is not the case, and where either the collection, or the transmission, or the screening

161

and evaluation of the information has broken down, or has never been adequately developed. Such systems perform well on occasion, but in the long run the odds should be heavily against them.

More generally, this line of thought suggests that *communication overload* or *decision overload* may be a major factor in the breakdown of states and government.[10] Similarly, attention overload may be an element in the troubles of our driven and often shallow mass culture with its spot news, capsule reviews, and book digests. Again, attention and communication overload may force a frantic search for a privileged status for their own messages upon many people in a prosperous and economically equalitarian democracy. Unless its citizens turn into "status seekers," they must fear that they will lack the social status—that is, the priority accorded in the social system to the messages they send—and that their attractive, interesting, or influential contemporaries will simply have no time to pay attention to them. If this is true, an economic democracy may turn into a jungle of frustrated snobs, starved for individual attention. The concept of communication overload may then be a key to the understanding of this cruel reversal of democratic hopes, and eventually to the amelioration of the underlying maladjustment.

Learning Capacity and Creativity in Politics: The Search for Cohesion and Values

Another kind of interest suggested by the stress on information might deal with the resourcefulness or "creativity" of political decisions. In Toynbee's analysis, referred to above, the failure of populations to imitate their rulers is viewed as a consequence of the failure of these rulers to invent and execute an effective new "response" to some new "challenge" presented to the state or the society by its environment. In this view, Greek valley farmers were challenged by invasions of plundering herdsmen from the hills, and responded to this challenge by the invention of the city-state. Later, the Athenians, when confronted with the "Malthusian challenge" of increasing numbers on insufficient soil, responded with the inventions of the "Solonic Revolution": oil culture and long-distance trade.

As we saw in our earlier discussion in Chapter 5, the ability of any political decision system to invent and carry out fundamentally new policies to meet new conditions is clearly related to its ability to combine items of information into new patterns, so as to find new solutions that may be improbable in terms of their likelihood of being discovered, but relevant once they are discovered and applied.

This ability to produce novelty, and to recognize relevant new solutions once they have been found, seems related to the combinatorial richness of the system by which information is stored, processed, and evaluated. This *creative intelligence function* in the society is not directly related to either enforcement or compliance, but it forms an essential aspect of the intellectual resources on which the survival of the political or social system may depend.

In addition to being invented and recognized, new solutions and policies must be acted on, if they are to be effective. Material resources must be committed to them, as well as manpower and attention. All this can be done only to the extent that uncommitted resources are available within the system. Such uncommitted resources need not be idle; what counts is the ease or probability with which they are available for unexpected recommittment. Here we may recall the concept of "learning capacity" from our earlier discussion of models. We may describe the "learning" of a system as any structural change within that system, which causes it to give a different— and thus possibly more effective—response to a repeated external stimulus. If learning thus consists in internal structural changes followed by changes in external behavior, the *"learning capacity"* of a system is related to the amount and kinds of its uncommitted resources. The larger the proportion of uncommitted to committed resources within a system, the greater the set of new kinds of behavior it can learn. Furthermore, the greater the set of uncommitted resources within a system or organization is, compared to the set of responses needed to solve a particular problem, or to meet a particular situation or challenge, the more adequate the learning capacity of the system will be to meet that challenge, that is, the greater will be its probability of actually meeting it within the available limits of time.

In a qualitative sense, many of these considerations are well known. Toynbee speaks of challenges as "adequate" or as "excessive," but gives no quantitative definitions of these terms. We all speak of the "flexibility" of organizations or governments, but this crude mechanical image is not very helpful for either structural or quantitative analysis. The notion of the "set of uncommitted resources," in contrast, permits questions about their number and dis-tribution, their proportions to the rest of the system, or the load likely to be imposed upon it. It has become quite possible to estimate in advance the problem-solving capacities of an electronic calculator, and even to do so for different stages of its run after a lesser or greater part of its facilities has become loaded up with other information. It should be possible to estimate, although far more roughly, the problem-solving capacity of a government or a society, as well as to estimate its ability for *innovation* (as distinct from invention)—that is, its capacity to put a new solution actually into operation. Questions of this ability to invent and to innovate, and of the "propensity" to do so, have long interested students of economic growth. Their applications range from the technical assistance program to the capacity of China, Japan, and Argentina to produce atom bombs by 1970. In their political applications, questions of innovating capacity should be of no less interest to students of political stability and of political power.

THE STRUCTURE OF FACILITIES FOR SOCIAL LEARNING

All these processes can be studied either in structural or in quanti-tative terms. From the viewpoint of structure, the study of existing facilities can lead us to estimate possible or probable performance. Thus the probability of novelty and the capacity for learning de-pend to some extent on the size of the ensemble of possible recom-binations of separate items of information, and material internal re-sources. In this sense learning capacity in organizations depends on the range of internally available recombinations of knowledge, man-power, and facilities; and these ranges should increase with the effectiveness of dissociations, that is, the extent to which information processing and storing facilities—and hence items of knowledge—could be subdivided into ever smaller independent pieces.

Unqualified, this statement would be a dangerous half-truth. For the smaller we make the items of information, and the vaster we make the ensemble of their possible new combinations, the longer it would take to scan these ensembles and the less would be the probability of extracting from them relevant or usable combinations within a limited time. As we saw in our discussion of game theory in Chapter 4, typing on a million typewriters by a million monkeys does offer a range of possible recombinations that does include the collected works of William Shakespeare, but the probability of obtaining them by this method within a limited time is infinitesimal. Learning through the recombination of large numbers of unrelated small items is therefore likely to be slow and may have to be guided heavily by additional selective criteria from outside the ensemble of recombinable items. This would correspond to the description of "infant learning" given by D. O. Hebb and to the same author's description of the learning of visual orientation by persons who acquired vision for the first time in adult life as the result of a corneal operation.[1] Hebb contrasts this with what he calls adult learning. This, in his opinion, consists in the recombination of a smaller number of larger subassemblies of memories or habits; and the principle would apply, *mutatis mutandis,* to recombinations of subassemblies of material facilities. Infant learning, in this view, resembles building a house from bricks; adult learning resembles assembling it from prefabricated panels. Infant learning thus is slower but richer in possibilities; adult learning is more rapid within the limits of combinations of the subassemblies that are given.[2]

Three problems suggested by this view are finding some optimum range between infant-type and adult-type learning; or of alternating between infant-type and adult-type learning at various stages within the same organization; and, finally, of establishing strategic criteria of interest for the selection of promising configurations from the large ensemble of infant-type learning for the purpose of developing the selected configurations more intensively by more nearly adult-type learning methods. All these problems will have to be discussed elsewhere.

From a structural point of view, the *learning capacity* of an organization is thus indicated by the amount of its uncommitted inner resources; by the extent of their possible dissociation into discrete items; and by the extent and probable relevance of its fixed subassemblies available for new recombinations. Somewhere between the extreme subdivision of items in infant learning, and the relative rigidity of a small ensemble of large fixed subassemblies, there probably exists a region of optimum solutions combining a high degree of richness and originality—that is, improbability—of new patterns, with a high degree of speed in their selection, and with a high probability of their relevance to the challenges offered to the organization by its environment.

POSSIBLE MEASUREMENT OF LEARNING AND INNOVATING PERFORMANCE

Structural data about learning capacity may be checked against observed data of learning performance. Here research might deal with adaptations of the concept of the learning curve to the behavior of organizations, industries, or countries. For a quantitative approach to the problems of learning and innovation in economic history, an outline of concrete research possibilities may be indicated briefly:

We might . . . measure the *imitative innovation rate,* that is the rate at which selected, standardized, technical innovations were accepted in given countries. We could select those cases for which sufficient records are available. Numerous examples suggest themselves: the linotype machine, the shoe machines of the United Shoe Machinery Corporation, the cash register, typewriter, ball-bearings, telephones, the Westinghouse railroad air-brake, and many like instances.

We might then try, let us say in the case of the linotype machine, to find out when and where these machines were first introduced on a significant scale, how long a time elapsed between the first introduction and the stage when more than one-third the total circulation of a country was printed with their aid, how much longer until the one-half and two-thirds marks were reached. Figures on the linotype machines might be obtainable from the corporation handling the license rights; data on newspaper circulation have been collected for some time now by the Editors' and Publishers' Year Book. A sample graph of the speed with which the printing of newspapers was modernized, in this respect, could be correlated with such "economic" factors as the total numbers of newspapers among which the entire circulation was divided; the capital investment in the newspaper industry; the volume of paid advertising; the profits of the business; and numerous other variables.

After some of these correlations have been made, it might be possible to see if there still remained any significant differences in the speed with which typesetting was being modernized in the United States, for example, as compared with, perhaps, France. This comparison could tell us for the limited subject of typesetting, not only whether French entrepreneurs were as quick (or slower) than their American counterparts in modernizing their plants, but also, if they had been slower, by just *how much* they had lagged behind.

Such figures as these for the linotype machine alone would mean little, but if the investigation is repeated for, let us say, the cash register (utilizing the records of the National Cash Register Company)—comparing the number of cash registers installed in a given country with the volume of retail sales, or with the number and turnover of retail stores above a certain minimum sales volume per store—the aggregate data would begin to take on significance. (The available figures in each case would, of course, vary with the obtainable statistics for each country.)

The outcome of a comparison of these several innovation rates in different countries with those found to have prevailed in the United States might show that the French retail grocers or department-store executives had a different rate of adoption of these techniques; that perhaps they were more quick to adopt one innovation than another; and, in the end, we might emerge with a quantitative measure of the differential rates of the acceptance of innovation.

This sort of data would be essential for any significant statements about the performance of French entrepreneurship as compared to the American variety, or about the innovating performance of small owner-managed firms as compared to large corporate enterprises; or, to look at the matter from another side, about the innovating performances of all types of business in the classical decades of free trade, say, 1846–1873, as compared with the classical period of capital concentration and protection, say 1890–1929.

Complementary to these investigations of imitative innovation would be an investigation of *initiative innovation*, that is, the frequency with which significant innovations originate and are first significantly applied in a particular country, or in special types of economic institutions. A study of imitative innovation might tell us how quickly American improvements in the technology of coal-

168

mining were introduced in Britain during the era of private enterprise in the 19th century as compared with the rate of such introductions in the 20th century before 1945, and with the rate of such innovations since that time under public management. A study of initiative innovation could tell us, at the same time, what significant innovations in coal-mining, if any, originated in Britan during each of these periods. Findings for both types of innovations could then be compared to similar data for coal-mining in France and Germany, with due allowances, of course, for the different geological and geographical conditions in each case.

It would be against this international background of comparison of the performance of both businessmen and officials in other countries that the contribution of American businessmen in various periods of economic history could be properly appraised, or the chances better estimated for stimulating further innovations in a given country by means of economic aid from the United States.[3]

Records of learning performance at successive times may themselves be made the basis for a second-order measurement of what Gregory Bateson has called "the deutero learning" of an organization.[4] Deutero learning is second-order learning; its measurement would measure the speed at which an organization learns to learn, that is, the rate of improvement in its performance when confronted with a succession of different learning tasks.

From a structural investigation of the learning facilities and the learning capacity of an organization, and from measurements of its learning performance, as well as of its second-order learning, we may derive a test for evaluating the major over-all learning and behavior patterns of the organization. Has the learning of the organization been *creative*, that is to say, has it increased its ranges of possible intake of information from the outside world and its ranges of possible inner recombinations? Or has the learning of the organization been merely viable, that is, neither adding nor detracting from the subsequent capacities of the organization for learning and self-steering? Or, finally, has the learning performance of the organization been pathological, that is, has the organization learned something that has reduced its subsequent capacity to learn, or its subsequent capacity to control its own behavior? It was suggested earlier that such self-destructive learning resembles what moralists call sin and perhaps what Socrates had in mind when he taught that no man would err willingly.

Any shift from infant-type to adult-type learning has on this showing at least a pathological aspect. As large subassemblies of information or resources are frozen, and as major pathways of habit and routine become fixed, the speed and probability of the responses of the organization will increase in relation to a limited range of currently probable or frequent stimuli. But this observable improvement in obvious competence in routine matters will have been bought at the price of reducing the range of available new recombinations within the organization, that is, at the price of reducing its inner resources of originality and creativity. The same process may have involved the hardening of routines in the selection of kinds of information for intake as well as in the allocation of priorities in its treatment, and in the attachment of secondary symbols to it for treatment in the feedback channels that carry consciousness. All this may result in narrowing the range of information that is permitted to enter the organization or that is likely to become effective in it. Thus the organization may come to run in blinkers of its own making, and cumulative losses of sensitivity may lead to partial blindness behind a façade of seemingly ever more mature performance. This pathological aspect of adult learning seems to have been known intuitively to the early Christians. Their injunction to men to "become like little children" must have shocked disciples of Platonic philosophy, which extolled perfection and maturity, but it should be recognized as a legitimate and significant insight by modern theorists of learning and organization.

Considerations of this kind have a direct bearing on the valuation of the evolution and learning performance of countries and societies. Several times in history we find a conspicuous decline and partial disintegration in the established routines and fixed subassemblies of formalized learning and established patterns of custom and civilization, coupled at the same time with a broad diffusion of some fundamental items of knowledge and technology and with the emergence of a larger number of smaller units or subassemblies of knowledge or of economic or political activity, offering a wider range of possible new combinations. The so-called "Dark Ages" in Western Europe between A.D. 500 and 1000 are an example of this process. The civilization of the American Colonies, and later the United States, between 1730 and 1850 is perhaps another. In both these cases we find numerous comments on the loss of any fixed traditions, institutions, or patterns of civilization summed up in eloquent complaints about a supposed new barbarism or cultural chaos. On closer inspection, these periods turn out to have been periods of great fundamental growth and of the enrichment of the ensemble of learning resources and possibilities, which then in turn led to the emergence of novel and temporarily more relevant patterns.

In the subsequent phase, these new patterns turn into temporarily fixed subassemblies. The subsequent age thus may impress observers with its apparent conservatism and stability, while at the same time embodying continued and important processes of change. These continued changes, however, are largely changes within the limits of adult-type learning, exploiting a limited range of recombinations or largely ready-made routines. Such adult-type learning may still be original and creative, as these concepts were defined above, but it has strict limits and it may end in deadlock or in a partial return to a seemingly barbarous or infant-type learning stage.

The demobilization of fixed subassemblies, pathways, or routines may thus itself be creative or pathological. It is creative when it is accompanied by a diffusion of basic resources and, consequently, by an increase in the possible ranges of new connections, new intakes, and new recombinations. In organizations or societies the breaking of the cake of custom is creative if individuals are not merely set free from old restraints but if they are at the same time rendered *more* capable of communicating and cooperating with the world in which they live. In the absence of these conditions there may be genuine regression; barbarism would then mean not merely the loss of prized traditions or routines; it would mean the relative dumbness and deafness to which the Greek word *barbaros* first referred.

POLICY ASPIRATIONS AND PROPHETIC LEADERSHIP

When genuine or supposed solutions to new problems have been discovered by some individuals or groups in the society, they must be proposed to others for acceptance and support, and for eventual execution. The kind of solutions invented and proposed will of course depend in large part upon the experiences, habits, and interests of the individuals and social groups among whom they originate or by whom they are accepted. This is a well-known point that has often been stressed by adherents of economic or sociological interpretations of history.

What this emphasis tends to overlook is the *combinatorial aspect* of invention. Even if a problem is known, all the elements of its solution are at hand, and the would-be problem-solvers are strongly motivated to find the solution as quickly as possible, there may be no way of telling how quickly an adequate solution will be found. When you or I try to solve a combination puzzle, or when cryptographers try to break a secret code, or when mathematicians seek for the solution to certain problems, the number of possible solutions may be very large, and the probable time for finding an adequate solution may also be large. As we found in our earlier discussion of the theory of games, in such situations very much may depend on the invention of suitable search strategies, shortcuts, or partial solutions that may make the finding of the total solution more probable and that thus may greatly cut down the total time of search. Since the finding of these immediate steps or solutions may in itself not be very probable, we could say that, from a combinatorial point of view, *creativity or invention means to produce a relevant combination here and now,* which on the basis of probability—including economic as well as cultural conditions—should have been found only in the more or less distant future.

In politics and social life, by the same considerations, solutions advocated by different individuals, interest groups, or social classes have to fulfill three quite different sets of tests.

First, the solutions must express to some extent the habits, preferences, beliefs, and perhaps the socially standardized personality structures of their proponents. If they completely fail to do this, they would not be proposed by these particular persons, or, in the extreme case, they would not be proposed by anyone at all. Some psychologists use such words as "cathectic" for this function of political ideas.

Second, the ideas and policies proposed may or may not represent adequate answers to the challenges confronting the state or the society. If they did not do so, they might still give emotional satisfaction to their supporters; they might even help them to get a large temporary share of the tangible or intangible rewards available in the society; but they would not be likely to prevent their supporters at a later stage from sharing the consequences of social breakdown or stagnation.

In the third place, the solutions proposed must be sufficiently acceptable to sufficient numbers of individuals and groups in the society, other than their original proponents and backers, to permit them to be actually carried into operation.

Ideally, a successful solution to a major policy problem should be strongly backed by an influential group in the society; it should be practically capable of solving a major problem confronting the society or state; and it should be sufficiently acceptable to a sufficient number of other members of the society to permit its execution.

In actual fact, of course, these three criteria need not coincide. Relevant solutions that are strongly backed by influential groups from the beginning would usually be solutions with the highest probability of being found, that is, solutions that are relatively obvious. Very serious challenges to the functioning of a society or state, however, may have only those solutions that are fairly unlikely to be discovered by means of the standardized and accepted memories, habits, preferences, and culture patterns existing in the society. If such solutions are found soon enough to be of political significance, they may be more likely to be found by some deviant members of the community—by persons whose memories, habits, or viewpoints may differ significantly from those of most other groups in their community or culture and who may have fewer habits and interests to sacrifice in identifying themselves with new ideas and new patterns of behavior.

These considerations may account to some extent for the well-known fact that new patterns of behavior in politics, economics, and culture are often originated or propagated in their early stages by social deviants, misfits, strangers, members of minorities, and "marginal men." It is also well known that persons of this type ordinarily are unlikely to form stable, cohesive, and influential social groups. Usually the best they can hope to do may be to persuade more powerful and more stable groups in the society to accept the policies they propose.

If the new policies involve only fairly limited but deep-going changes in previously accepted policies and patterns of behavior, a peculiar type of situation may result. The new ideas may be so unusual that it may take unusual or marginal men to propagate them. Men of this type become their prophets or their agitators. Eventually these ideas are accepted by influential groups in the society, but they are accepted without the individuals and groups who originally propagated them. Finally the policies are put into operation by the "ins"; and the "outs" are left, either to disperse or to continue as a sect complaining about the imperfect execution of their principles. The story of the Cobden's Free Trade agitation and British commercial policy in the mid-nineteenth century, or the story of William Lloyd Garrison and the abolition of slavery, or the role of Tom Paine in the American Revolution, or the story of Edmund Burke and the actual consolidation of conservative power in England at the turn of the eighteenth century may be examples of such cases.

All these persons in one sense were leaders. All of them were successful in the sense that some of their major ideas were accepted. Yet, while many of their "policy aspirations" were eventually fulfilled, none of these men attained real power, whether or not they ever seriously sought it. The well-known distinction between "policy aspirations" and "power aspirations" seems confirmed by situations of this kind. The two kinds of political aspirations are often distinct in their psychological and social background and in their probabilities of fulfillment; and this distinction may remain effective regardless of the intentions of the aspirants.

Prophetic leadership of this kind appears as the opposite of the "continuing leadership" discussed in an earlier section.

What has been stated in these pages is a combinatorial and probabilistic view of creativity in general, and of political creativity in particular. It considers creativity as the outcome of a sequence of steps of information processing that can be described, in principle, with some precision. The main steps in this sequence are selection, abstraction, storage, dissociation, recombination, selective critical recognition, and new application of information patterns. Each of these operations can be traced in the teamwork among scientists, in the history of science, probably in the development of folk art, folk literature and folk music, and, in principle, in the minds of individuals, ranging from the creativity of the child to the creativity of the young or mature artist, scientist, or prophet. Creativity is thus a property of certain complex information-processing systems ranging from individuals to societies and cultures. It is found at different system levels; and it can be described, in principle, in its main sequential steps, inner structure, and favoring or inhibiting external and internal conditions, in some detail.

This view is in some respects the opposite of the one long held, and recently reaffirmed, by Arnold Toynbee. Toynbee's contribution to the understanding of creativity has been strategic rather than tactical. He has presented a formidable and indeed persuasive case for the crucial importance of creativity in history and politics. In so doing, he has pointed to such processes of creativity as one of the most important targets for historical and political analysis and understanding. The fact, pointed out in an earlier chapter of this book, that Toynbee indicates little or no inner structure for these processes of creativity, or for the persons or groups who carry them, is then an omission of the tactical task of attaining and securing these intellectual targets. It detracts in no way, however, from the very great significance of his strategic contribution.

There is nonetheless something of the occupational risk of the prophet in Toynbee's renewed assertions that creation is a "mysterious action," that "novelty is logically unintelligible," and that "to say that a cause need not act uniformly is to deny causal connexions altogether."[5] The last of these three statements was made obsolete long ago by the acceptance of probabilistic rather than of deterministic ways of thinking. Situations where highly determinate causal connections are actually found to exist can be treated easily as special cases of high probability, much as cases of relative "rest" in physics can easily be treated as special cases of relative motion. It is only the obsolete metaphysical frameworks of absolute rest and absolute determinism that made the treatment of motion and probability—including concepts of genuinely true coins and of randomness—seem so difficult and paradoxical.

Once combinatorial probability, rather than rigid determination, can be accepted as part of our intellectual frame of reference, it is not difficult to treat novelty and creativity as combinatorial phenomena. This is indeed what many recent students of creativity have done; and, in the same decades during which Toynbee has held to the belief that creativity and novelty were "mysterious" and "logically unintelligible," increasingly specific discussions of these combinatorial processes have been appearing.[6]

COMMUNICATION, COHESION, AND THE LIMITS OF STATES AND FEDERATIONS

Many political scientists are inclined to accept as given the political units, states, nations, or federations with which they deal. Sometimes, however, such states break up; inhabitants of certain regions, members of certain nationalities, or adherents of some political or religious faith may try to secede, and may be successful in doing so. In other cases, previously separate states or peoples try to federate, or to unite in some other form in a common political unit. What conditions govern the success or failure of such enterprises? While we must call on the whole range of social sciences, including history, in our search for an answer, the study of information and communication can, perhaps, make a major contribution.

Briefly, we may consider a *people* a community of social communication habits. Its members usually have common habits of speech, such as language, or common cultural memories permitting them to understand one another's ideas, even if they are expressed in two different languages, as among the German-speaking and French-speaking Swiss. The ability of the members of such a people to transmit information to each other over a wide range of topics; the ability to form efficient patterns for teamwork for a wide variety of purposes; and perhaps their ability to form new patterns of teamwork for new purposes—all these may be estimated or measured by methods ranging from the judgment of well-informed observers to the more refined experimental techniques of social psychologists. Data on all these points measure, as it were, the invisible communications equipment the members of a population carry in their minds. From it, inferences can be drawn not only as to the cohesion of an already existing people, and of the membership of particular individuals or groups within it, but also as to the presence or absence of a minimum of cultural compatibility and mutual understanding, sufficient to permit common political or economic institutions to weld different populations in a gradual process of social learning into one people or one nation.

The survey, or measurement, of communication habits must be supplemented by a survey or measurement of actual communication experiences. What are the concentrations of population, the patterns of settlement, the volumes of traffic and migration, the distribution of radio audiences and newspaper readership, the frequency and range of face-to-face contacts? And what are the status positions of each of these kinds of communication experiences in terms of the social structure and the cultural values of the populations concerned? Answers to such questions can indicate a major part of the setting in which proposals for Pan-Arab unity or Western European Federation would have to be evaluated.

Surveys of communication habits indicate one class of the difficulties of social learning that a political integration process must surmount. Surveys of communication experiences, and of the cultural and social status assigned to them, indicate the essential material

177

with which any political integration process has to work, as well as some major sources of its potential strength. Political leadership in a process of integration or federation of several countries or regions into a new state can be evaluated in terms of what it attempts and what it accomplishes in the face of the opportunities and obstacles revealed by such data.

Moreover, changes in the basic data of communication habits or communication experiences may be indicative of later changes in the social functions of existing political units. In terms of the new patterns of social communication, actual or possible, the existing political unit or nation-state may now appear to be too large, or possibly too small. From considerations of this kind we may derive an approach to the social as well as the political dynamics of federation and secession, as well as to the dynamics of nationalism and colonial dependence. A number of studies utilizing this approach are currently in print or in progress.[7]

PREFERENCES, AUTHORITY, AND VALUES

In any communication system, except the very simplest, several messages may have to compete for the same communication channel, which may not have sufficient capacity to carry all of them at the same time. Wherever several communication channels meet, as in a telephone switchboard or in any social or political organization, the probability of occasional "logjams" of messages will be considerable. No communication system of any complexity, therefore, can function without a set of operating preferences or priorities. Telephone operators must know that calls to the fire department have precedence over ordinary conversations. Values determine in society or politics, as well as in individual life, which messages and types of information should take precedence over other kinds in our attention and in the transmission to other persons.

In its crudest and simplest form, a "value" is a repetitive preference for a particular class of messages or data that is to be received, transmitted, or acted upon in preference to others. The class of messages specified by any such value may be quite narrow or quite broad, and it may be specified in terms of the content of the messages or in terms of the source from which they originate.

A *source* of messages that receives habitual preferential treatment as regards attention, transmission, and obedience in politics or social life may be said to possess *authority*. In the extreme case, authority consists in the successful claim for the preferential treatment of messages originating from a particular source, regardless of their particular content; or, alternatively, the claim for preferential treatment of messages originating from a particular source— such as the Japanese Emperor in August, 1945—regardless of their particular content; or, alternatively, the claim for preferential treatment of messages accompanied by some particular symbol of authority—such as England's Great Seal of the Realm in the sixteenth century—again regardless of their particular content. *"Intrinsic authority"* might then refer to messages that command preferred treatment in social communication because of the merits of their particular content, even though they may neither originate from a preferred source nor be accompanied by preferred symbols.

In actual situations, external or formal authority in terms of sources or symbols and intrinsic authority in terms of actual content may be interwoven to varying degrees. As a source of high authority or prestige continues to emit messages of low intrinsic relevance or merit, men may learn to regard its messages less highly; and as a source of low authority, status, or prestige continues to emit messages that appear relevant and valuable to the recipients, the latter may learn to give it more consideration. Generally, external authority tends to be stressed where there is not time for the evaluation of the intrinsic merits of its messages, as in emergencies or military situations; or in cases where such evaluation would be too costly in resources; or where the recipients, because of their ignorance or cultural or social bias, are expected to be unable to evaluate these merits; or, finally, and not infrequently in politics, in cases where these merits appear doubtful, sometimes even to the originators of the messages themselves.

Some of these considerations have led to a good deal of "debunking" of authority in political writings. More recently, there have been some attempts to reverse this operation and to restore to the authority concept some of its lost prestige. No complete restoration of the *status quo*, however, seems likely. The potential cleavage between the external authority of a source of communications and the intrinsic merits of the messages originating from it cannot be completely obscured again, once awareness of it has become widespread.

While skepticism of formal authority may thus to some extent persist, we may infer from the study of communication that a set of operating preferences is indispensable for all organizations. There can be, therefore, no politics without values, and no viable political decision system without a set of values characterized by a minimum level of consistency.

In a more extended sense, the term "value" often connotes in social science an operating preference that is linked to other preferences, as well as being linked to important memories and emotional reaction patterns in the individuals who hold it. Values in this extended sense may turn out to be repetitive or persistent clusters of the simple operating preferences discussed earlier in this section. No matter which of these notions of value we adopt, however, we still find that the crucial problem is posed by the relation of several values to each other. It is impossible to understand the function of any single value except in terms of the set of other values that are relevant to it. Just as words have meaning only in the context of sentences and sentences in the context of language, so the function of any value can be described only in terms of a value system in which it occurs.

Here we meet two cognitive pitfalls. The first consists in our propensity to confuse values with value images—that is, to confuse what people say or think they prefer with what they actually do prefer in action. The second pitfall is another version of the old mechanistic fallacy that the behavior of a system can be completely predicted from the behavior of its parts. A set of values described singly may fail to describe the functioning of the value system formed by all of them together, much as a description of the stop-and-go signs at a number of intersections may fail to tell us whether all of them together will result in a traffic jam or in an easily functioning rotary pattern of traffic.

Certain important configurations of values can be described in very simple terms. One configuration particularly significant for politics and government is the feedback pattern, and we shall discuss this pattern as an aid to the understanding of purpose and autonomy in political organization.

II

Government as a Process of
Steering: The Concepts of
Feedback, Goal, and Purpose

Let us recall that our word "government" comes from
a Greek root that refers to the art of the steersman. The same underlying concept is reflected in the double meaning of the modern word
"governor" as a person charged with the administrative control of a
political unit, and as a mechanical device controlling the performance of a steam engine or an automobile. On closer investigation we
found that there is indeed a certain underlying similarity between
the governing or self-governing of ships or machines and the governing of human organizations. Steering a ship implies guiding the
future behavior of the ship on the basis of information concerning the past performance and present position of this ship itself in
relation to some external course, goal, or target. In such cases, the
next step in the behavior of the system must be guided in part by
information concerning its own performance in the past.

We have already met the concept for the common process underlying all operations of this kind, which is known as *feedback*. It may
be useful here to refer to a description of its essentials by Norbert
Wiener:

> This control of a machine on the basis of its *actual* performance
> rather than its *expected* performance is known as *feedback*, and in-

volves sensory members which are actuated by motor members and perform the function of *tell-tales* or *monitors*—that is, of elements which indicate a performance. . . .

Something very similar to this occurs in human action. If I pick up my cigar, I do not will to move any specific muscles. Indeed in many cases, I do not know what those muscles are. What I do is to turn into action a certain feedback mechanism; namely, a reflex in which the amount by which I have yet failed to pick up the cigar is turned into a new and increased order to the lagging muscles, whichever they may be. In this same way, a fairly uniform voluntary command will enable the same task to be performed from widely varying initial positions, and irrespective of the decrease of contraction due to fatigue of the muscles. . . .

It is my thesis that the operation of the living individual and the operation of some of the newer communication machines are precisely parallel. Both of them have sensory receptors as one stage in their cycle of operation: that is, in both of them there exists a special apparatus for collecting information from the outer world at low energy levels, and for making it available in the operation of the individual or of the machine. In both cases these external messages are not taken *neat*, but through the internal transforming powers of the apparatus, whether it be alive or dead. The information is then turned into a new form available for the further stages of performance. In both the animal and the machine this performance is made to be effective on the outer world. In both of them, their *performed* action on the outer world, and not merely their *intended* action, is reported back to the central regulatory apparatus. This complex of behavior is ignored by the average man, and in particular does not play the role that it should in our habitual analysis of society.[1]

SOME APPLICATIONS OF NEGATIVE FEEDBACK: OPPOSITION TO OVERSHOOTING THE GOAL

As we know, applications of this feedback principle in modern control engineering surround our lives. The thermostats in our homes, the automatic elevators in our office buildings, as well as the automatic gun directors in antiaircraft batteries, and the guided missiles now under development, all represent application of this principle.

In all these cases, an electric or mechanical system first of all is given a major internal imbalance or disequilibrium that functions as its *drive,* in the sense that the system tends to move toward a state in which this internal disequilibrium will be reduced, or more loosely expressed, in which its internal "tension" will be lowered. Moreover, this inner disequilibrium must be of a particular kind, such that it can be reduced by bringing the whole system into some particular situation or relation vis-à-vis the outside world. This situation of the system to the outside world we may call a *goal situation,* or briefly, a *goal:* once the system has reached such a goal its inner disequilibrium will be lower.

Second, in order for the system to approach the goal effectively, the feedback condition must be given. The system must receive information concerning the position of the goal and concerning its own distance from it; and it must receive information concerning the changes in its distance from the goal brought about by its own performance. The messages are often negative in that they *oppose* the previous actions of the system, so as to oppose overshooting of the target.

In the third place, the system must be able to respond to this information by further changes in its own position or behavior. With these facilities, and given sufficient freedom, the system will therefore tend to approach its goal.

Finally, if these changes are effective and the system reaches the goal, some of its drive or inner tension usually will be lowered.

As we saw earlier, there is an obvious similarity between these steps in the process of goal-seeking, and the concepts of "drive," "cue," "response," and "reward," which are familiar from the psychology of learning.

Similar patterns of behavior have been found in the performance of the nervous system of animals and human beings. Feedback processes seem to represent the particular machinery of *homeostasis* by which certain essential states or functions of an organism, such as body temperatures or breathing rate, are maintained at an even level. The maintenance of even states, and the seeking and approaching of external goals, are thus performed essentially by the same configuration of processes.

184

The similarity of these processes of steering, goal-seeking, and autonomous control to certain processes in politics seems striking. Governments may seek goals in domestic or foreign policies. In order to approach these goals they must guide their behavior by a stream of information concerning their own position in relation to these goals; their remaining distance from them; and the actual, as distinct from the intended, results of their own most recent steps or attempts to approach them.

In addition to seeking goals, governments or political organizations may try to maintain some state of affairs they deem desirable, such as prosperity in economics or tranquillity in politics. In so doing, they must receive information concerning the extent and rate of disturbances in order to guide the magnitude and speed of their countermeasures. If they react too little or too late, they will not stop the disturbance. If they react too much or too soon, they will overshoot the mark and themselves create a disturbance in the opposite direction. To the statesman, guiding a difficult program to success may thus resemble the art of driving an automobile over an icy road: his problem is to anticipate the skids quickly enough so that he can still control them by small corrections at the steering wheel, where slowness of the action or oversteering would provide worse skids and might wreck the car.

AN ALTERNATIVE TO THE "EQUILIBRIUM" APPROACH

In its application to politics, the feedback concept permits a more sophisticated approach than does the traditional mechanistic concept of equilibrium, and it permits a far wider range of analysis and measurement.[2] If we think of a political system in terms of a classic mechanistic equilibrium, we are forced to think in terms of a system that is isolated from its environment and that receives nothing important from the outside except disturbances. If these disturbances are small, the equilibrium will simply be restored through the automatic reaction of the system. If the disturbances are somewhat larger, we should expect them to elicit proportionately greater reactions tending to restore the same *status quo.* If the disturbances are too great, we can only imagine that the system will somehow be overthrown or destroyed, but the equilibrium concept gives us little or no information as to just what will happen from then on, except vague indications of disaster. In short, the equilibrium concept is incapable of describing an important range of dynamic phenomena and it can indicate no time path for substantial change. With no help from the equilibrium concept in analyzing major processes of social change, statesmen would either have to hope that "every action must be followed by an equal and opposite reaction," or they must rely on general experience or intuition.

To be sure, some of the more sophisticated dynamic theories of processes of change also speak of "equilibrium," but they are using the word as a description of a certain state of equilibrium that may be achieved or lost; but unlike classic mechanistic theory, they no longer envisage equilibrium itself as a process by which this state is maintained or restored. Rather they are describing this process in other terms—for example, through differential equations—and are then asking under what conditions a state of equilibrium will be one of its results.[3] In short, where classic mechanism often thought of equilibrium as a suitable over-all description of an entire large system, the concepts of equilibrium and disequilibrium are now most useful as descriptions of temporary states of small components of such systems, while the systems themselves are recognized as engaged in dynamic processes of change which go well beyond the classic equilibrium image. It is this classic image, however, that often lingers on in the folklore of social science and political thought and even in minds of statesmen trying to defend or restore some classic image of the balance of power.

At first glance the process of goal-seeking that we described above may seem similar to the process of restoring simple equilibrium. Actually, it is very different in at least four ways. First of all, in feedback processes, the goal situation sought is outside, not inside, the goal-seeking system. Second, the system itself is not isolated from its environment but, on the contrary, depends for its functioning upon a constant stream of information from the environment, as well as upon a constant stream of information concerning its own performance. Third, the goal may be a changing goal. It may change both its position, as a flying bird or an airplane, and even its speed and direction, as a rabbit pursued by a dog. Suitable feedback processes could in principle catch up with a zigzagging rabbit, just as in principle suitable automatic gun directors can track and shoot down an airplane taking evasive action. In the fourth place, a goal may be approached indirectly by a course, or a number of possible courses, around a set of obstacles. This problem resembles our notion of *purpose:* a major or strategic goal, preference, or value that is to be pursued through a set of intermediate movements toward intermediate goals, or avoiding intermediate obstacles. In a simple form this problem has appeared in the design of automatic torpedoes and guided missiles. In politics, it appears as the problem of maintaining a strategic purpose throughout a sequence of changing tactical goals.

In addition to these four differences between feedback and the equilibrium concept, feedback analysis permits us to identify and in principle to measure a number of elements in either goal-seeking or homeostatic processes. We can evaluate the efficiency of a feedback process in terms of the number and the size of its mistakes, that is, the under- or over-corrections it makes in reaching the goal. If the series of such mistakes should increase rather than decrease, the goal, of course, will not be reached at all. The system will go into a series of increasing oscillations, and may break down. Whether this will happen, or whether, on the contrary, the goal will be approached successfully through a number of diminishing mistakes depends on the mutual relationship between four quantitative factors. Some of these were mentioned briefly in an earlier section, but they may be worth reviewing here at greater length:

1. The *load* in terms of information, that is, the extent and speed of changes in the position of the target relative to the goal-seeking system. In the cases of a moving ship or airplane, or of a darting rabbit, this load may be quite high.

2. The *lag* in the response of the system, that is, the amount of

time between the reception of information concerning the position of the target and the execution of the corresponding step in the goal-seeking behavior of the system. This is the time between the reception of the information concerning the position of an enemy airplane and the actual pointing of the antiaircraft gun barrels to the spot designed for interception; or it might correspond to the time between a dog's seeing the hunted rabbit change its course, and the corresponding change in the course of the dog. Clearly, this lag may be influenced by a number of factors, such as slowness in the reception of target information, or in its interpretation or transmission; or by delays in the response of parts of the system in executing the new course; by the inertia of the system; and so on. The greater its lag in relation to its load, the less likely is a system to reach a changing goal or moving target.

3. The *gain* in each corrective step taken by the system, that is, the amount of actual change in behavior that results. Thus, the further we turn the steering wheel of an automobile during a given time, the greater should ordinarily be the gain in the resulting change of the course of the car. A high rate of gain increases the probability of *oversteering*, that is, of departing from the correct course in the opposite direction.

4. The *lead*, that is, the distance of the accurately predicted position of the moving target from the actual position from which the most recent signals were received. In this manner, sportsmen "lead" flying ducks and clay pigeons: they fire at the target's predicted rather than at its perceived position by aiming somewhat ahead in the direction of its previously observed course. The greater this lead, the greater is the probability of hitting the target or reaching the goal. The amount of lead, in turn, depends on the efficiency of predictive processes available to the goal-seeking system, and on the amount of inaccuracy that can be tolerated. For this reason, duck hunters use duckshot rather than bullets, and antiaircraft guns fire their shells in a pattern calculated in terms of probability.

The chances of success in goal-seeking are thus always inversely related to the amounts of *load* and *lag*. Up to a point, they may be positively related to the amount of *gain*, although, at high rates of gain, this relationship may be reversed; and they are always positively related to the amount of *lead*.[4]

A feedback model of this kind permits us to ask a number of significant questions about the performance of governments that are apt to receive less attention in terms of traditional analysis:

1. What are the amount and rate of change in the international or domestic situation with which the government must cope? In other words, what is the *load* upon the political decision system of the state? Similarly, what is the load upon the decision system of particular interest groups, political organizations, or social classes? What is the intellectual load upon their leadership? What is the load upon the facilities to ensure participation from their members?

2. What is the *lag* in the response of a government or party to a new emergency or challenge? How much time do policymakers require to become aware of a new situation, and how much additional time do they need to arrive at a decision? How much delay is imposed by broader consultation or participation? How much time is required to transmit a series of changing orders to the officials, soldiers, and citizens who are to execute them, and how much time do these persons require to readjust their previous behavior patterns, habits, and values, so as to be able to comply effectively? What is the corresponding lag in the response of particular political parties, interest groups, or individuals? What is the lag in the response to new information that is brought into the political decision system through one channel rather than another, for example, the lag in the reaction to information that is reported more or less "straight to the top" (as the possibility of an atomic bomb was reported to President Roosevelt in 1940), in contrast to the information that is first accepted among some particular social or occupational groups? What is the relationship between the accessibility of a government to the amount of lag observed in its reactions? If it is known that armies and totalitarian governments can cut down their rate of lag by ensuring the quick transmission of orders from the top *down*, to what extent is this advantage lost, and the amount of lag increased, by possible difficulties in such systems in getting new information *up* to the top? What attempted solutions for this problem have been

adopted in practice in various countries? What differences in this respect can be observed in the structure and performance of different dictatorships, such as Spain and Nazi Germany, or of, say, Yugoslavia, Cuba, Poland, China, and the USSR? What differences in this respect can we observe among various democracies, such as France, Great Britain, and the United States?

3. What is the *gain* of the response—that is, the speed and size of the reaction of a political system to new data it has accepted? How quickly do bureaucracies, interest groups, political organizations, and citizens respond with major recommitments of their resources? To what extent do authoritarian regimes have an advantage in enforcing a massive response to new policies, once they have been adopted? To what extent can democracies have a high rate of gain? What factors account for the vast and quick response of the United States to Pearl Harbor—a response utterly unexpected by the Axis governments?

4. What is the amount of *lead*, that is, of the capability of a government to predict and to anticipate new problems effectively? To what extent do governments attempt to improve their rate of lead by setting up specific intelligence organizations, strategy and planning boards, and other devices? What is the effect of free public discussion, including freedom for unorthodox opinions, upon the predictive efficiency of a political decision system? What is the relationship of the institutions, organizations, or practices that produce forecasts to those that control their selection, evaluation, and acceptance for action?

The over-all performance of political decision systems will depend upon the interplay of all these factors. Since gain is related to power, governments or organizations with little power may have to try to compensate for their low rates of gain by trying to increase their foresight and the speed of their response, that is to say, to cut down their lag and to increase their lead. Great powers, on the other hand, may often succeed in coping with a situation by the sheer size of their response, even though their reactions may be slow and their predictions poor. Again, governments or political organizations, whose rates of lag, gain, and lead were sufficiently adjusted

190

to each other for dealing with moderate rates of change in their environment, may find themselves unable to control their behavior effectively in times of rapid change that may put an excessive load upon their decision-making system.

Considerations of this kind may be of some help in the long and seemingly unpromising debate concerning the "superiority" of this or that political system. Such debates have often been held in terms of a vague all-round superiority, in which cultural, ethical, religious, and political values were inextricably mixed and which tended to end as exercises in ethnocentrism. At the other extreme, attempts could be made to evaluate political systems operationally in terms of a single function, in which case the outcome depends largely upon the selection of the function. If we assume, however, that all governments are trying to maintain some control over their own behavior, to maintain as long as possible the conditions for the existence of their political systems, and to get nearer to, rather than further away from, the goals that they have accepted, then it would be possible to evaluate different configurations of political institutions in terms of their capacity to function as a more or less efficient steering system.

While the evaluation of political systems as steering systems ought to be technically possible, it would be quite one-sided. Both Pericles and John Stuart Mill might remind us that states should not merely be evaluated in terms of their ability to function efficiently as states, but far more in terms of the types of personality and character they produce among their citizens, and of the opportunities they offer to all their citizens for individual development. In the last section of this paper we shall deal with some of these broader concepts of growth in relation to individuals as well as to communities and government. At this point, let us note only that over-all steering performance is an important aspect of political decision systems but that it is by no means an exhaustive one.

Another word of caution should be added. Thus far our discussion has been in terms of *goals* and not of *goal images*. We defined goals in terms of the actual configuration of the steering or decision system, and in terms of the configurations of its environment. In this manner we discussed the goals the system appears to be seeking in its observable behavior, as in the case of a ship steered by an automatic pilot. In the case of a ship steered by a single human pilot, we would have to treat the memories of the pilot as part of the ship. A psychiatrist dealing with the personality and the nervous system of an individual might similarly look for the goals that he might in fact be pursuing, as distinct from the goals that the patient contemplates in his imagination. The goals actually sought and the goal images carried in the minds of some or all of the participants may of course coincide, but they need not in fact do so. Wherever one's goals are pictured in goal images that are distinct from the actual process by which goals are sought, information derived from such images may be fed back into the steering process and influence its outcome. This aspect of goal images and other kinds of conscious behavior will be discussed in a later section.

SOME APPLICATIONS OF AMPLIFYING FEEDBACK: AUTOMATIC REINFORCEMENT OF RESPONSE

Thus far, we have discussed patterns of negative feedback. In all these, information concerning the performance of a decision system is returned to it and may serve to negate, oppose, or reverse its current action if that action had been leading the system away from its goal. In other situations, however, we may meet positive or amplifying feedback patterns. In cases of amplifying feedback, information about the response of the system serves to reinforce that response in the same direction, and information about this reinforced response may produce further reinforcement of this behavior. Panics in crowds, market panics, cases of runaway inflation, armament races, or the growth of bitterness in an extremely divided community are examples of amplifying feedback systems in social or political life. The sequence of military mobilizations by the various powers in July–August, 1914, showed the features of an amplifying feedback system on a grand scale—features that to some extent came as a surprise to all participants.[5] Since amplifying feedback situations may under certain conditions get out of control, and may damage or wreck the system in which they arise, their better understanding should be of great interest to social scientists.

Perhaps the decisive quantitative consideration in evaluating the probable behavior of an amplifying feedback system, or the course of an amplifying feedback sequence, is the increasing or decreasing character of the series of increments in response to the mutual stimuli at each cycle of operation. If the sequence of reinforcements of behavior, due to the feedback phenomenon, forms a uniform or even an increasing series, then the total response must grow until it exceeds the limits of the system and ends in some form of breakdown. If, on the contrary, this sequence of reinforcements forms a decreasing series, so that, on the whole, each new reinforcement tends to be smaller than the ones that went before, then the total reinforcement will tend to approach an upper limit that need not be beyond the capacities of the system. In this latter case, amplifying feedback would bring the system up to some maximum level of performance, and would tend to keep it there. In the earlier case of uniform or increasing amplifying feedback, there would be no such upper limit within the system: performance would increase without limit until stopped by breakdown, external constraint, or exhaustion.

Situations of bitter domestic or international conflict may easily assume the characteristics of amplifying feedback situations. Each side may feel obliged to answer the threats, encroachments, or insults of the other by reprisals in kind, or by precautionary measures that are in fact competitive and are interpreted as threats by the opponent. If each side is convinced that it must have a margin of superiority over the other, amplifying feedback may result for the whole system of which the two contending groups or states are parts. The course of the resulting amplifying feedback sequence could be forecast and perhaps even controlled, however, by observing and, if possible, controlling the growth or decline of the amount of gain at each cycle, that is, the size of successive increments in performance, of which it is composed. If gestures are answered by more vigorous gestures, and threats with more vigorous counterthreats, but if care is taken to keep the competitive increase at each stage somewhat below the increase during the stage that preceded it, then it should be possible for both contending sides to "keep themselves covered" at each step, and, without ever accepting inferiority to the rival, to reduce the sequence of wage-price rises, military threats, and so on, to some foreseeable and perhaps tolerable maximum level. President Kennedy's announcement in March, 1962, that the United States would respond to the earlier series of Russian nuclear weapons tests in the atmosphere with a *smaller* series of such tests of its own, unless a nuclear test ban should be agreed on within a short time, may have represented an attempt to use such tactics of "underretaliation," or of decreasing increments, in the amplifying feedback situation of the nuclear weapons race.[6]

If no control over the increments is possible, then the uniformity, or increase, or decrease, in the observable rate of gain of the system could be used for predictive purposes. Many amplifying feedback processes depend on some external supplies or facilities in maintaining their rate of gain, such as forest fires that require fuel, or arms races that require economic resources. In such situations we may find a phase of constant or increasing gain, and thus accelerating performance, followed by a phase of slowly or rapidly decreasing gain, as the limits of available supplies or facilities are approached. The resulting sequence of behavior may be pictured somewhat in terms of the well-known "logistic" curves of growth. These S-shaped curves show a slow rise in growth or performance, accelerating later to a phase of very rapid growth, and decreasing gradually in the end so as to remain below a definite upper limit.

Some aspects of conflict situations can be analyzed in terms either of an amplifying or of a negative feedback process. The interchange of threats, or acts of retaliation, has been a topic of study by a number of theorists of "deterrence."[7] One might conceive, for instance, of a deliberate policy of "underretaliation," which would aim at inflicting on the opponent only four-fifths or nine-tenths of the damage one's own side has received, in the hope that the subsequent counterretaliation of the enemy will again remain limited to four-fifths or nine-tenths of one's own action, so that the series of moves will quickly converge to a new and tolerable level.

SOME IMPLICATIONS OF GOAL-CHANGING FEEDBACK: CONTINUING DECISION SYSTEMS

Thus far we have discussed goal-seeking and steering systems in which the goals were assumed as fixed. If the thermostat in our home has been set for 68 degrees, the heating or air-conditioning system will then go through a series of operations to maintain this temperature. In the preceeding section we discussed, in principle, the ability of such a system to seek one particular goal, or to maintain one particular state, such as this one temperature under rapidly changing weather conditions outside.

It is, however, quite possible for the goal itself to be changed. This may occur gradually, through a drift in the characteristics or behavior of some parts of the system. Gradual changes in the culture patterns or personality structures of a population, or in the personnel of a political elite, may thus change the goals sought by a political decision system. Studies of the political effects of changes in the "national character" or in prevailing personality patterns, such as the change toward "other-directedness" suggested by David Riesman, might be developed in this direction.[8]

In some organizations, goal-changing is a part of the pattern of feedback processes itself. In such cases, if goal A has been approached to the extent of a given threshold value, the reaching of the threshold will trigger a rearrangement of some elements in the communication system, so as to give priority to another feedback circuit steering the system in the direction of another goal B. If B is reached, the system may return to the search for A, or go on to a third goal-seeking circuit steering it toward goal C; and so on. In this manner, animals may alternate between hunger and thirst, and machines have been built that move toward sources of light as long as their own energy supply is high, but move toward sources of energy when their own energy supply falls below a certain level.

Isolated instances of goal-changing are well known in politics. Literature is replete with descriptions of the changes in the behavior of former political "outs" that have become "ins," or of new men who have "arrived" and who, as the French say, "do not send the elevator down." How, when, and how quickly goals are changed by individuals, groups, and organizations might be a fruitful subject for political research.

A more specifically political problem arises in situations where a major strategic goal must be achieved through a sequence of intermediate or tactical goals. According to Adolf Hitler's view of mass psychology, the art of mass leadership in such cases consists in the ability to make each intermediate goal appear as the ultimate one, and to convince the rank and file that everything depends upon their ability to gain this particular objective here and now, regardless of all else. Only ultimate goals, in this view, have the capacity to elicit the total commitment of all available resources from large numbers of persons. Despite vehement disagreement with other theories of Adolf Hitler, Communist agitation often shows a similar pattern: each particular and transitory goal is represented for the time being as the be-all and end-all of political activity, until it is replaced by another. Similar psychological strategies have been employed to some extent by democratic governments in wartime, and in some of the protracted contests of the "cold war."

Despite their occasional empirical usefulness, such psychological "all-out" tactics are fraught with serious political costs. Thucydides early noted one of their drawbacks: since each tactical goal is represented as all-important, and virtually as ultimate, all disagreement about tactics becomes treason. Since, moreover, the most recklessly chosen tactical objectives can be most easily represented as ultimate goals, or as equivalent to victory, the most reckless tactics may seem to be the most appealing; and since, at the same time, they may evoke a larger measure of dissent, they may form an excellent pretext of purges of dissenters. Under suitable conditions, such as those prevailing in Athens during certain stages of the Peloponnesian War, the most reckless foreign policy or military tactics thus tended to be selected by the political decision process. The gradual hardening of war aims in modern wars involving mass participation, such as the last two world wars, may be related to a similar political process.[9] It might be worth investigating to what extent totalitarian dictatorships are subject to this process, and thus to the danger of the loss of control over their own strategy, and whether, and to what extent, and by what devices, different regimes of this kind have succeeded in dealing with this problem.

Exalting each of a series of changing tactical goals to the temporary status of a final goal may also exact a somewhat subtler price. Both Hitler and Lenin drew a technical distinction between the mere adherents of political parties, who agreed with the party's announced objectives, voted for its candidates, and possibly gave it some limited support, and the fully active members of the organization—sometimes called the "activists"—who committed to the party a major part of their time, resources, and imagination. Within the ranks of those "activists," in theory, little further distinction was made. If a political party, however, demands all-out commitment to a succession of changing tactical goals, and at the same time invites persons to become activists, it is apt to impose precisely upon those activists an almost intolerable psychological strain. They must commit themselves completely to each transitory goal. They may find it impossible, therefore, to devote much time and attention to considering the strategic course of which the goal may be a minor part, and thus to considering the probability of a change in the goal in the future. Many of them may well feel "let down" when this change in fact arrives. Since this experience is repeated every time the goal is changed, such parties are apt to have a high turnover of disgruntled former activists. These activists may eventually leave their party almost regardless of the supposed intrinsic merits of each change in policy, even in terms of their own previously held ideology. They may leave the movement, not because the particular change in tactics was iniquitous, but rather because for each of them personally it was one change too many—the straw that broke the camel's back.

In addition to producing a high turnover, this "idolization of ephemeral goals"—if we may adopt one of A. J. Toynbee's terms again—may have a peculiar effect on the type of persons who remain faithful to the parties or governments that resort to such tactics. On the one hand, there will remain a larger or smaller number of eternal activists, who accept each change without question, and who give their all to each goal in its day. On the other hand, the functions of planning strategy, of choosing sequences of tactical goals, and of timing the switches between them must still be fulfilled. Since many of the unquestioning activists may become psychologically unsuited to fulfilling this second group of functions, another structure may have to be developed to fulfill it: a strategic party or "inner circle"—a group of "insiders" who commit their own attention in part to data inconsistent with the all-out policy of the moment, and who carry on among themselves some of the deliberation and discussion needed for its future change.

Parallels to this functional split may even occur in business organizations. The folklore of sales organizations and advertising staffs is full of the distinction between the "Boy Scout" or "eager beaver" type of employee who commits himself completely to every sales campaign, and the "insider" or "executive type" who does his bit in a respectable fashion but who avoids all undue enthusiasm about tactical goals he knows will soon be changed.

Where democratic governments use tactics on an all-out scale, as they did during the Second World War, they may face the risk of a similar split between cynics and believers, with a gradual increase in the number of cynics as time goes on. David Riesman's assertion that the "inside dopester" may have replaced the crusading reformer as the political model for many persons in our time may not be unrelated to this problem.[10]

Most elements of this analysis should lend themselves to research. How sharp a change in goals or policies has been imposed on how many people, in how short a time, and with what consequences? How noticeable is the split between outsiders and insiders in a particular political party or government? What methods and devices have been adopted to control this type of disintegration, and with what success?

One possible way of controlling this split between tactical and strategic goals, and the corresponding split between outsiders and insiders, has been suggested to the writer by Professor Franklin Scott. If it were possible to publicize at all times the strategic goal of the government or organization, and to publicize the particular relation of the day's tactical goals to that strategic goal, then it might be easier for citizens or soldiers, or for the members of an organization, to maintain their emotional commitment to the strategic goal and to avoid emotional commitment to the changing tactics, while at the same time giving full operational support to these tactics, not for their own sake, but for the sake of the strategic goal they are held to serve. This, it will readily appear, represents to some extent a more elaborate disguise for the well-known "means-ends" problem; but the actual extent to which such methods have been used, or could be used, in politics might be an interesting topic for research.

A last aspect of goal-changing feedback might involve fundamental changes in goals. An organization, having pursued one kind of goal, might come to pursue a very different kind of goal. In this manner, the Swedish political system changed from the pursuit of military power in the seventeenth century to the pursuit of neutrality and social welfare in the twentieth. This may involve more than the change of just one or several values. Rather, where such changes in major goals occur, we may find at work a process of long-range reconstruction; and where they occur in a relatively short time we may face the phenomena of renovation, reformation, revolution, or conversion. All these involve a major change in over-all function and behavior, as well as major structural rearrangements of the political decision system, and usually of the rest of the society. If we ask, "How likely are such major changes to occur in a particular political or social system? And how likely are they to occur without self-destruction on the part of the system?"—then we have gone beyond the problem of simple goal-changing feedback. We are asking about the learning capacity or innovating capacity of that society. This problem was discussed in an earlier section, but we shall return to it later.

12

Political Self-Awareness, Autonomy, and Sovereignty

In an earlier section it was noted that goal images could be stored in a goal-seeking system and that such stored information could then be applied to the further behavior of the system. We then made this notion more general, and distinguished two classes of messages or symbols, primary and secondary, that may move through a decision system. *Primary messages* were taken to be those referring to events outside the system; and *secondary messages* were taken to be those referring to primary messages, or to other secondary messages up to any level of regress. In terms of a primary message, we said, a decision system might "know" of an external fact; by means of secondary messages it would "know" that it "knows." This, it was suggested, is perhaps the most simple pattern of what is called consciousness.

SECONDARY SYMBOLS IN ORGANIZATIONS

In everyday life we do something similar, when we "register" a letter at the post office: we ask the post office to attach a secondary symbol to the letter, and to keep secondary records of its mailing and transmission, so as to be able in case of loss to trace its course among the millions of mail items carried daily. In effect, we are making the post office particularly conscious of this letter. The post office has physical possession of the information contained in the letter as soon as it has possession of the letter, but it needs secondary symbols to become aware of this specific letter among all the others. In peacetime, most post offices in democratic countries are forbidden to let anyone except the addressee read the letters entrusted to them, but in situations of wartime censorship, where certain letters may have to be read, they may again have to identify them by secondary symbols, such as watch lists, or lists of particular addresses, or categories of mail to be censored.

In governments or intelligence organizations, the distinction between primary and secondary messages can be empirically observed. Such organizations as, for instance, the United States State Department may receive a large amount of reports concerning events in the outside world. Secondary symbols are then attached to these incoming reports, perhaps in a Document Control Center, so that the organization "knows" of each report that it has received and where it can be found. Other secondary symbols implement the decisions concerning the routing of the primary reports, and their subsequent filing, as well as the class of persons permitted to see them in terms of a "security classification." Finally, summary sheets and evaluation sheets are attached to the reports, so as to reduce the amount of detail that is transmitted to the higher levels of decision. The policy committees or program committees at the top of such a research or decision-making organization may then deal only with abstracts, summaries, project descriptions, and the like, and with policy or action papers condensing and evaluating large amounts of primary information. Without this functional division between primary and secondary information, it would be almost impossible to keep control of the flow of large amounts of information, to identify the most important items, and to utilize them within a limited time for decisions and action.

Perhaps the most important function of secondary symbols may

201

be to permit decisions to be reached on the basis of large amounts of information. The capacity of every information-carrying system is limited. This is as true of every human brain as it is of every committee, and of any electronic calculator. In all these, only limited numbers of data can be held for simultaneous inspection or interaction. Only by using secondary symbols at a high level of abstraction is it possible to utilize at one and the same time information drawn from a wide range of primary data. In a somewhat extended sense, we may call *consciousness* the specific process of simultaneous, or nearly simultaneous, interaction of a number of different secondary symbols, drawn from different ranges of first-order information.

In its most extended sense, we may use the term *consciousness* for the entire process of deriving and using secondary symbols in a decision system, from the moment of attaching them to primary messages through their confrontation and recombination on the highest decision levels all the way to their reapplication to action. In this sense, consciousness is the set of feedback processes of secondary symbols.[1]

Consciousness may permit great precision in steering. If fed back into the control and redirection of the intake facilities or "sensory organs" of the decision system, it may serve to fix or to change the interest and attention of the organization, that is, to identify the kinds of information to be picked up and transmitted in preference to others.

Consciousness cannot, of course, be achieved without cost. It requires facilities and resources; it ties up manpower and materials; and it imposes delay upon decisions. "The brain," as the Austrian labor leader, Victor Adler, used to tell his followers, "is an organ of inhibition." Consciousness may increase the accuracy and relevance of decisions by taking into account a wealth of information and by treating several potentially interdependent items at nearly the same time. It may also produce, however, very nearly the opposite result. It may increase the probability of wrong decisions by using secondary symbols that misrepresent the distribution of primary data. It may pass by the most relevant items of primary information in favor

202

of unrepresentative items that appear preferable on the basis of some previously acquired criteria of acceptability.

Consciousness may thus become false consciousness. A government, a social group, or a political organization may live in part in a world of dreams, as did some of the southern leaders before the American Civil War, or as did some of the Japanese military on the eve of Pearl Harbor. In less dramatic situations, many organizations, governments, or individuals operate with self-images of their own behavior that may differ widely from what they actually are doing.

Whether true or false, accurate or misleading, however, consciousness may be a powerful engine of control. By changing the amount of attention and secondary reporting given to certain kinds of social or political facts and events, their eventual impact on the entire society or political system can be greatly changed. Control of the social institutions of mass communication, and generally of the storage and transmission of information, is an obvious major component of power.

What is less obvious, but perhaps no less true, is that the potential power exercised through the feedback processes of social consciousness depends not merely on the size of the information-transmitting institution (such as perhaps a multimillion dollar newspaper), but sometimes even more decisively upon the extent of *condensation* of primary data and the *strategic location of control* at some bottleneck point in the flow of secondary information. The vast number of possible historical facts poses such a bottleneck problem, and if the national past is held to be at all relevant for current political decisions, a small number of historians may wield a surprising amount of long-run influence. This is not to say that historians alone could have restored the prestige of Napoleon in the first half of the nineteenth century, or that historians and journalists alone could hope at some future date to restore the prestige of Adolf Hitler.[2] In both cases, the presence of a large receptive public, and thus of certain social, economic, and political conditions, would be essential. However, even with such conditions prevailing to a limited extent, much could be done to hasten or hinder the process, or even to help to reverse it in some precariously balanced situations of decision.

The concept of consciousness as the feedback and simultaneous confrontation of secondary symbols suggests some research problems in the study of governments and political organizations.

What kinds of primary data are most likely to be picked up and reported to higher levels of the decision system? What kinds tend to be neglected or screened out? To whom are secondary data reported, and how far upward do they go in the organization before being used for decision?

To what extent are abstracts from different ranges of information and experience inspected *simultaneously*, or confronted with each other in reaching a decision? Or, on the contrary, to what extent does the right hand not know what the left hand has been doing?

How accurate and how representative—and, hence, how realistic —are the secondary data used? How realistic are the self-images and the images of the surrounding situation that are used at various levels of decision? To what extent can major distortions in these images, and thus major instances of "false consciousness," be traced to particular points or channels in the information-carrying and decision-making system?

What is the operating efficiency and what are the costs of the organized treatment of secondary information?

To what extent is all the most relevant secondary information carried in the head of any single individual? To what extent, therefore, is the information simultaneously presented in the plotting room of an antiaircraft defense center, or in the "Situation Room" in the United States Department of Defense, larger than, or different from, that carried by any single individual? To what extent, accordingly, do the consciousness, the situation images, and the decisions, carried by a whole committee, staff, or organization, differ from those carried by any individual? To what extent may the "thinking" of this or that government thus be different from the thinking of each of the single individuals who compose its personnel?

Finally, what use is made of the secondary data and of the "consciously made" decisions? Do they delay the primary reactions of the organization to the point where the latter become "sicklied o'er with the pale cast of thought, . . . and lose the name of action"? Or do they come too late or with insufficient status to affect the organization's actual behavior, so that persons with an accurate consciousness of the real situation must look on powerless as did Cassandra at the fall of Troy?

Almost every one of these questions has been asked at one time or another in qualitative terms, and sometimes answers have been suggested in similar terms of qualitative judgment or description. The communications approach to the study of organizations might permit us to ask these questions in terms of more clearly identifiable structures and substructures, and of distinct and potentially quantifiable functions. We shall continue to need insight and perceptiveness in this field, perhaps even more than in many others, but with the help of communication analysis we may learn someday to organize these insights in such a manner that they can be more often compared and verified.

An extremely crude diagram of some basic information flows and control functions in the foreign policy process of a government, as presented in the Appendix (see p. 258), may help to locate some of these questions in their relation to each other, and to the governmental decision-making system as a whole.

BOUNDARIES AND AUTONOMY

Some of the aspects of communication discussed thus far may lead us to the study of autonomous organizations in political or social life. The limits of an autonomous organization can be described in terms of a *communication differential:* among members or parts of an organization there should be more rapid and effective communication than with outsiders. This differential between internal and external communication may serve in turn as a means of identifying membership in borderline cases. A high differential between inner and outer communciation may let an organization appear relatively cohesive vis-à-vis its social environment; whether such an organization will also be functionally or operationally cohesive, however, will depend far more on the effectiveness of inner communications measured against the tasks imposed on them, rather than upon the mere difference between inner and outer communications. If the former are poor, the fact that the latter are still poorer may serve as a test of separateness rather than of viability. Attempts to increase the distinctive identity of an organization, group, party, or people by reducing their communications to nonmembers, instead of increasing the communications among their members, may thus lead to superficial success but may eventually reveal themselves as attacks at the wrong end of the problem.

Within the organization, lesser communication differentials might provide a measurable test for the difference between "insiders" and ordinary members, and permit a study of cliques, influence, and corruption from this aspect.

Among the most important of the patterns of inner communications, channels, and preferences that hold an organization together are the feedback loops that include *memory facilities* as parts of their pathways. By memory facilities are meant any kind of facilities available to the organization by means of which data from the past are stored and held available for recall and applications to recombination or to action. Such memory facilities for an organization exist most obviously in the heads of some of its members. In addition the organization may include other facilities: filing systems, libraries, or special organizations dealing with the maintenance of available knowledge, such as reference staffs, policy groups, overseers, and the like.

Whatever its physical form, memory is essential for any extended functioning of autonomy. Indeed, we might define autonomy above the simple feedback level as the feeding back of data *from* some form of *memory*, and thus from the past, into the making of present decisions.

Autonomy, in this view, depends on the balancing of two feedback flows of data: one from the system's performance in the present and in its environment; the other from the system's past, in the form of symbols recalled from its memory. "Freedom," Jean-Jacques Rousseau once said, "is obedience to the law which we prescribe to ourselves." The "we" in this statement, and the whole notion of self-rule implicit in Rousseau's words, require memory as an essential element: without it, the self-imposed law could be neither formulated nor remembered. Without traditions and memory, would-be self-steering organizations are apt to drift with their environment. Without openness to new information from their environment, however, self-steering organizations are apt to cease to steer themselves and to behave rather like mere projectiles entirely ruled and driven by their past. Paradoxically, selfhood in individuals and organizations is lost with the loss of information from outside one's own closed system and "one's own" time.

Autonomy in an organization is thus a function of the whole system. It is not located at any one point in the system, but there may be one or more points of particular importance for it. These crucial points for the autonomy of an organization are the points at which a flow of data recalled from the past enters the flow of data used for the making of current decisions. The location within an organization of its major memory facilities, and the points or channel patterns by which these memories are used for steering and decision-making, may tell us much about the probable functioning as well as about possible structural weaknesses and vulnerabilities of the organization.

The splitting of one organization into two, as well as the merging of two organizations into one, can be studied in these terms. In the case of split or secession, we should be able to trace the increase in communication differentials within the organization and the development of at least two "inside" areas that become "outside" areas relative to each other. Such communication differentials may arise quite unexpectedly, as by-products of intensive development in some particular region or part of the organization; yet if such regional communication should outgrow communication with the whole to a critical extent, its effects may prove divisive. The development of separate memories and memory facilities, separate feedback loops in communication, and the like, may represent other aspects of the process of secession. The opposite of this development, the process of political and organizational integration, might also be investigated in terms of declining communication differentials among the merging units, and the development of common memory facilities, major communication channels, and steering systems.

The foregoing remarks suggest that we may sometimes expect to find several organizations with limited autonomy vis-à-vis each other within a larger autonomous organization, which in turn may have some limited autonomy vis-à-vis some other large organization on its own level, and so forth. Politics indeed may be studied as the cooperation and conflict of such autonomous or semiautonomous groups. The widespread image of the political process as the pushing, pulling, and clashing of interest groups tends to slight, perhaps, this aspect of autonomy, and to leave unexplained the curious fact that there are not more bitter conflicts among all the different groups than we actually find in practice. It might, perhaps, be more realistic to think of political parties and interest groups as organizations with at least limited ability to steer themselves, with leaders and decision-making facilities that permit them to take warnings from their environment, to receive signals concerning the limits of practicable or safe action, and to maneuver accordingly with the aim to avoid damaging collisions at least as much as to reach particular goals in a short time.

Political conflicts could then be studied not merely from the aspect of their having been desirable for one or another contender or necessary and irrepressible from the viewpoint of the system within which they occur, but they could also be studied in terms of the efficiency or the failures of the steering facilities, the limit signals, and the maneuverability of the organizations and groups involved. Instead of looking simply for a "strong central power" to prevent conflicts—a power that conceivably may become precarious in certain domestic political conflicts and that in international politics does not as yet exist—we might rather ask how much central authority together with what distribution of autonomous organizations and what levels of efficiency in self-steering would be required to keep the frequency and intensity of group conflicts below the danger level for the whole system.

The analysis of policy aspiration groups and power aspiration groups might also be supplemented from this aspect of their steering capabilities and performance. To what extent do leaders and members of such groups know how far to go in any specific situation —perhaps to go to the brink of recession or of inflation or of war— and what is their ability to stop exactly there? The ability of political systems to combine individual freedom and a propensity to innovate with internal peace and stability may be not unconnected with the answers to such questions.

THE CONCENTRATION OF DECISIONS: SOVEREIGNTY AND VULNERABILITY IN POLITICAL SYSTEMS

Any major decision system is likely to include a considerable number of feedback processes and of the corresponding loop patterns of communication channels. Each of these feedback loops may contain one or several critical stages or *decision points*, at which either the behavior of the feedback can be changed or at which the behavior of one feedback loop produces a critical change in the behavior of another. Points at which feedbacks of stored information from memory facilities interact with feedback processes based on current outside information are decision points of this kind.

The set of important decision points in a system may show a lower or higher degree of concentration, and perhaps of hierarchy. If all important decisions are concentrated at one point, and if decisions made at that point tend to govern or override all decisions made elsewhere in the system, the performance of the system may resemble the situation of concentrated sovereignty, familiar from the absolute monarchies of seventeenth- and eighteenth-century Europe.

The concentration of decisions in such a system corresponds to some extent to the concentration of symbols of legitimacy, and the imputation of responsibility to the individual princes, ministers, or rulers. If the political system follows a series of decisions that leads to disaster, the actions or omissions of these few persons tend to be viewed as its causes.

An even more essential characteristic of sovereignty is the absence of any recognized input channel of controlling or overriding information from outside the system. In the theory of sovereignty no outside organizations, as well as no outside preferences or values, may be permitted to interfere with the working out of the internal decision probabilities of the system.

Finally, the concentration of all overriding decisions at a single point implies that no autonomous subsystem is permitted to function within the larger political organization, at least not with any degree of autonomy sufficient to modify or override the decisions made at the top.

Although these principles of organization were practiced by the absolute monarchies of Europe from the days of Machiavelli to those of Frederick of Prussia, they have been inherited to a large extent by the modern unitary state. To be sure, in such states the concentrated sovereignty inherited from absolute monarchs may be distributed among a small number of high-level institutions according to some pattern of constitutional arrangements. In practice, however, most of the important decisions still appear to be highly concentrated. A few dozen ministers, officials, and judges and, perhaps, a few hundred legislators seem to be holding among them the entire concentrated power of the state. According to widespread belief, this small circle of decision-makers is, or ought to be, impervious to all outside influences, particularly to influences from abroad, as well as highly resistant to special regional or sectional pressures.

The decisions of such a political system are believed to be "ultimate" or "final," in the sense that there is no further instrumentality for modifying or changing them after they have reached a particular stage, point or institution in the system. Each of these points or institutions functions in the manner of a court of last resort for the class of decisions entrusted to it, and is held to have the power of "*ultimacy*" or *finality* in respect to them. Even though this power of ultimacy is no longer concentrated in the hands of a single person, as it was in the days of absolute monarchy, it is still concentrated in what looks like a small and easily identifiable region, and it is believed to inhere in the state as a whole.

Despite its seeming plausibility, this scheme may represent a highly imperfect description of the actual state of affairs. Studies of domestic politics may show that the actual workings of the decision-making process are far more impersonal; that the resulting decisions may often be unpredicted and may even seem unpredictable; and that all attempts to allocate responsibility for major decisions to particular individuals may end up in a maze of alibis, in which each decision-maker may sincerely believe and plausibly show that he did only what he had to do in the circumstances of the time. In the field of political decisions concerning war and peace, both the debate about the guilt for World War I and the war-crimes trials after World War II have demonstrated the degree of complexity and impersonality to be found in present-day political decision systems.

Overestimating the concentration of decisions at a single point is apt to lead to an overestimation of the importance of particular offices or persons. If only Minister X could be converted or assassinated, if only the "right man" could be put into Ministry Y—so runs the argument—then soon all would be well, or at least the worst could be prevented. Usually such notions prove to be mistaken, both because the social setting may produce new officeholders very similar to the former incumbent and because the actual range of discretion permitted to each particular office or decision-maker may prove much smaller than imagined.

The same consideration may well apply to the problem of estimating the vulnerability of governments to the destruction of crucial points or institutions in the decision system by aerial bombardment, or to infiltration by adherents of a particular ideology or agents of a foreign power. The higher the actual degree of concentration of decisions, the greater the actual degree of vulnerability is apt to be; and the greater the imagined degree of such concentration, the greater may be the fear of infiltration or destruction.

Realistic estimates of the actual situation can be made only on the basis of a careful mapping out of the distribution and configuration of decision points, the extent of their mutual support and control, and the presence or absence of reserve facilities for taking over the functions of decision points and partial decision systems that have been temporarily incapacitated or destroyed. A not wholly dissimilar problem has long existed in a field seemingly far removed from politics. Problems of damage control in battleships has involved precisely such questions as to how a ship is to continue in operation after its captain has been lost or its bridge destroyed or its steering assembly incapacitated. A study of the "damage-control characteristics" of a given political system might well prove worth undertaking in our atomic age.

The naïve assumption of concentrated sovereignty may even be more misleading in international politics. The emphasis on sovereignty may tend to divert attention from the very real limits that constrain the decisions of even the most powerful nations. No state is omnipotent or disposes of unlimited resources, nor can any government expect unlimited sacrifices from its population. If we are to analyze the actual working of political autonomy under these conditions, it may be useful to distinguish three categories:

1. *Limit probabilities*, that is, the probability that the behavior of the government, or state, will run into a physical, social, economic, or military limit, such as overwhelming resistance, external force, or inner difficulties.

2. *Limit signals*, that is, signals, data, or information announcing the approaching or the presence of such a physical or social limit. Such limit signals must be received by the decision system, interpreted, and applied to the control of its further behavior in a more or less efficient manner.

3. *Limit images*, that is, images of such physical or social limits, of their configurations, and of the probability of meeting them under particular conditions. To be effective, such images would have to be stored in the memory facilities of the system, as well as recalled and fed back into the control of its behavior. Such limit images may, of course, be elaborate or crude, precise or vague, realistic or misleading; and they may or may not be used effectively by the system.

Effective behavior on the part of any autonomous organization requires the organization to remain within its limits of action or survival, and thus to satisfy its limit probabilities through the use of limit signals and limit images. Sovereign states face the same task in this respect as do other autonomous organizations, but they face it with an added difficulty. While their behavior is subject to limits and limit probabilities, and while they usually receive some limit signals, *sovereign states as a rule exclude limit images*. They teach their citizens, as well as many of their lawmakers and officials, to reject as unreal, or at least as illegitimate, all constraints or limits upon their own decisions or upon the behavior of their country. In addition to the absence of institutionalized limit images, sovereign states may also be endangered by the low status, both in terms of prestige and of treatment in communication, of such limit signals as they actually may receive. Facilities for the reception, treatment, and use of limit signals may be extremely deficient, and may leave the government in danger of running sometimes head on into some actual limit to its power.

The similar effect in domestic politics of the loss of limit images, and of the neglect of limit signals where it may lead to extreme group conflict and civil war, has been discussed in an earlier section.

CHAPTER

13

The Self-Closure
of Political
Systems

This chapter can offer merely a brief note on some recurrent difficulties of governments, and some aspects of the relationship between morality and politics, as well as on a possible mode of thinking about them. More than once in the development of the social sciences a change in the manner of thinking about a problem area has preceded the sharp formulation of specific questions and the mobilization of resources to answer them. The emphasis on emotion in the writings of Rousseau, the traditionalism of Burke, or the pragmatic attitude of William James and John Dewey each served in its time to direct attention to areas and aspects of problems that previously had been slighted. This chapter attempts to approach the ancient problem of morality and politics from the viewpoint of the study of communication and organization, and particularly of the concept of autonomy. If it succeeds in pointing out the political and psychological process of self-closure as a problem in its own right, and in suggesting specific problems and questions for other investigators, it will have fulfilled its task.

The basis of autonomy, it was suggested earlier, consists in a particular pattern of treating information. Since much of this information is transmitted by means of symbols, autonomy involves certain

214

ways of treating such symbols. If there are strong tendencies toward eventual failure inherent in all autonomous organizations, and particularly in governments—as many pessimistic theories of politics allege—then such difficulties of governments can perhaps be traced to their propensity to prefer self-referent symbols to new information from the outside world.[1]

SOME OPTIMISTIC VIEWS OF POLITICS

Many early views identified politics with good, or at least suggested that politics could be morally good and therefore ought to be so. The concepts of law and right, of freely acknowledged leadership, and of instituted authority became separated only gradually in the course of history. Even when men made the discovery of *summum ius summa iniuria*, and realized that the law need not mean either right or justice, they often explained this experience in terms of a lost "golden age" of brotherhood, a past period free from the present tension between morality and power, in which compulsion was either absent and unnecessary or in which it was invariably good and just.

While some men dreamed of a golden age of authority and justice in the past, other men projected it into the future, or at least into the realm of the ideal and perhaps the partially possible. Political utopias, from Plato and Thomas More to our day, picture societies in which compulsion and obedience are either absent or in which they correspond closely to some positive and explicit system of morality.

Another group of thinkers even went so far as to describe the coincidence of politics and morality as probable in human life. John Locke and Adam Smith considered the world as inhabited by rational men and women who would be led by their experience to institute a just system of natural rights in politics and a system of natural liberty in economics. Once established, these just systems would endure; if they should be temporarily disturbed by folly or ambition, an inevitable reaction, or the renewed impact of ex-

215

perience, would sooner or later restore a natural and just state of affairs.

Other thinkers were willing to grant that the discovery and establishment of a just political and social system might take a longer time. They devoted some attention, therefore, to the time path or to the actual sequence of steps by which this desirable state was to be reached. Accordingly, they developed theories of progress. The pace of such progress might be agonizingly slow or its path might lead through temporary reverses, dark ages, catastrophes. Yet, according to the vision of Condorcet, in the end knowledge would come out of ignorance, and freedom would replace oppression. In Kant's view of world history, peace would replace war, and the power of scientists might replace that of princes, as consciousness gradually came to replace blind strife. Economic abundance, the abolition of classes, and the withering away of the state, acording to Marx and Engels, were to replace capitalism and oppression. A high plateau of permanent prosperity, supported by the associated activities of enlightened businessmen, according to Herbert Hoover, was to bring about the abolition of poverty, first in the United States and perhaps gradually in the rest of the world.

All these views pictured the world of politics as being at bottom actually or potentially good. However, all these views had at the same time to explain the current existence of injustice and evil. Since the bad features could not be inherent in the nature of politics itself, they must be due to special causes. Once these special causes of evil were identified and destroyed, goodness would reign unchallenged.

The theories of political optimism are thus in one sense potential theories of crusading. Once the guilty parties, the obscurantists or the princes or the capitalists or the government bureaucrats or the radical agitators, have been eliminated from society, all will be well. Of course, men of good will may differ about the exact causes of evil: Should only the German officers and Junkers be destroyed, many Americans asked each other in 1944, or does the guilt rest with the entire German people? It is thus possible that the wrong group of persons or conditions might be identified as sources of evil. If so, the mistake would have to be rectified as far as possible in the next attempt to strike at the right target; and if irreversible damage has been done, there is nothing for it but to try and do better next time.

The outline given in the preceding paragraphs has been so simplified as to approach a caricature. Like a caricature, however, it may bear some resemblance to some salient features of the object it portrays. If we are willing to grant such a resemblance, we may perhaps understand more readily the continued appeal, as well as the most recent vogue, of the opposite group of theories of politics: the conceptions of politics as inherently tragic or inherently evil.

POLITICS AND EVIL

The tradition of regarding politics as actually or potentially tragic or evil goes back to St. Augustine, and echoes of this "Augustinian" view of politics can be found in the thought of Martin Luther, John Calvin, and Sören Kierkegaard. Some of this tradition has remained discernible in the work of such thinkers as Max Weber and Karl Jaspers, and some of its echoes may be found in the recent political or historical writings of such men as Hans J. Morgenthau, Reinhold Niebuhr, and George Kennan.[2] In substance, this view suggests that the sphere of politics is intrinsically evil, for it is inextricably mixed up with the practices of force and deception. Power corrupts, it is granted, and there is no politics without power. Individuals of good will can do little except withdraw, or else play this unholy game as best they may. To behave in politics in a way that is morally good, and yet pragmatically successful, is either held to be impossible, or it is held to be possible only by means of grace, that is, of events beyond the foresight and control of human beings. To be sure, the views of none of the writers we have cited agree exactly with this summary; but its fundamental pattern is perhaps discernible in the thought of all of them.

Once one assumes the incompatibility of realistic politics with the great moral traditions of mankind, different emotional attitudes may be adopted. One may reject much of traditional morality as irrele-

217

vant, as did Machiavelli, or as outrightly undesirable, as did Nietzsche, and attempt to derive a new set of values and enjoyment from the active conduct, or at least the enthusiastic contemplation, of the merciless political struggle.

Alternatively, hardboiled politics may be accepted as inevitable but also as inevitably doomed to eventual failure and disappointment. Such a view of politics may then be borne with resignation, as it is in the philosophy of Schopenhauer, or the inevitable decline of each culture may be contemplated with an attitude of gloomy heroism, as it is suggested in the works of Oswald Spengler.

A number of attitudes of reasonable compromise between optimism and pessimism in regard to the relationship of morality and politics has been attempted. The political theories of Aristotle, of St. Thomas Aquinas, of Edmund Burke, and perhaps of Benjamin Disraeli and of Winston Churchill, all suggest that politics and morality cannot be completely reconciled and that, as Mr. Churchill once put it, "a robust conscience" is an essential part of the equipment of the statesman. Yet the dangerous and doubtful means employed by statesmen who, like Kipling's Queen Victoria, must be "wise in terrible things," are believed to be capable of producing, with prudence, a discernible net gain for good. This class of views should appear on the whole both reasonable and appealing. That it does not appeal to many in our day may merely be a symptom of the temper of the age; or it may be an indication that such views do not impress us as adequate for the crisis of our time. We may suspect that these moderate and conservative views may be tinged with a good deal of the temper of that very liberal optimism they ostensibly oppose. We may suspect that they overestimate both the frequency and the probability of situations in which the good and the expedient may coincide and in which political power and the pursuit of moral ends will prove compatible. Failures of rulers and statesmen to predict even the pragmatic outcome of their political decisions, let alone their moral and spiritual effects, may turn out to be not the exception but the rule; and the Augustinian despair of the possibility that politics could be anything but evil may take hold once again of men's imagination.

There may be more to this problem than the misgivings of a generation haunted by the memory of atomic explosions and weary of crusades. Perhaps some may suspect that there are some deeper insights contained in the ancient religious tradition of "original sin" and that there is perhaps some truth in the qualitative and intuitive statements of the eternal insufficiency of man, which contrast so strongly with the "if only" approach of the philosophies of optimism.

Is there perhaps a paradox in the nature of autonomy, in the self-steering and the self-rule of each individual personality, as well as of each autonomous human organization? Autonomy is impossible without openness to communication from the outside world; but at the same time autonomy is impossible unless the incoming flow of external information is overridden to a significant extent by internal memories and preferences. What can go wrong in this precarious pursuit of an ever-changing balance, and how great is the probability of the eventual failure and self-destruction of every autonomous organization?

AUTONOMY AND ITS MODES OF FAILURE

Autonomy, or self-steering, is a characteristic of organizations that are guided in their behavior by a loop sequence of decisions that feeds back upon itself. A simple organization of this kind may receive information concerning some external objective or goal, and may be driven by its own inner disequilibrium to approach it; and it will be guided in the next stage of its performance by the receipt of information concerning both the goal and its own behavior and position relative to it. In this manner, it will receive information concerning its own distance from the goal, or the extent to which it has already overshot the mark; and under certain conditions this information may serve to correct its approach and to guide it through a series of diminishing mistakes until the goal is reached. An extended organization of this kind may be able to alternate between the pursuit of a series of goals, or to rearrange under certain con-

219

ditions parts of its own inner structure in such a manner that it may come to seek new goals.

To be truly autonomous, such extended self-steering organizations must also carry with them a wide range of stored data from the past, and they must govern the recall of such items from memory by means of feedback processes similar in essence to those by which they obtain information from the outside world. Autonomy thus involves the feeding back of a stream of data recalled from memory into a stream of decisions regarding current behavior. The points at which these two kinds of communication channels meet are strategic points in the decision system. If we ask where within a large organization the core or the "self" of the organization is located, we are asking in essence about the location of the points that are most critical for its vulnerability or its control.

The main concentrations of memories (which may of course be concentrated in the heads of a few individuals in the organization), and the main junctions of communication channels at which these memories are brought to bear upon current decisions, are strategic *decision points* in this sense. The distribution of such decision points may be important in the process of learning. Seen from the outside, *learning* on the part of an organization involves an observable change in its behavior in response to the repetition of some unchanged stimulus. Seen from the inside, such a repetitive change of behavior can be accomplished only by a change in inner structure. Usually such a change in inner structure is likely to involve either the content and distribution of memories, or the location and sequence of decision points, or both.

Individuals, as well as large social or political organizations, can thus learn to remake their current behavior. They can redirect their attention; they can change particular preferences; and they can change the structure and consistency of larger parts of their preference system. Anything they do in the external world at any moment will be an expression of the probabilities of behavior implicit in their inner structure at that time. In this sense, it is said of persons that they act "in character," or they act out their inner needs, drives, and personality patterns. It is said of political parties or governments that they are acting out the political and social preferences of the organizations and social groups of which they are composed, or from which they draw support; and it is sometimes asserted of sovereign states that their domestic politics tend to govern their foreign relations.

Our picture of the working of self-governing organizations may suggest that these views are only partially true. Every self-governing organization must receive significant information from its environment, and modify its own overt behavior accordingly. At the same time, however, it must report back to itself the outcome of its own behavior as it has been modified by the environment. The greater the extent of its autonomy, the greater has to be the extent and effectiveness of the facilities for memory of which it disposes; and the more effective these facilities for memory, the more faithfully they will store information derived from the organization's changing environment, and from the organization's changing responses to it. Every self-governing system must therefore remake its own memories and inner structure as it acts. These inner changes may be small or large at any particular step, but their cumulative effect is apt to be considerable. If sociologists like Don Luigi Sturzo have applied the image of a collective "personality" to peoples and states, we may perhaps apply to this "personality" the suggestion of Jean-Paul Sartre, that we act out our personality at every moment of our life but that we inescapably remake it in so doing with every decision taken.

Every autonomous decision system, on this showing, eventually is likely to rearrange its own inner structure, and these changes may be either viable or pathological ("functional" or "disfunctional" in Robert K. Merton's terminology), depending on whether they increase or decrease the probability of the future successful functioning of the system, and particularly of its future learning performance. The failures or pathologies that may develop quickly or gradually in this process may perhaps be divided into six broad groups:

1. The loss of *power*, that is, the loss of resources and facilities required to make the behavior of the system prevail over obstacles in its environment;

2. The loss of *intake*, that is, the loss in the effectiveness of previously existing channels of information from the outside world, or the loss of entire channels, or the loss of the ability to rearrange such intake channels and to develop new ones;

3. The loss of *steering capacity* or coordination, that is, the loss of control by the organization over its own behavior, or of the ability to modify behavior with sufficient speed and precision;

4. The loss of *depth* of memory, that is, not merely the loss in the over-all storage capacity of memory facilities, but particularly any loss in the effectiveness of the facilities for the recall and recombination of data, and for the screening and identification of the most relevant of all the many possible combinations, by means of some search criteria and search devices; in everyday language, this category would thus include losses in memory, in imagination, and in judgment;

5. The loss of capacity for partial *inner rearrangement*, and correspondingly, for the learning of limited new patterns of behavior; this is sometimes loosely described as the "rigidity" or "flexibility" of an organization, thus diverting attention from the combinatorial aspects of learning and structural change;

6. The loss of capacity for comprehensive or *fundamental* rearrangement of inner structure, and thus for comprehensive changes in behavior; in different contexts of discourse this is sometimes called "restructuring," "personality change," "reformation," "resolution," "rebirth," or "conversion."

Each of these types of loss is likely, of course, to be followed in time by other losses; and the probabilities of each of these types of loss, as well as of several types of loss occurring together, may form the set of probabilities of pathological learning, that is to say, of the eventual self-crippling or self-destruction of any self-governing organization.

Among all such autonomous organizations, political systems assume a special place. Politics deals essentially with the manipulation of overriding preferences and priorities in social life through the operation of threats of enforcement and habits of compliance. In this sense, politics represents in present-day societies a major sphere of decision. An inquiry into the probabilities of the six types of failure or self-destruction in political systems may therefore throw some light upon the relationship of politics and evil, and its possible relevance for the study of the political process.

THE PROBABILITIES OF FAILURE

The six kinds of failure outlined in the preceding section all involve in one way or another the overvaluation of particular data or memories in a decision system. The probability of each particular kind of failure may depend therefore on the probability with which the system will produce such overvaluations in the course of its operation.

The first mode of failure is the failure of power. This involves the pursuit of actions or policies that tend to dissipate or destroy the material and social resources required for their own continuation. Even Machiavelli warned princes that temporary gains in power from a financial policy of liberal spending would be purchased at the cost of dissipating the financial resources without which they could not be continued. As Max Weber and other writers have pointed out, the acceptance of ethics emphasizing thrift and accumulation have had much to do with the rapid growth of Western economic and political power during the past four centuries. More recently, British writers have commented on the contrast between the largely consumer-oriented economies and political systems of France and Britain, on the one hand; and, on the other hand, the far greater stress on economic accumulation characteristic of the present economies of both the United States and Russia. Despite the greater emphasis on thrift and accumulation, individual or collective, in modern industrial economies, the tendency toward waste has not lost its significance. We find it in the tendency to destroy natural resources; to exhaust soils, forests, and mineral reserves; to divert large amounts of manpower and resources to unproductive ends; and, occasionally, to substitute values of quick gain and conspicuous consumption for those of long-term development.

Another facet of this attitude is perhaps the tendency to consider human beings essentially as liabilities rather than as assets, and to focus time and attention more on attempts to arrest the growth of population than on attempts to increase the rate of growth of economic resources and educational facilities.

Perhaps the tendency underlying all these attitudes is the tendency to overvalue the present over the future, and to place a heavy discount on the latter. We do this directly when we cut down forests for timber without replanting, or when we let the soil erode. We do it more indirectly when we refuse to face the probability of continuing population growth for the next thirty or fifty years in most areas of the world, and avoid the responsibility for formulating our political, social, and economic policies accordingly. What matters here is not so much the importance of these particular errors of commission or omission, but rather the tendency of individuals, social groups, and political organizations to overvalue the present, and to produce repetitive errors of this kind in the absence of any special provisions or policies designed to avoid them.

The second mode of failure is the failure or the gradual narrowing of intake of information from the outside world. This failure involves the overvaluation of memories over current ranges of intake, of internal over external messages, and of current ranges of intake over new data and new ranges of information. Overvaluations of this kind are favored by several conditions inherent in the operation of most or perhaps all autonomous systems. Information already stored within the system, or coming in through well-established channels, is apt to have shorter communication lines and simpler routines of access to the strategic points and areas of decision in the organization. Stored memories and routine types of information may therefore tend to receive operational priorities in the actual workings of the system, even regardless to some extent of their status in its imagery. Autonomous systems may thus tend to imprison themselves in an invisible rut of their own making. We may find an example of this tendency in the familiar process by which a newspaper or an intelligence agency adopts a policy, and sends out men to report on facts pertinent to it; then selects the reports and the men that are most favorable to the policy; and then receives from these men further reports still more favorable; and so on.

A broader category of examples may be found in the well-known tendency toward ethnocentrism: the overvaluation of the notions and folkways of one's own people and culture. To some extent this latter tendency may be produced by the sheer frequency of contacts; as a region becomes densely populated and a relatively homogeneous culture develops among its inhabitants, there may be left only an ever smaller proportion of time and attention for contacts outside that area. Before we rejoice about the speed of modern airplanes that have shrunk global distances for a few paying passengers, let us reflect that today a smaller proportion of mail crosses national boundaries, or is addressed to citizens of other countries, than was the case fifty years ago. Let us find out whether a larger or smaller proportion of our population has been engaged in peaceful travel; whether we devote a smaller or larger proportion of our newsprint to news from abroad, and to the opinions and actions of other nations. Let us ascertain whether a larger or a smaller proportion of our population can read or speak a foreign language; and whether a larger or smaller proportion of our reading is composed of the works of foreign authors, even in translation. Data of this kind have nothing to do with the frequency or scarcity of overt symbols of nationalism. Individuals and groups may become most thoroughly self-centered when they are least aware of it. What such data would indicate would rather be the possibility of an automatic isolationism brought about by the gradual shrinking of the channels of openness and intake, or the gradual drowning of their messages in the flood of competing internal information. A tendency toward such self-narrowing or self-isolation may be rather general in autonomous systems, and it may take specific devices and policies to counteract it even to a limited extent.

The third mode of failure is the decline or degeneration of steering capacity or coordination. This process may involve the overvaluation of structure over function, or of machinery over performance. As an autonomous system grows more complex it may increase the length of channels and the number of stages through which messages must go before resulting in decisions.[3] Ordinarily this may mean increased delay and slowness of response to changing information from the environment. The speed of such effective responses, however, relative to the speed of changes in the target or environment, is an essential factor in steering performance. A big dog has a poor chance to catch a zigzagging rabbit if its own rate of turn is slow; and the difference between speed and maneuverability is a well-known problem in the design of fighter aircraft. Where and if autonomous organizations tend to a greater slowness of response as they grow bigger, any growth in the power of each particular response would be likely to offer only very imperfect compensation. Strong responses that come late are characteristic of oversteering, in the manner of the novice automobile driver who barely avoids the lefthand ditch by turning his car toward the righthand one. If slowness of response to outside information is accompanied by greater complexity of inner communication channels, and therefore greater slowness of inner communication and coordination, steering performance is apt to degenerate still further.

A particular form of the loss of such steering or coordination in the behavior of an individual or an organization is the loss of coordination between behavior and memory. On the one hand, communication among different memory facilities may still be good; large amounts of data may be recalled and recombined in various fashions; but few data may come in from the outside, so that the thinking process occurs, in Francis Bacon's vivid image, as "in a spider" who draws his web out of himself. On the other hand, communication may degenerate between memory and action; relevant data may be recalled and recombined, and new outside information added to them; but the whole process may remain poorly connected to decisions about action, so that such decisions either do not take place at all or are long delayed or take place substantially unaffected by it.

The fourth mode of failure, the loss of depth of memory, is related to this process. It involves the overvaluation of established routines for recalling and recombining data, and of established criteria of relevance and interest in the screening of new combinations for more intensive development. The overvaluation of established ways of

226

performing these functions may involve, of course, the overvaluation of the particular structures currently performing them. The result in any case may be an increase in shallowness of thought. A set of new combinations of symbols has been created by established criteria of interest. Sooner or later any such set searched in terms of unchanging criteria is apt to approach exhaustion as far as those particular criteria of interest are concerned. The contrast we so often feel intuitively between originators and epigones in literary or scientific thought may be related to this pattern of intellectual decline. The only answer to this type of gradual failure seems to be inner re-arrangement, partial or comprehensive, of the facilities for memory, recall, and recombination, as well as of the criteria for search and relevance in finding the new combinations worth pursuing. But it is precisely this capacity for inner rearrangement that may decline in the course of the operations of an autonomous organization.

The fifth and sixth modes of failure bear on this point. They are the loss of capacity for partial inner rearrangement and of limited learning capacity, on the one hand, and the loss of capacity for comprehensive structural rearrangement, on the other. Both of these involve the problem of *commitment*. The more rigidly the structures and resources of an organization are committed to any particular set of functions or purposes, the less readily available are they for recommitment, and the less are thus the chances for any rearrangement in the system. In political and social organizations, and perhaps in the life of individuals, this rigidity of commitment is linked to the problems of challenge and success. The more serious the challenge, or the greater the danger, the greater may be the need to commit our resources to meet it on pain of destruction; but in meeting such an "excessive" challenge, in Toynbee's usage of the word, the ability to recommit resources later to new functions may be lost. The greater the success in meeting a crisis, the greater, simi-larly, may be the rewards for, and the prestige of, the particular tactics, institutions, and patterns of commitment of resources, that served to win it. The sequel of success may thus be the tendency, in Toynbee's term, "to rest on one's oars," or the outright "intoxication of victory." In either case, the degeneration of steering performance

COMMUNICATION MODELS AND POLITICAL DECISION SYSTEMS

and learning capacity may be the direct consequence of survival and success themselves.

It is evident that attempts to avoid all commitment will not avoid degeneration. The way of apathy, of withdrawal, and of absolute detachment has been sought at many times. Where it has not ended in self-destruction, it has ended in isolation. Even where it promised contemplation and compassion for the needs and sufferings of others, it has ended in self-centeredness if its compassion bore no fruit in action. If withdrawal and detachment were followed by return to action, on the other hand, this return again involved commitment, and with it the three kinds of risks: to perish in glorious failure; to continue in a new well-meaning routine; or to risk the intoxication of success.

Taken together, the six modes of failure present every self-governing organization, as well perhaps as every responsible individual, with a serious danger of eventual self-induced stagnation or of partial or total self-destruction. Obviously, men have sought for ways to counter these dangers. To some extent even the optimists who thought those dangers small and the pessimists who held them to be almost overwhelmingly large may have agreed that the dangers were real, and they even may have agreed on some of the ways to meet them. Few if any of these persons, however, have put their thoughts in the shape of an explicit theory of organization; rather we may have to turn to the great philosophic and religious traditions of mankind for some indications of their insights.

HOW CAN AUTONOMY BE PROTECTED AGAINST FAILURE?

Most of the traditional suggestions for preserving autonomy and avoiding self-destruction have been expressed in terms of policy, or preferable patterns of behavior, rather than in terms of particular institutions or devices. Even where particular institutions or values were suggested, the emphasis has frequently been that the spirit—the second-order strategy for choosing among values and value

228

systems—would be decisive that would be found at work at any particular practices or pathways likely to lead beyond it toward self-destruction. Finally, most of these suggestions have been addressed to individuals rather than to states, peoples, or organizations. This emphasis is relevant as individuals carry a large part of the decision function in all these larger groups. Individuals do not, however, carry all of this decision function. A good many decisions depend in part on the configuration of the communication channels and decision points in the political or social system in which they occur, and individual discretion left to them should not be overestimated. In such situations, insights applicable to the pathology of the decision system of an individual personality may offer at least some general policy suggestions for preserving and safeguarding the autonomy and long-run existence of larger organizations, and particularly of the political community.

The suggestions we shall discuss may seem couched in language unfamiliar to the political scientist, though not to the person interested in religion. It has sometimes been the fashion to reject out of hand all propositions expressed in religious terminology as allegedly "irrational" and "unverifiable," and some spokesmen for religion have indirectly supported this practice that seemed to promise them a sanctuary from inconvenient critics. All that will be asked is that the policies to be discussed should be evaluated for their rationality and soundness in terms of politics, and perhaps in terms of the broader study of organizations. If they fail by these standards, let their language give them no protection; but, until then, let it not bar them from a hearing.

THE CONCEPTS OF HUMILITY AND OF THE SIN OF PRIDE

All six modes of failure of autonomy that we discussed turned out to be related to the overvaluation of the near over the far, the familiar over the new, the past over the present, and the present over the future. They involved overestimation or overvaluation of the organization compared to its environment, of its past methods and commitments over new ones, and of its current will and inner structure over all possibilities of fundamental change.

The injunction to humility, common to several of the great religions, seems to be aimed directly at many of these sources of failure. In its essence, humility is perhaps an attitude toward facts and messages outside oneself; and openness to experience as well as to criticism; and a sensitivity and responsiveness to the need and desires of others. Its opposite has traditionally been called "the sin of pride," the sin, as G. K. Chesterton once called it, of "seeing oneself out of proportion to the universe."

In its extended sense, humility has perhaps implied the avoidance of overestimating not only the importance of oneself but also the importance of one's immediate environment. Though it may have been thus far the source of all one's experiences and problems, this environment itself is small in every sense, compared to the concept of God or of the Universe.

Finally, humility involves a profoundly skeptical attitude toward one's own ability to achieve it, or to maintain it for any length of time. Insufferable conceit has been noted in men who had convinced themselves that they were humble.

Taken together, the attitudes indicated by the concept of humility, and by their contrast to the sin of pride, are attitudes favorable to new learning, to maintaining and extending the channels of intake of outside information, and to the readiness for inner rearrangement.

In addition to being taught by religion, attitudes of humility have been important in science and in politics. "In the face of a fact," P. W. Bridgman has said, "the attitude of the scientist is one of humility which is almost religious." Centuries earlier, Isaac Newton likened his discoveries to the pebbles picked up by a child playing on the shores of the ocean of truth, and insisted that his own measure of success had been due to the fact that in his work he had stood "on the shoulders of giants." The willingness to be humble in the face of experimental fact, and to respect the work of others, but to remain unimpressed by show or pretense, has played an important part in the growth of modern science.

In politics, the attitude of humility perhaps has been expressed best in the ideas and the personality of Abraham Lincoln. Its classic statements are perhaps his Second Inaugural Address and the Gettysburg Address, as well as his suggestion that "we should be less concerned whether God is on our side, and more concerned whether we are on His." Lincoln carried some of this attitude into political practice in his openness and sensitivity to the needs of others, including even his defeated enemies. Humility in this sense extends beyond goodwill: more than one leader of goodwill may have been more willing to do good to others according to his own views than to be sensitive to theirs.

THE CONCEPTS OF LUKEWARMNESS AND FAITH

Commitment involves the risk of rigidity, and the loss of ability to meet the next challenge. Once this is discovered, what would be more natural than to avoid all commitment wherever possible? In economic life, the "investor" who keeps his money under his mattress avoids all the possible risks of committing it to a bank; the investor who keeps it in a cash account shows his "liquidity preference" as against all the potential troubles of industrial investments; and the investor who insists on keeping his funds in readily salable debt certificates of foreign governments, as so many French investors did during much of the past hundred years, may still enjoy his ability to jump quickly in every direction that market changes may indicate. But an economy in which everyone prefers liquidity is sick; and a political system becomes unstable if nobody wants to be burdened by convictions and if everybody wants to be what David Riesman has called an "inside dopester," who always knows which opinions to have next. To avoid commitment to any policy or action means to value one's resources more highly than their use, and to value one's self more highly than anything that one might do. In organizations as well as in individuals, the continued refusal of commitment thus represents one particular variety of self-centeredness and of self-overestimation. As it is exactly this self-overestimation which in the long run tends to destroy autonomy and learning capacity, there may be perhaps some good evidence for the truth of the biblical prediction that he who would keep his life shall lose it, but he who would lose his life shall find it.

As the opposite of lukewarmness, *faith* is perhaps a concept of commitment. How deeply do we commit our personality and our resources to a policy or course of behavior based on a particular proposition? Faith in this sense is a different concept from what might be called belief. The latter implies the refusal to consider the possibility that a proposition might be wrong, but it says nothing about the amount or proportion of resources that are to be committed to it. Faith, on the other hand, may be faith in "fear and trembling" that the proposition might be incorrect, or that one's understanding of it might be wrong, or that the behavior in question might not in fact be demanded by it, or that it might prove impossible to perform with the resources at hand. None of these would matter, as long as all one's resources are in fact committed to the proposition. In the imagery of the racetrack, dogmatism could be measured by the size of one's bets in proportion to one's resources. In the Western democracies, and particularly in the United States, many of us have expressed our belief in the justice of policies of racial equality, or in the wisdom of a technical assistance program of economic aid to underdeveloped areas, but we have been less numerous in urging ourselves, as well our legislators, to express our faith in these propositions.

The concepts of faith and humility exist to some extent as opposites in mutual tension. Faith implies commitment to some judgment of our own, even if it were only our judgment in choosing the right authority or the right book to obey; but humility might advise us to distrust our judgments even in such cases. Taken together, the two concepts offer us no model of a perfect working arrangement, but rather indicate two boundary conditions between which a viable pattern must be sought. To combine humility with faith, to be capable of rapid and thorough commitment without losing the openness to alternative information and the capacity for rearrangement and possible recommitment to other goals, or to a different understanding of some of the goals previously sought—that is, perhaps, a requirement for all autonomous systems that are to have a good chance of extended survival.

THE CONCEPTS OF REVERENCE AND IDOLATRY

If humility implies a warning not to put too high a value on inner or routine information, reverence perhaps implies the complementary injunction to put a higher value on outside information and on information that is new. In this sense, both Erich Fromm and Jacques Maritain have suggested in their writings that love for a person is not possible without respect, that is, without a high value put on the integrity and autonomy of the loved person and on the needs, desires, and messages of the loved one. What is true in human love would apply no less strongly to the vaster environment in which we live. Whether it is formulated as "reverence for nature," or, with Albert Schweitzer, as "reverence for life," or in terms of religion as reverence for God, reverence always implies the openness to, and the higher value put on, any information concerning that which is outside and greater than ourselves, that which is the not-I or the not-we but which has its own integrity and its own patterns of existence and behavior. In its extended sense, reverence involves the refusal to pay more respect to the lesser than to the greater, or to the smaller rather than the larger context.

This refusal is made explicit in the many religious injunctions against idolatry. To prefer the familiar over the infinite, the local over the universal, and more, to treat the familiar and the local as if they were absolute, as if they were the be-alls and the end-alls of value—this is perhaps the basic meaning of idolatry. Its practice has been no less frequent in the pathology of history and politics than it has been in the pathology of religion. To worship the letter above the spirit, to worship traditional rights before human rights, and established interests above human needs—all these practices have endangered, and in some instances destroyed, civilizations. The "idolatry of ephemeral institutions," as Toynbee has called it,

233

has been one of the characteristic ways in which past civilizations have gone to their breakdown.

THE CONCEPT OF LOVE AND ITS TWO OPPOSITES: THE DILEMMA OF COSMOPOLITANISM AND NATIONALISM

The self-preservation of autonomous organizations involves the perpetual pursuit of a set of balances. Messages from outside must not be overvalued too highly over data from within, or else the organization will drift with its environment. But data from within must not be overvalued against the outside world, or the organization will wreck itself through power, willfulness, and pride. Perhaps it is not fanciful to think that this problem of balance is expressed with precision in the commandment "Thou shalt love thy neighbor as thyself." It is a command that at the same time indicates the twin opposites of love: self-abasement and self-idolization. No individual, no culture, no people, and no state can endure without self-respect, and without placing a positive value on its own memories and its own character. Yet neither individual nor state can maintain self-control if they idolize their current memories and preferences beyond the possibility of development and change under the impact of experiences and information from outside.

In the politics of nationalism, this fundamental problem has appeared time and again since the eighteenth century in the quarrel between nationalism and cosmopolitanism. Many persons in that century asserted that their home was wherever they could be most prosperous, and they placed a low value on the mass of their countrymen who were poorer, less skilled, or less well educated than they were themselves. As for themselves, they preferred to be at home in an international guild of the prominent, be it an aristocracy of birth and talent, or a group of master craftsmen in the specialized techniques of some art or science, protected by standards of performance that would effectively keep out many of their less accomplished countrymen.

The reaction against the "horizontal" exclusiveness of cosmopolitanism often took the shape of the "vertical" exclusiveness of nationalism. No art, no science, no ideas, and no leadership were to be tolerated that had not grown from the national soil. The command of the great monotheistic religions, "Thou shalt have no other gods before me," found a strange echo in the claim of the nation-state and of the nationalists who soon professed to speak in its name: "There must be no ism but our nationalism!"

Both of these views, cosmopolitanism and nationalism, the underestimation as well as the idolization of one's own country, would be likely in the long run to damage the autonomy and integrity of the political communities in which they might persist, and thus to damage the national interest that at least the nationalists profess to serve. Both views are far removed from the concept of love: to appreciate and respect and love one's neighbors as oneself, and to love one's neighbor countries on this planet as one loves one's own. Love in this sense means respect as well as self-respect; it means openness to needs of the wider as well as of the smaller circle; it involves the readiness to active commitment in response to them; and it involves therefore conflicting claims on limited resources of attention, thought, and action. It may well seem therefore to be almost impossible to live up to in practice.

To escape the tension of the perpetual search for an almost unattainable balance, and in order to maintain at least a small area of expectability around ourselves, most of us have decided to give in all cases of doubt some definite preference to the problems and persons nearest to us, and thus to our own family and our own country. This is what in fact we do, but in so doing we again incur all the dangers of blindness, idolatry, or lukewarmness to the need of those who are most distant. The solution we adopt is thus at best a short-run solution, and it leaves us with all the long-run dangers the pessimistic philosophers of politics have pointed out. To perpetuate a truly autonomous political organization with the means contained in it at any time may well be, we are tempted to conclude, an impossible task.

THE OUTSIDE WORLD AS A RESOURCE:
THE CONCEPTS OF CURIOSITY AND GRACE

Curiosity is an empirically observable behavior trait in human beings and in many of the higher animals. Experiments have indicated the existence of an "investigatory reflex" in many animals that prompts them to turn their attention to new stimuli. The curiosity of small children is notorious, and inhibition of curiosity in adults is a feat accomplished only by a limited number of cultures. Curiosity has been essential for the growth of science, and as interest in the affairs of others it may have been important as an indirect factor in the development of morality. Yet there is an element of reserve in the treatment of curiosity on the part of many ethical or religious thinkers.

Curiosity may lead to drifting; the new discoveries or data are accepted as highly important regardless of their probable consequences for the integrity and autonomy of the individuals or organizations who acquire them. Rapid increases in knowledge, reinforced sometimes by rapid increases in power, may overload the steering arrangements and steering capacities of the individuals, families, or groups to whom they come. The result is the partial or total loss of self-determination in situations that rapidly get out of control: once the jinn has been freed from his bottle, once Pandora's box has been opened, once the sorcerer's apprentice has ordered the broom to walk, once the poor fisherman has been given the power of three wishes, all that the individuals or families can hope for is at best to get back to their initial situation with the least possible damage.

On the contrary, curiosity may involve the treatment of new data as if they had no claim on us at all. Whatever we discover or experience is then treated as a mere instrumentality, a source of pleasure or excitement, or a mere tool for the accomplishment of goals it can neither set nor change. This is in a sense the "cold curiosity" of some investigators, or the esthetic thrill of the mere spectator.

236

Under neither of these two manners of treatment are outside information or the experience of outside conditions likely to be of much help in meeting the almost insoluble dilemma of autonomy: to meet with limited resources at one and the same time the current internal needs of the individual personality, or the social or political organization, without permitting them to override in a pattern of self-centeredness the equally indispensable claims of the wider and less obvious environment, and of the potential and as yet undeveloped new inner patterns of thought and behavior.

The concept of grace may perhaps differ from the attitude of curiosity at this essential point. In terms of grace we may regard information or events originating from outside ourselves as answers to our innermost problems of self-determination. They are available to us neither as mere instruments to preconceived and narrow goals nor as overwhelming forces that drag us helplessly along with them. Rather they are available to us as improbable events or data that may offer us the missing pieces to our puzzles, the particular crucial elements needed to resolve a particular inner crisis of our decision system. In this sense, unforeseen or improbable events from the outside may make the difference between success or failure in the pursuit of a difficult balance between competing sets of decisions; they may furnish additional resources, material or intellectual, at a critical time or point; and their impact may decide between success or failure in a fundamental process of inner structural reorganization.

The concept of grace may thus imply the treatment of the world beyond the self, or beyond any particular group or organization, as the potential source of aids or resources in goal-setting and learning. Such resources cannot be predicted but they can be prepared for. To find the right aid at the right moment may clearly be improbable in every concrete situation. Yet there may well be a difference between the capacity for continued autonomy and survival of organizations that are ready to seek for, and to respond to, new potential resources, in contrast to organizations that seek no new data from outside themselves, or seek them for nothing but instrumental purposes.

While the concept of grace has found its greatest elaboration in religious writings, it finds some limited but interesting parallels in the history of science. The biologist Walter B. Cannon has coined the term "serendipity" for the ability of scientists to pick up new, unexpected insights and data in the course of some preconceived investigation in pursuit of some entirely different object. A good deal of the discussion of this process has been carried on in terms of the significance and probability of the so-called "accidental discovery" in the development of science, and so historians of science have been inclined to agree with the judgment of Louis Pasteur that accidental discoveries favor "only the prepared mind." It will be noted that, even when the scientist's mind is prepared in Pasteur's sense, the actual making of a significant accidental discovery is improbable and unpredictable but that it will be even far more improbable if the scientist's mind is not prepared, for in the latter case the discovery would be quite unlikely to be followed up even if it should occur.

The concept of grace thus involves three basic attitudes:

1. The acknowledgment that in the long run some unpredicted events or data from outside will be essential for the solution of some of the decisive inner steering problems of every autonomous organization. In other words, no autonomous organization can remain indefinitely self-sufficient by means of the data and resources it commands at any one moment, or even by means of the set of data and resources it has got into the practice of receiving at any one time from its environment. In this respect the concept of grace implies the eventual insufficiency of all current, as well as of all predictable, routines for the preservation of autonomy.

2. The expectation that the universe does in fact contain the essential data and processes that may be necessary for the solution of the steering problems of the organization but are missing from its current inner resources. This implies the expectation that all limited problems of self-responsibility and self-government have answers, that the finding of those answers in time is possible, although it is improbable, and that it is apt to depend in part on processes beyond the control of the autonomous organization. Thinkers who stress

the probability of finding such solutions may tend to speak of a "friendly universe," or in religious language of the "benevolence of Providence" or the "fatherhood of God." Thinkers who are impressed by the improbability of finding such solutions in time to avoid self-destruction, however, may emphasize the images of predestination, and the Deity as a sovereign and to human eyes irresponsible ruler. Some images of this kind may play a role, at least implicitly, in the Augustinian and Calvinist traditions.

3. The assumption that an attitude of readiness and receptivity toward crucial new experiences and new data will nevertheless increase the probability of their being found and acted on in time to forestall self-destruction. The test of receptivity would consist in using these new data not merely as instruments for preconceived ends but also to let them come to bear upon the decisive points of the decision process, and even upon the decisions concerning the possibility of its own fundamental inner rearrangement. In this sense the test of receptivity is the willingness to commit both structures and resources to the responses to the new data. If one recalls our discussion of the connection between the depth of commitment and the concept of faith, it may appear that some such notion may be involved in certain aspects of the Lutheran tradition.

Thus far the concept of "grace" has been discussed in connection with a possible attitude to processes and messages coming from outside an autonomous system. Any extended autonomous system, however, that has more complex facilities of memory, also contains within itself a lesser universe of combinatorial possibilities and ways in which its remembered data could be recombined into new patterns. As the range of such combinatorial possibilities is likely to be vast, the discovery and identification of a relevant answer to a self-steering problem from among the possible ideas of that system may also be quite improbable, and the concept of grace as an attitude of readiness to receive information that is improbable but relevant may apply to that extent also to the area of novelty and initiative possible within the system. In this sense, perhaps, Heraclitus asserted the possibility of specifying the limits of the mind, on the grounds that it had "so deep a logos"; and prophets, mystics, and some religious leaders have urged men to harken to their "inner voice." A large social or political organization, comprising perhaps millions of individuals, may similarly be thought of as containing a vast internal universe of possible patterns of thought and behavior. Nevertheless, the vastest internal universe we can imagine for any individual or organization is still bound to remain small compared to the universe surrounding it. While the attitude of grace may thus well include receptivity toward inner initiative and insight, it will nevertheless be predominantly directed toward the outside world.

ECLECTICISM AND THE CONCEPT OF SPIRIT

How is it possible for an autonomous organization to accept outside information in the making of its most crucial inner decisions without losing its own identity? To accept the impact of outside information in a sequence of decisions may lead to decisions incompatible with one another. To accept it in the rearrangement of inner structures may leave the system with a collection of partial inner structures among which little or no communication and coordination may be possible. In such cases the effect of indiscriminate receptivity may be the destruction of autonomy or even the destruction of the system. Even where the system as such survives and retains a measure of autonomy, its steering performance and its capacity for further growth may be substantially lowered. It is perhaps this that is implied in our reproach against *eclecticism*, the acceptance of diverse features and patterns from a variety of different sources and their combination in a system in which no or few significant second-order patterns can be discovered. A second-order pattern, in this sense, is somewhat similar to a "style" in art, or a "recursion formula" in mathematics: it is a pattern or sequence that can be abstracted from two or more first-order sequences or patterns and that can be shown to apply to the description and possible extension of both of them.

If we think of a value as a pattern of decisions, for a particular class of problems, we may conceive of spirit as the set of second-order values that might describe a pattern of decisions by which first-order values are chosen. Spirit in this view would represent a consistent strategy of values, as distinct from the "tactical" values that govern particular classes of decisions. Spirit, so conceived, would be the opposite of eclecticism, but at the same time it would be the opposite of the "letter" of intolerance or narrowness. As a strategic value pattern, it would be preserved by alternative patterns of "tactical" or first-order values. The search for such strategies of values, as well as their identification in existing structures, might form a significant aspect of our understanding of the presence or absence of integration in an autonomous system.

In politics and social life, larger autonomous systems are characteristically composed of smaller units that themselves have autonomy and that may have a higher degree of autonomy than the larger unit of which they are a part.

Hobbes' Leviathan, a giant whose body is made up of smaller men, may thus be more slow-witted than his components, even though his circle of vision is wider than theirs. Large political systems are inferior to the marvelous brain structures of the individuals of which they are made up, in regard to the ability to think, compute, and decide rapidly, but these individuals usually lack the comprehensive information available to governments. In politics, wide ranges of information most often are at the command of slow bureaucracies, while quick-thinking individuals are hampered by a lack of crucial ranges of knowledge.

The autonomy, complexity, and range of the self-steering performance of the individual human personality is thus vastly greater than the autonomy and steering performance of any social organization, even though the larger organizations may perform some particular limited functions more effectively. The problem of political and social integration is thus essentially one of the integration of sets of autonomous units with their own strategies of value; and the success or failure of political integration could also be evaluated in terms of the presence or absence of a second-order strategy of value, or a "common spirit," that could be identified in the different value patterns and steering systems of the smaller autonomous units. This approach to the study of integration could by no means be the only one; but together with the study of inner structures, communication, steering performance, and social learning behavior, it might help us to gain a more realistic picture of the integration process.

As regards the eventual chances of survival of any autonomous system, we found them to depend to a decisive extent on its range of relationships to events and information from outside its own limits. In the long run, these chances may thus depend in good part on its ability not only to continue to remake and restructure itself but also to achieve integrative relationships with others.

SOME IMPLICATIONS FOR THE STUDY OF POLITICS AS A SPHERE OF SOCIAL DECISION

As the preceding discussion has suggested, the preservation of individual or group autonomy, or even the preservation of some measure of autonomy for whole nations, or for all mankind, is not limited to problems of politics alone. Rather, the preservation of autonomy involves the whole range of individual and social learning, from scientific discoveries and economic innovations to the most subtle changes in culture, ethics, values, or religion. Nevertheless politics occupies a special position within this range.

Politics involves the steering or manipulation of human behavior by a combination of threats of enforcement with habits of compliance. Such habits of compliance may range from mere fear or apathy to full-fledged convictions of legitimacy and personal identification with decisions; and the threats of enforcement may range from mere marginal policing to all-out foreign military occupation. What is characteristic of politics is that threats of enforcement and habits of compliance will appear in combinations and that in such combinations they may be capable of overriding or modifying many other goals, habits, or preferences that exist in the society.

Politics may be considered as a decisive sphere of social learning, or as a major sphere of social decision, precisely because it is characterized by this power to override other kinds of preferences.

Politics is thus a decisive instrumentality by which social commitments can be produced, preserved, or changed.

For all these reasons it may prove rewarding to study politics from the point of view of autonomy, steering performance, resourcefulness, and power, learning capacity, and self-preservation. What major facilities of communication and memory, what machinery for self-steering, what channels of intake and foci of attention, what operational reserves available for recommitment, and what major patterns of values are found in a given political system?

If we are interested in the future effectiveness or survival of such a system, we may now be able to ask for more than the mere data bearing on crude power. We may ask: What are its facilities and rewards for the encouragement of criticism, its transmission to decision points, and for the responsiveness of the system to it? What are the learning responses of the system, and what are its strategies of commitment? What attempts and arrangements are made in the system to preserve its freedom from idolatry, to avoid the intoxication of success and the worship of ephemeral practices and institutions? What provisions or attempts are made to ensure openness on the part of the system to the needs of outsiders, and readiness to learn from changes in its environment, as well as from new sources of initiative within itself? What is the status of any practice or institution designed to treat the social and physical environment of the system not merely as a source of either obstacles or tools, but as a potential source of challenge, guidance, and vital information? What are the instances of integrative behavior on the part of the system observed in the past, and what are the prospects and instrumentalities for such behavior in the future?

If we could make a political survey in these terms, we might be able to assess more realistically the present and prospective decision-making capacity of a particular government or state.

Eventually we might be able to take part more effectively in the continuing debate between the optimists and pessimists in politics. Conceivably, we might emerge with the Augustinian viewpoint that the probabilities are still heavily against the survival, and for the eventual self-destruction, of every autonomous system. Or we might arrive at the belief that an attitude of awareness of these odds in favor of destruction might in itself be a factor in changing them for the better and that the universe contained enough new resources to offer a chance of extended survival to all those autonomous systems that succeed in maintaining themselves in readiness to respond to them. In any case, we might emerge from such an inquiry with the impression that the warnings of the pessimists are more than a mere expression of fearfulness or gloom and that they refer to very real tendencies inherent in the operation and structure of all autonomous systems; and we could begin to ask how in any particular, historically given political system these tendencies toward self-destruction could be modified in favor of survival.

At the present time we are at best barely beginning to understand a little of the working of human personalities and human organizations. In our search for understanding, it may not be safe to disregard the individual and social insights of thousands of years, laid down in the great philosophic and religious traditions of mankind. The day may come when social scientists who refer to some elements in these traditions will no longer automatically be suspected of obscurantism, or of a breach of professional standards. Perhaps we may look forward to the time when all that is claimed to be true will be permitted to enter the ongoing process of scientific verification, even though that process may fall far short of exhausting it; and when the study of the growth of autonomy, and of the responsibility of persons and groups, will be carried forward with the help of all the sources of relevant knowledge available to mankind.

14

The Politics of Power
and the Politics
of Growth

In discussing autonomy and memory, we discussed some aspects of political aspirations. Any autonomous system of memories and self-steering decisions is apt to have its own set of internal probabilities in terms of which it will not merely behave at any one moment but also project or propose its behavior for the future. As P. W. Bridgman once put it in my hearing, "The future is a program"; that is, the future may be viewed as a set of probabilities implied by the present distribution of resources and environmental factors. In this sense every autonomous system tends to act out the future implicit in the distributions of its memories and in the configurations of its communication channels; and insofar as its behavior leads it to acquire new memories and to change some of its internal communication patterns by learning, it will remake itself and its future to a limited extent at every such step. If the system has consciousness, if it monitors its own behavior, and derives and remembers images of itself that it applies to its own actions, then it may well also derive and use images projecting its behavior into the future. It will thus use goal images and entertain explicitly formulated aspirations.

THE CONCEPT OF POLITICAL WILL

When do such political aspirations harden into political will? The literature of political science is rich in references to political will, but far less rich in attempts to analyze the meaning of the term.[1] From the viewpoint of communication, it was suggested earlier, *will* may be taken to consist in the putting into operation of data proposed from the past of a decision-making system in such a manner as to override most or all of the information currently received from its environment. In its extreme form, it was suggested, will in politics functions somewhat like the deadline in a newspaper or the departure of a train. It assesses the relevance of events and messages in terms of time: information received before the moment of decision may be treated as relevant, but later messages are not. Will in this sense implies the operational priority of predecision data over postdecision data. Emotionally, it may mean to individuals and groups the acting out of their own preferences, personality characteristics, and culture patterns, unburdened by the task of having to reassess or revise them in terms of ever new data from the present.

Since will implies the ability to stick to a decision, it may thus appear as an escape from the psychological burden of further decision-making. In groups or governments where a decision may have been reached only after considerable difficulties, persisting, for example, in a foreign-policy decision and freezing the policies designed to execute it may have an important advantage—not having to reopen the original problem, and thus avoiding renewed domestic conflict. Similarly, in situations where decisions involve conflicts between different values, persistence may prove easier than revision.

In cases of major decisions, will may involve the commitment of major resources to decisions that must not be revised. In this sense, it may involve the suspension or abandonment of the learning process, and may imply the desire not to learn, or at least not to learn anything that may prove incompatible with what has been willed.

In the poetry and folklore of extreme political movements, this type of will has found its appropriate symbol in the image of the dead man who returns from his grave in order to act out some political aspiration or decision, single-minded and impervious to all distractions or blandishments of the world of the living. In such imagery, the dead hero serves as a symbol of escape from all compromises and frustrations, and the frequency and appeal of the symbol of the irresistible army of the dead—the appeal, as it were, of the "death urge" in politics—may perhaps tend to increase with the amount of the fears and frustrations experienced in social and political life and in the ordinary political process.

THE PROBLEM OF POLITICAL POWER

The notion of a will that is not merely inflexible but actually irresistible implies the notion of power. By *power* we mean, in everyday language, the ability to get "our way" or to get "our" will. As we have seen, power implies the ability to act out with little or no modifications the behavior implicit in our memories and in the configurations of our personal preferences and values. Power thus means for persons and groups the ability to act "in character," whatever that character may be.

In this simple sense, power is a quantitative concept. It could be measured in each case, in principle, by the extent of modification of overt behavior accepted by a person, a group, or a decision system in response to its environment (and perhaps particularly in response to the behavior of other autonomous systems) compared to the extent of modification imposed on the environment. In this sense, power corresponds to the notion of hardness among minerals, or of a peck order among chickens. In all these situations power is epitomized in the answers to the questions: Which process can impose the greater modification on the other? And which process imposes greater modifications upon all others?

If "will" implied the desire not to learn, "power" may imply the ability not to have to do so. In this simple sense, both will and power may form aspects of the pathology of social learning, and the ceaseless warnings of moralists, philosophers, and theologians against both will and power may be understood in this context. By pathological learning in the case of an individual or an organization we may understand a learning process, and a corresponding change in inner structure, that will reduce rather than increase the future learning capacity of the person or organization. Will and power may easily lead to such self-destructive learning, for they may imply the overvaluation of the past against the present and future, the overvaluation of the experiences acquired in a limited environment against the vastness of the universe around us; and the overvaluation of present expectations against all possibilities of surprise, discovery, and change.

If carried to extremes, the simple forms of will and power may destroy the decision systems in which they become dominant. However, power may be quantitatively measured in a less primitive way. In an extended sense, we might define *power* (or "strength," if another word is wanted) as the ability to act out a particular preference in behavior, or to reach a particular goal, *with the least loss of ability to choose a different behavior,* or to seek a different goal. Power in this extended sense is thus related not merely to the absence of imposed modification of behavior but also to economy of commitment, and to the capacity for alternative commitments in the future.

If we bear in mind the simple and extended meaning of power in politics, we may be able to study not merely the pathology of power; we may also be able to think of will and power as elements in the politics of growth.

THE POLITICS OF GROWTH

It is often said that it is the task of politics to promote the "public interest" or the "common good" of a nation or of a larger society over and above all special or lesser interests. If we admit that there can be such a common good and that social life is not exhausted by group conflicts, we must ask what this good is. Despite wide differences in cultures and values, we may assume provisionally that one of the most widely accepted values is the *survival* of the family, community, people, or nation. In terms of their probability of survival, we may divide all political systems or organizations into four categories:

1. *Self-destroying systems*, which are apt to break down eventually even in relatively favorable environments.

2. *Nonviable systems*, which are unlikely to survive under the range of difficulties found in most environments (though they need not be likely to be self-destructive).

3. *Viable systems*, which are likely to preserve their original probability of survival over a limited range of environmental conditions; and

4. *Self-developing or self-enhancing systems*, which are able to increase their probability of survival and their ranges of possible action over an increasing variety of environments.

While social organizations are radically different from organisms, the last three of these categories happen to parallel somewhat the medical notion of "health," and to parallel closely the biologist's concept of "evolutionary progress."[2] This latter concept is also based on the notion of probable long-run survival and on the probability that in the long run most environments may change very considerably, so that only self-changing and self-enhancing systems and organizations are apt to survive eventually, thanks to their ability to cope with many different environments and to increase their relative independence from any one of them.

Neither the biologist nor the social scientist need deny that there may arise on occasion some nonviable organisms or some nonviable or self-destructive organizations. All they need say is that such highly self-destructive organizations will tend in fact not to survive, even though they may function as a dangerous environment for those organizations and individuals committed in some way to the values of life and survival. In the legislative control of the behavior of individuals, we similarly draw up laws on the assumption that most persons value life, and desire the survival of individuals and communities dear to them; and we treat suicide and attempts at

249

suicide as exceptions that, though real, are not likely to change the basic rules of the game for the survivors.

The consequence of these notions, from Emile Durkheim's notion of social health to Julian Huxley's concept of evolutionary progress, is the recognition of growth, of adaptability, and of learning capacity as essential for the survival of societies and cultures. What are the dimensions of this growth, and what can politics contribute to it?

DIMENSIONS OF GROWTH

As the first dimension of growth of a political system, we may count the growth of *manpower* and population included in it, as well as gains in their physical and mental health. In the second place, we may count *economic growth*. Without trying to summarize the literature on economic growth, we may merely note that this would include particularly the amounts of disposable factors of production, such as capital goods, land, and labor, as well as the growth of skills and technical knowledge. A further condition would be that the rate of growth of the second category, economic resources, should exceed in the long run the rate of the growth of population. The meeting of these conditions requires the maintenance of rates of savings and of investment in capital-goods industries, which without government aid have been attained only in a few countries, and only for limited periods, and which often may require political decisions.

In the third place, we may list the criteria of growth that bear on the availability of material and human resources for recommitment to new uses. Particularly we may list here the development of *operational reserves* in the system that may be committed to the pursuit of new goals or to the meeting of new stresses or new challenges from the environment.

The fourth group of criteria of growth refers to the growth of autonomy, or *self-determination*. This implies, on the one hand, a growth in the resources and functions that bear on social cohesion, that is, the growth, range, speed, and effectiveness of internal communications, both among individuals and among institutions or parts of the society or the political system. On the other hand, it implies growth in the steering performance of the system, in the effectiveness of its use of data recalled from memory, and of information received from outside. It will require, therefore, a growth in the facilities of memory and recall, and thus of institutions of learning, record-keeping, and the like; a growth in the variety and effectiveness of channels for the intake of new ranges of information from the outside world; an improvement in goal-seeking operations, through increases in the gain and lead, and through the cutting down of lag by reducing the delays due to either slowness of communication or to inertia or inner resistance in response.

A possible fifth criterion is implied in the fourth. A growing organization, and hence also a growing state or government, must be able to change its own patterns of communication and organization, so as to overcome the results of the "scale effect," familiar from our earlier discussion. It must resist the trend toward increasing self-preoccupation and eventual self-immolation from its environment; and it must reorganize or transform itself often enough to overcome the growing threats of internal communication overload and the jamming up of message traffic. One of the most effective responses to these threats—highlighted by such writings on politics and administration as "Parkinson's Law"—consists in *strategic simplifications*.[3]

Often in history, growth in organization and progress in technique appear to imply just such a simplification of some crucial link or coupling in the chain of interlocking and self-sustaining processes by which the organization is kept going. Thus the maintenance of an ever-growing written tradition is facilitated by the invention of increasingly simple alphabets and increasingly simple methods of writing and, eventually, printing. The many tasks of modern languages are facilitated by the sloughing off of many of the ancient inflections and the replacement of their semantic functions by means of word position and context. Other examples of this process of strategic simplification are the replacement of trolley tracks by rubber tires; of telegraph wires by radio; and many other processes of this kind, ranging all the way to the increasingly simple symbol structures of the central theories of physics from the cumbrous models of Ptolemy and Copernicus to the simpler and more general formulations of Newton and Einstein.

Cases of this sort are cited by A. J. Toynbee, but the interpretation proposed here is somewhat different from his. In none of the cases of simplification which he cites do we find a simplification— or a reduction in the number of elements—for any of the systems cited *as a whole*, be they systems of transportation, communication, or theoretical physics. On the contrary, each system as a whole is becoming more complex; what is becoming simpler are particular links in it, which are crucial or strategic. Thus a modern radio station is a far more complicated piece of electric equipment than the original wire telegraph of Samuel Morse; but its ability to transmit signals without telegraph wires permitted man to put its increased complex of resources to other and more fruitful uses. With this qualification, however, there seems to be a good deal of evidence supporting Toynbee's surmise that some such strategic or crucial simplifications may well be essential for any extended process of growth.

An important special case of such strategic simplifications might perhaps be seen in the replacement of gross operations or experiments with major physical resources by much simpler and quicker operations or experiments by means of symbols. An increasing shift from operations with gross resources toward a growing proportion of operations by means of symbols is thus another possible criterion of growth; and most of the cases of what Mr. Toynbee has called "etherealization" as an important aspect of growth could be brought perhaps under this heading.

All these elements of growth, taken together, may go far to meet one of the tests for growth once proposed by Simon Kuznets: the ability of an organization, an economy, or a state to approach the goals it happens to have chosen. In this sense, growth as the ability to approach previously chosen goals is closely related to the increase in the will and power characteristics of the system. The more rigorously the system is able to exclude all outside resistance in its way, the more likely it may be to reach the particular goal chosen. In this sense, will and power represent the ability to harden and deepen the temporary commitment of attention and resources, and are essential instruments of short-run steering performance, autonomy, and growth.

The sixth group of criteria deals with long-run growth. These include increases in *goal-changing* ability, in the range of different ends the society, culture, or political system is able to choose and to pursue. Here we find learning capacity, not merely in terms of limited operational reserves but also in terms of the capacity for deep rearrangements of inner structure, and thus for the development of radically new functions. Here we list the growth in the possibility of producing genuine *novelty*, of applying some of the resulting new combinations of information to the guidance of behavior as *initiative*, and of producing eventually new patterns in the physical or social environment in processes of *creativity*.

Thus far, all criteria derived from our growth model have applied primarily to the decision system as a whole. However, an essential characteristic of any human organization, in contrast to an anthill, is the interplay between the dimensions of growth of the organization and the growth of the individuals and of the more or less autonomous subgroups that compose it. In this sense, the growth of human organizations is always the growth of several levels of autonomous systems, and the autonomous growth and enhanced self-determination of individuals is one of its touchstones. To a lesser but still very real degree, this may apply to the growth of lesser autonomous organizations within the system. The growth of the whole decision system may thus also be "measured" in terms of progress in articulation and multiple autonomy, and thus as progress in what some psychologists have called "integrative behavior." Gains in the capacity for integrative behavior—which does not destroy the autonomy of the units integrated—may in turn be related to the ability of a society or state to deal with other societies or states without suicide or mutual destruction. A combined growth in power and in the awareness of limits; in depth of memory and in openness to new ranges of information; in social, intellectual, and emotional resourcefulness and creativity; and in the capacity for *integrative behavior;* these, taken together, may well be most conducive to survival in international politics.

THE TASK OF POLITICS:
ACCELERATING NEEDED INNOVATION

If we accept provisionally this sketch of the criteria of growth, politics can contribute much to fulfill them. Within the general field of social innovation and social learning, politics can function as the sphere of decision. If we define the core area of politics as the area of enforceable decisions or, more accurately, of all decisions backed by some combination of a significant probability of voluntary compliance with a significant probability of enforcement, then politics becomes the method par excellence for securing preferential treatment for messages and commands and for the reallocation of human or material resources. Politics thus appears as a major instrument for either retarding or accelerating social learning and innovation, and it has been used in both functions in the past. Politics has been used to increase the rigidity of already semipetrified social systems, and it has been used to accelerate ongoing processes of change.[4]

Examples of the conservative function of politics can be found in many cultures. Perhaps it has been a peculiarity of Western politics to have developed a range of significant techniques for accelerating innovation. Perhaps three of the most important of these techniques are majority rule, the protection of minorities, and the institutionalization of dissent.

In an earlier section it was suggested that autonomous organizations may be prone to overvalue internal or parochial information, as well as familiar data from the past, as against data and information derived from new or wider ranges of experience. Resistance to change and innovation may thus be one of the "occupational risks" of autonomous organizations. Political patterns requiring unanimity —as does much of Oriental village politics—may tend to slow down the rate of change to a very low level. Majority rule in the Western manner permits, on the contrary, a change to be carried out much

254

earlier and thus much faster. At the same time, Western traditions for the protection of minorities may prevent majority-imposed rates of change from disrupting the integrity and dignity of dissenting individuals or groups, or of breaking the bonds and communication channels of social cohesion. Finally, the institutionalization of dissent, and the provision of acceptable channels and modes for the expression of criticism and self-criticism, of counterproposals and of new suggesstions, protect not merely the majority of yesterday but also provide potential growing points for the majorities of tomorrow. Taken together, majority rule, minority protection, and institutionalized dissent, reinforced by highly conscious, analytical, critical and combinatorial modes of thought, provide Western societies and political systems with an unusually wide range of resources and instrumentalities for rapid social learning and innovation. Even though other cultures may not copy these institutions in their Western shape, they will have to provide by some means for the functions of wide exploration and rapid recommitment these Western institutions have performed.

Politics, like all techniques of making and implementing decisions, is not an end in itself. Indeed, we have a range of generous visions, from early Christianity to H. G. Wells, envisaging a state of social development where all social compulsion, and with it all politics, will become obsolete. Whatever one may think of these hopes, politics in the world of today is an essential instrument of social learning. It will be more likely to function as an instrument of survival and growth, rather than destruction, if it is guided by cognitive insights. All studies of politics, and all techniques and models suggested as instruments of political analysis, have this purpose: that men should be more able to act in politics with their eyes open.

This perspective is no less relevant to those among us who see politics chiefly as a contest rather than as a process of awakening. Competition in world politics in the second half of the twentieth century resembles less a tug-of-war than a race; less a hundred yard dash than a marathon; less a marathon than a slalom; and less a slalom than a combined course in survival, and persuasion, as well as in learning and discovery. In this contest, too, government and politics will long remain indispensable instruments for accelerated social learning, by which mankind in its various subdivisions, still organized in states, can adapt more quickly to the dangerous but hopeful tasks of growing up.

APPENDIX

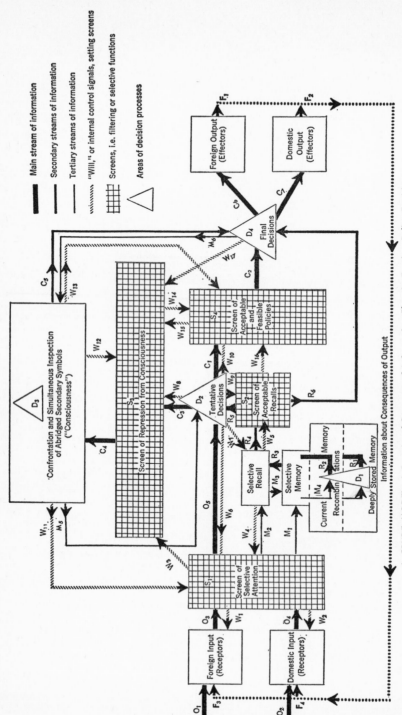

Legend:

— Main stream of information

— Secondary streams of information

— Tertiary streams of information

— "Will," or internal control signals, setting screens

▦ — Screens, i.e. filtering or selective functions

△ — Areas of decision processes

Foreign Output (Effectors) F_1

Domestic Output (Effectors) F_2

D_4 Final Decisions

C_6 C_7

M_6 W_{17} C_2

C_5 W_{13}

Confrontation and Simultaneous Inspection of Abridged Secondary Symbols ("Consciousness") D_3

W_{12}

C_4

S_2 Screen of Repression from Consciousness

W_{14} W_{15}

S_4 Screen of Acceptable and Feasible Policies

C_1 W_{10} W_{16}

W_8 D_2 Tentative Decisions

C_3 S_3 Screen of Acceptable Recalls R_6

W_{11} M_5

W_1 R_5

W_9 W_5

R_4 R_3

Selective Recall M_3

Selective Memory M_2

Current Recombinations M_4 R_2 Memory R_1

Deeply Stored Memory D_1 R_1

O_5 W_6 W_4 M_1

W_3

S_1 Screen of Selective Attention

O_3 W_1 $Ó_4$ W_2

Foreign Input (Receptors)

Domestic Input (Receptors)

O_1 F_3 O_2 F_4

Information about Consequences of Output

A CRUDE MODEL: A Functional Diagram of Information Flow in Foreign Policy Decisions.

APPENDIX

MAIN INFORMATION FLOW (heavy arrows)

I. Current Information from outside the decision system

O_1 Current general information about foreign countries (part of external intelligence)

O_2 Current general information about domestic politics (part of internal intelligence)

O_3 Current foreign information, as selected by receptors

O_4 Current domestic information, as selected by receptors

O_5 Current foreign and domestic information, screened and combined

II. Past Information, recalled from storage within system

R_1 Information recalled and recombined from deep memory

R_2 Information recalled and recombined from recent or current memory

R_3 Combined information from memory

R_4 Combined information from memory, as selectively recalled

R_5 Recalled information from memory, screened for acceptability in terms of culture, values, personalities, cognitive dissonance, etc., and transmitted to area of preliminary decision

R_6 Acceptable memories, transmitted to area of final decision

III. Combined Information, of memories and outside data

C_1 Combined selected data and acceptable memories, moving toward final decision (e.g., "action papers")

C_2 Combined selected data and memories, as screened further for feasibility and acceptability as policies

C_3 Abridged combined data, transmitted toward area of confrontation and simultaneous inspection

C_4 Abridged combined data, screened for acceptability to consciousness

C_5 Abridged data and memories, selected and combined at the level of conscious confrontation, and transmitted to area of final decision

259

C_6 Final policies selected and transmitted to effectors in foreign policy area

C_7 Final policies selected and transmitted to effectors in domestic policy area

Note: Policies need not always be consistent between C_4 and C_5, nor within C_4 or C_5, respectively. Thus the United States Congress may vote a foreign policy resolution demanding greater anti-Communist efforts in the Western Hemisphere, and at the same time cut economic aid funds for Latin American countries; or the West German government could call upon Britain to aid in the defense of West Berlin while at the same time threatening British Trade with exclusion from the European Common Market.

Such inconsistencies might show up in advance in the recombinations and symbolic projection of information at the level of abridged simultaneous inspection and "consciousness"; or else they might be reported back only later in the feedback of information about the results of the first inconsistent actions taken under these policies in the outside world, but still early enough to permit correction of these policies at later stages.

IV. Feedback Information about the consequences of the actions of the system on its relations to the world outside it

F_1 Feedback information about the results of foreign policy actions

F_2 Feedback information about the results of domestic policy actions

F_3 Feedback information gathered by foreign area receptors

F_4 Feedback information gathered by domestic area receptors

V. The "Will" System

MAIN SCREENS

S_1 Screen of selective attention to current information

S_2 Screen of acceptable recalls from memory

S_3 Screen of acceptable summary information for confrontation and simultaneous inspection ("consciousness")

S_4 Screen of acceptable and feasible policies

MAIN INFORMATION FLOWS, ADJUSTING SCREENS

W_1 Information which sets attention focus or "tracking" pattern for foreign area receptors

W_2 Information which sets attention focus or "tracking" pattern for domestic area receptors

W_3 Outside information, changing the screen of acceptability to consciousness

W_4 Recalled information, changing screen of attention

W_5 Selectively recalled information, changing screen of subsequent acceptable recalls

W_6 Information about tentative decision, changing screen of attention (e.g., "self-confirming policy")

W_7 Information about tentative decision, changing search pattern for selection of interesting recalls from memory (e.g., "search for precedents")

W_8 Information about tentative decision, changing screen of acceptability to consciousness

W_9 Information about tentative decision, changing screen of acceptable recalls

W_{10} Information about tentative decision, changing screen of acceptable and feasible policies

W_{11} Information about results of simultaneous confrontation and inspection ("consciousness"), changing the screen of attention to outside information

W_{12} Information about results of simultaneous confrontation and inspection ("consciousness"), changing screen of acceptability to consciousness

W_{13} Information about results of simultaneous confrontation and inspection ("consciousness"), changing screen of acceptable and feasible policies

W_{14} Information about results of simultaneous confrontation and inspection ("consciousness"), via screen of repression from consciousness, to screen of acceptable and feasible policies ("unthinkable")

W_{15} Information about feasibility and acceptability of policies, changing screen of acceptability to consciousness

W_{16} Acceptable recalled information, changing screen of acceptable and feasible policies

W_{17} Information about final decision, changing screen of repression from consciousness

VI. Minor or Secondary Information Flows

M_1 Selected outside information, transmitted to memory for storage and possible recall. This is a minor flow only as regards the making of immediate decisions. Its actual volume of information may be large

M_2 Selected outside information, changing probabilities of recall ("that reminds me . . .")

M_3 Orders for recall, to memory

M_4 Orders, or associative trails, or chain reactions, within memory

M_5 Information about results of simultaneous confrontation and inspection ("consciousness"), transmitted to area of tentative decision

M_6 Abridged information about final decision, which is being fed back to the area of simultaneous confrontation and inspection

VII. Consciousness

Feedback cycle C_5–M_6, on repeated run-throughs, would make the final decision "conscious"

VIII. Areas of Decision

D_1 The area of dissociative and combinatorial memory is an implicit area of decision, since the forming of certain combinations, and the omission of others, functions indirectly as a series of partial decisions. Such combinations include not only data but also their patterns of configuration; they also include images and values

D_2 Area of preliminary decision, where combinations between memory data and current intake function as explicit preliminary decisions

D_3 The area of simultaneous confrontation and inspection, which functions indirectly as a decision area, since certain combinations between the simultaneously presented data are formed, while other possible combinations are not, and the successful combinations have the effect of partial decisions

D_4 The area of explicit final decision—which may, however, already have been prejudiced in its outcomes by the events at the earlier decision areas, D_1–D_3

NOTES

NOTES

PREFACE

1. Cf. Arnold Brecht, *Political Theory*, Princeton, Princeton University Press, 1960; Charles E. Merriam, *Systematic Politics*, Chicago, University of Chicago Press, 1945; David Easton, *The Political System*, New York, Knopf, 1953; and the forthcoming studies by Carl J. Friedrich, *Systematic Politics*, and by Talcott Parsons, *Society and Polity*.

2. Cf. Bruce M. Russett, *Community and Contention: Britain and America in the Twentieth Century*, Cambridge, M.I.T. Press, 1963.

3. Cf. the forthcoming study by Richard Merritt, "Symbols of American Community, 1735–1775," Ph.D. dissertation, Yale University, 1962, and a study in progress, by the same author, on the changes in community relationships between West Berlin and East Berlin since 1945.

4. Cf. Benno Wasserman, "The Failure of Intelligence Prediction," *Political Studies* 8, June, 1960, pp. 156–169.

5. Cf. Leroy N. Rieselbach, "The Basis of Isolationist Behavior," *Public Opinion Quarterly* 24, Winter, 1960, pp. 645–657, and Bruce M. Russett, "Demography, Salience, and Isolationist Behavior," *Public Opinion Quarterly* 24, Winter, 1960, pp. 658–664. Cf. also, Leroy N. Rieselbach, "American Isolationist Behavior, 1938–1958," Ph.D. dissertation, Yale University, in progress.

CHAPTER 1

1. I heard this notion first expressed at a lecture by Norbert Wiener at M.I.T. in 1947; cf. also J. B. Conant, *On Understanding Science,* New Haven, Yale University Press, 1948, pp. 19, 24–25, 101–103, 137 n. 4, 138 n. 8, and *passim;* and *Science and Common Sense,* New Haven, Yale University Press, 1961, pp. 24–25, 31–33, 97–98, 162, 289–291, and *passim.*

2. Cf. P. W. Bridgman, *The Logic of Modern Physics,* New York, Macmillan, 1927; Philipp Frank, *Foundations of Physics,* in *International Encyclopedia of Unified Science,* Chicago, University of Chicago Press, 1946, Vol. I, No. 7, pp. 1–78.

3. For a discussion of the concept of understanding, see also K. W. Deutsch, "The Limits of Common Sense," *Psychiatry: Journal for the Study of Interpersonal Processes,* 22:2, May, 1959, pp. 106–107; and "The Place of Behavioral Sciences in Graduate Training in International Relations," *Behavioral Science,* 3:3, July, 1958, pp. 278–280.

4. Paul Lazarsfeld at a meeting of the Columbia University Seminar on Methods in the Social Sciences, March 12, 1951.

5. Cf. Conant, *On Understanding Science,* and Bridgman, *The Logic of Modern Physics.*

6. For the concept of heuristics, see G. Polya, *How to Solve It,* Princeton, Princeton University Press, 1945, pp. 102–103, 118–123.

7. For the relationship of prediction to time series, cf. Norbert Wiener, *Extrapolation, Interpolation and Smoothing of Stationary Time Series,* New York, Wiley, 1949. In the natural sciences, a yes-or-no prediction might answer a question like this: Will this paper burn or not? A qualitative prediction might answer the question: Will it burn with a bright yellow flame? A quantitative prediction might answer the question: In how many seconds will it heat the contents of a test tube to 400° Fahrenheit?

In economics or politics, yes-or-no questions might be: Will the Jones Corporation build a new plant? Will the Blank party put on a political drive? Qualitative questions might be: Will the Jones Corporation build a large and modern plant? Will the Blank party put on a drive for clean government? Quantitative questions might be: How large a plant will they have built by what date? How many meetings, posters, radio appeals will the Blank party use before next November, and when will the drive reach its climax? The spectrum formed by these different kinds of questions might well be continuous.

8. Cf. S. S. Stevens, "Mathematics, Measurement and Psychophysics," in Stevens, ed., *Handbook of Experimental Psychology,* New York, Wiley, 1951, pp. 1–49.

9. For the concept of a "language game," cf. also Ludwig Wittgenstein, *Philosophical Investigations*, Oxford, Blackwell, 1958, pp. 5–50.

10. Cf. Werner Jaeger, *Paideia: The Ideals of Greek Culture*, London, Oxford University Press, 1939, I, 103–111, 151–161; V. Gordon Childe, *What Happened in History*. New York, Penguin Books, 1946, pp. 208–209.

11. Peter B. Neiman, "The Operational Significance of Recognition," unpublished B.S. thesis, M.I.T., 1949. Colin Cherry, *On Human Communication: A Review, a Survey, and a Criticism*, Cambridge–New York, M.I.T. Press–Wiley, 1957, Chap. 7, "On Cognition and Recognition," esp. pp. 256–280. A similar requirement of correspondence or coincidence applies to the operation of certainty. "Thus we pay for certainty by foregoing information that fails to agree with other information. No machine man ever made uses so many parallel channels or demands so much coincidence as his own brain, and none is so likely to go right."—W. S. McCulloch, "Machines That Think and Want," in Ward C. Halstead, ed., *Brain and Behavior, Comparative Psychology Monographs*, 20:1, serial number 103, pp. 39–50, Berkeley–Los Angeles, University of California Press, 1950, p. 41. For a brief description of a possible model for the physical arrangements by which the brain may recognize a chord regardless of the pitch, see W. S. McCulloch, "Brain and Behavior," in *Current Trends in Psychological Theory*, No. 5 in the *Current Trends in Psychology* series, Pittsburgh, University of Pittsburgh, 1951, pp. 165–178, esp. 176–177.

12. Cf. Max Weber, "Ueber einige Kategorien der verstehenden Soziologie," in *Gesammelte Aufsätze zur Wissenschaftslehre*, Tübingen, Mohr, 1922, pp. 403–450, esp. 403–414. For Weber's further distinction between subjectively goal-oriented (or "purposively rational") and non-goal-oriented but psychologically conditioned types of action, see *ibid.*, pp. 408–411. Cf. also Max Weber, "Methodische Grundlagen der Soziologie," *op. cit.*, pp. 503–523, esp. pp. 507–510.

13. Cf. Wilhelm Dilthey, "Ideen über eine beschreibende und zergliedernde Psychologie," in *Gesammelte Schriften*, Vol. 5, Leipzig–Berlin, Teubner, 1924, pp. 139–240; William Kluback, *Wilhelm Dilthey's Philosophy of History*, New York, Columbia University Press, 1956; and Herbert Arthur Hodges, *The Philosophy of William Dilthey*, London, Routledge & Kegan Paul, 1952.

14. Cf. Talcott Parsons, *The Social System*, Glencoe, Ill., The Free Press of Glencoe, 1951, p. 7.

15. P. W. Bridgman, *op. cit.*, pp. 80–91.

16. R. M. MacIver, *Social Causation*, Boston, Ginn, 1942.

17. W. W. Rostow, *The Process of Economic Growth*, New York,

Norton, 1952, pp. 12–54, and esp. 24–26 and 35; cf. also an earlier and somewhat different formulation in K. W. Deutsch, "Innovation, Entrepreneurship, and the Learning Process," in A. H. Cole, ed., *Change and the Entrepreneur: Postulates for Entrepreneurial History*, Cambridge, Harvard University Press, 1949, pp. 24–29, esp. 25–27; and in more elaborate form, K. W. Deutsch, "Innovation Curves in Politics and Economics," *PROD*, 1, September, 1957, pp. 4–7.

18. Cf. Hermann Weyl, *Philosophy of Mathematics and Natural Science*, Princeton, Princeton University Press, 1949, pp. 146–147, 155–157. "What is decisive is this: the farther the analysis progresses, the more detailed the observations become and the finer the elements into which we dissect the phenomena, the simpler—and not the more complicated, as might be expected—become the basic laws, and the more completely and accurately do they explain the factual course of events."—*Ibid.*, pp. 146–147. Cf. also Ernst Mach, "The Economy of Science," reprinted in Philip P. Wiener, *Readings in Philosophy of Science*, New York, Scribner's, 1953, pp. 446–452.

19. The work of Professor Laszlo Tisza on the structure of theoretical physics suggests that theories of greater generality—such as relativistic physics or quantum mechanics—often may be more complex, and include more terms in their equations than do more restricted theories—such as Newtonian mechanics—which are included in the general theories as special cases but which can be described more economically by simpler models in which some of the terms of the more general equations can be neglected. Laszlo Tisza, Communication, M.I.T., 1961.

20. W. S. McCulloch, "A Recapitulation of the Theory, with a Forecast of Several Extensions," *Annals of the New York Academy of Science*, 50, Art. 4, "Teleological Mechanisms," pp. 259–277, October 13, 1948, p. 267.

21. Philipp Frank, *Relativity—A Richer Truth*, Boston, Beacon Press, 1950, p. 133. The differing view, given in the present text, suggests that the concept of probability is quite compatible with that of a dependable and knowable order. For a recent discussion of some similar problems, see also Henry Margenau, *Open Vistas: Philosophical Perspectives of Modern Science*, New Haven, Yale University Press, 1961, *passim*.

CHAPTER 2

1. Cf. Derek J. de Solla Price, *Science Since Babylon*, New Haven, Yale University Press, 1961, pp. 17–21.

2. For a recent retelling of that archetypal Greek legend, see Mary

Renault, *The King Must Die*, New York, Pocket Books, 1960, pp. 268–269.

3. Cf. Price, *op. cit.*, pp. 1–2, 9–22.

4. A. Rosenblueth and N. Wiener, "The Role of Models in Science," *Philosophy of Science*, 12, 1945, p. 318.

5. J. W. Goethe, *Faust*, I, i, trans. C. F. MacIntyre, Norfolk, Conn., New Directions: "... thus working on the roaring loom of time, I weave God's living garment." Copyright 1949 by New Directions.

6. H. T. Pledge, *Science Since 1500*, New York, Philosophical Library, 1947, p. 29.

7. Cf. Norbert Wiener, *Cybernetics*, second revised and enlarged edition, Cambridge-New York, M.I.T. Press-Wiley, 1961, pp. 30–44. I am indebted to Professor Wiener for letting me use the page proofs of the new chapters 9 and 10 of this edition.

8. The latter terms refer to "any improvement or deterioration in value position or potential" of an actor, and not merely to those changes that could be described readily "in hedonic terms." Harold D. Lasswell and Abraham Kaplan, *Power and Society*, New Haven, Yale University Press, 1950, pp. 61, and 61, n. 6.

9. Philipp Frank's comments on K. W. Deutsch, "Higher Education and the Unity of Knowledge," in Lyman Bryson *et al.*, eds., *Goals for American Education*, New York, Harper, 1950, p. 131, n. 1; italics mine.

10. *Ibid.*, pp. 131–132.

11. Immanuel Kant, "Idea of a Universal History on a Cosmo-Political Plan," translated by Thomas De Quincey, in *Speculations Literary and Philosophic*, Edinburgh, Adams and Charles Black, 1862, pp. 133–152.

12. The actual—though limited—possibilities of "de-differentiation" in real organisms, such as embryonic tissue, were usually ignored in this classic model. I am indebted to Professor J. B. S. Haldane for this point.

13. Ralph W. Gerard, "Neurophysiology: an integration (molecules, neurosis and behavior)," in V. E. Hall *et al.*, eds., *Handbook of Physiology*, III, Washington, D.C., American Physiological Society, 1960, pp. 1919–1965, esp. pp. 1931–1932, 1939, 1949–1956. Cf. also the same author's "Becoming: The Residue of Change," in Sol Tax, ed., *Evolution After Darwin*, II, *The Evolution of Man, Mind, Culture and Society*, Chicago, University of Chicago Press, 1960, pp. 255–267.

14. "Spirit," i.e., breath, became a model for these "ineffable" parts, at a time when neither the chemistry nor the physiology of breathing was well understood. To this was added the confusion of the fleeting "spirit" of breath in a living body, with the evaporating "spirit" of ether or alcohol in distillation, fermentation, and intoxication—all of them not understood themselves. The orginal simple physical imagery of the words

"spirit" and "spiritual" has long been less than adequate for the subtle and important processes of mental and emotional communication they were intended to describe, except for the generalized secondary connotations these words have acquired from long tradition. For a discussion of a possible operational meaning of "spirit" in terms of present-day knowledge, see pp. 240–242, below.

15. Cf. E. Heimann, *History of Economic Doctrines*, New York, Oxford University Press, 1945, pp. 132, 177. Erich Roll, *A History of Economic Thought*, 3rd ed., Englewood Cliffs, N.J., Prentice-Hall, 1956, pp. 217–231.

16. Cf. Oswald Spengler, *The Decline of the West: Form and Actuality*, London, Allen and Unwin, n.d. (1926?), pp. 5–6, 25, 38–39, 94–97, 104–105, 117, etc. Cf. also George Terborgh, *The Bogey of Economic Maturity*, Chicago, Machinery and Allied Products Institute, 1945, pp. 2–3.

17. Heraclitus; italics mine. Cited in Bertrand Russell, *A History of Western Philosophy*, New York, Simon and Schuster, 1945, p. 43. "All things are an exchange for Fire, and Fire for all things, even as wares for Gold and gold for wares," *ibid.*, p. 44. On Heraclitus' coining of the words *synapsis* and *harmonia*—"contiguity" and "harmony"—see Werner Jaeger, *The Theology of the Early Greek Philosophers*, Oxford, Clarendon Press, 1947, pp. 119–120.

18. R. G. Collingwood, *The Idea of History*, Oxford, Clarendon Press, 1946, pp. 46–52.

19. Migne, *Patrologia Latina*, 50, 667; cited in Eugen Rosenstock-Huessy, *The Christian Future*, New York, Scribner's, 1946, p. 75, n. 1.

20. A. J. Toynbee, *A Study of History*, 2nd ed., London, Oxford University Press, 1945–1961, esp. Vol. 3, pp. 112–390; Eugen Rosenstock-Huessy, *Out of Revolution: Autobiography of Western Man*, New York, Morrow, 1938.

21. In the latest volume of his work, Mr. Toynbee says that this particular lack "is inevitable, considering my belief that novelty is logically unintelligible." A. J. Toynbee, *A Study of History*, Vol. 12, *Reconsiderations*, New York, Oxford University Press, 1961, p. 254. The point is further discussed on pp. 175–176, below.

22. Simon Kuznets, "Measurement of Economic Growth," in *Economic Growth, A Symposium: The Tasks of Economic History*, Supplement VII, 1947, *The Journal of Economic History*, New York, New York University Press, 1947; and *Six Lectures on Economic Growth*, Glencoe, Ill., The Free Press of Glencoe, 1959.

23. Teilhard de Chardin, *The Phenomenon of Man*, New York, Harper, 1961, p. 78.

24. I John 3:2 (King James Version). It should be noted, however, that Père Teilhard himself did envisage human evolution—and indeed the entire evolution of the earth—as tending toward a single goal, or relationship, which he designated symbolically as "Point Omega." Cf. Teilhard de Chardin, *op. cit.*, pp. 257–263, 267–272, and *passim*.

25. To the extent that the opposite assumption was made—the assumption that "it is the spirit which builds the body for itself"—organism could not be used consistently as a model.

CHAPTER 3

1. N. Rashevsky, *Mathematical Theory of Human Relations: An Approach to a Mathematical Biology of Social Phenomena*, Bloomington, Ind., Principia Press, 1947, pp. 127–149, and esp. pp. 148–149.

2. On the distinction between elite and mass opinion, see K. W. Deutsch and L. J. Edinger, *Germany Rejoins the Powers: Mass Opinion, Interest Groups, and Elites in Contemporary German Foreign Policy*, Stanford, Stanford University Press, 1959, *passim;* and on the crucial middle group of "politically relevant" or "mobilized" strata, and its distinction from the underlying population, see K. W. Deutsch, "Social Mobilization and Political Development," *American Political Science Review*, 55:3, September, 1961, pp. 493–514; and *Nationalism and Social Communication*, Cambridge-New York, M.I.T. Press-Wiley, 1953, Chap. 6, pp. 97–126.

3. For recent examples of various more sophisticated models, applied to the study of conflicts, see, e.g., Anatol Rapoport, *Fights, Games, and Debates*, Ann Arbor, University of Michigan Press, 1960, pp. 15–106; and Kenneth E. Boulding, *Conflict and Defense: A General Theory*, New York, Harper, 1962.

4. See N. Rashevsky, "Two Models: Imitative Behavior and Distribution of Status," in P. F. Lazarsfeld, ed., *Mathematical Thinking in the Social Sciences*, Glencoe, Ill., The Free Press of Glencoe, 1954, pp. 67–104.

5. Cf. James S. Coleman, "An Expository Analysis of Some of Rashevsky's Social Behavior Models," *ibid.*, pp. 105–165.

6. George Kingsley Zipf, *National Unity and Disunity: The Nation as a Bio-Social Organism*, Bloomington, Ind., Principia, 1941; and *Human Behavior and the Principle of Least Effort*, Cambridge, Addison-Wesley, 1949.

7. Cf. John Q. Stewart, "Empirical Mathematical Rules Concerning the Distribution and Equilibrium of Population," *The Geographical Review*, 37:3, July, 1947, pp. 461–485, and esp. 462–471.

271

8. George Kingsley Zipf, *National Unity and Disunity*, pp. 196–197 and Figure 18.

9. Cf. Herbert A. Simon, "Some Strategic Considerations in the Construction of Social Science Models" in Lazarsfeld, *op. cit.*, pp. 388–415, and Herbert A. Simon, *Models of Man: Social and Rational*, New York, Wiley, 1957.

10. Note, however, Simon's important and suggestive paper "Notes on the Observation and Measurement of Political Power" in *Models of Man*, pp. 62–78. For further developments in the analysis of this particular problem, see Robert A. Dahl, James G. March, and D. Nasatir, "Influence Ranking in the United States Senate," paper presented to the American Political Science Convention, September, 1956, and Robert A. Dahl, "The Concept of Power," *Behavioral Science*, 2, July, 1957, pp. 201–215.

11. Cf. Herbert A. Simon, *Administrative Behavior: A Study of Decision-Making Processes in Administrative Organization*, 2nd ed., New York, Macmillan, 1957; and James G. March and Herbert A. Simon, *Organizations*, New York, Wiley, 1958.

12. Lewis F. Richardson, "Generalized Foreign Politics: A Study in Group Psychology," *British Journal of Psychology*, Monograph Supplement No. 23, Cambridge University Press, 1939. Cf. also his *Arms and Insecurity*, Chicago, Quadrangle Press, 1960, and *Statistics of Deadly Quarrels*, Chicago, Quadrangle Press, 1960; and the summaries in Quincy Wright, *A Study of War*, Chicago, University of Chicago Press, 1942, Vol. II, Appendix 42, pp. 1482–1483; Kenneth J. Arrow, "Mathematical Models in the Social Sciences," in Daniel Lerner and Harold D. Lasswell, eds., *The Policy Sciences: Recent Developments in Scope and Method*, Stanford, Stanford University Press, 1951, p. 137; and in Rapoport, *op. cit.*, Part I.

13. For some examples of correctly used coefficients, see, e.g., Boulding, *op. cit.*, pp. 35–37, 128–130; and Rapoport, *op. cit.*, pp. 15–106.

14. Cf. K. W. Deutsch, "On Communication Models in the Social Sciences," *Public Opinion Quarterly*, 16:3, Fall, 1952, pp. 356–380, and especially pp. 364–367. Few serious investigators should find it hard to choose between the difficulty of having to admit that one has been less than completely right in the past and the pleasure of being able to think that one may have learned a little in the meantime.

15. Talcott Parsons, *The Structure of Social Action*, New York, McGraw-Hill, 1937, pp. 604–605. Cf. also Weber's essay, " 'Objectivity' in Social Science and Social Policy," in Max Weber, *The Methodology of the Social Sciences*, trans. by E. A. Shils and H. A. Finch, Glencoe, Ill., The Free Press of Glencoe, 1949, pp. 49–112, esp. 89–110, ". . . there are certain relationships between the 'idea' in the sense of a tendency of prac-

tical or theoretical thought and the 'idea' in the sense of the ideal-*typical* portrayal of an epoch constructed as a heuristic device. An ideal type of certain situations, which can be abstracted from certain characteristic social phenomena of an epoch, might—and this is indeed quite often the case—have also been present in the minds of the persons living in that epoch as an ideal to be striven for in practical life or as a maxim for the regulation of certain social relationships. . . . Thus the causal relationship between the historically determinable idea which governs the conduct of men and those components of historical reality from which their corresponding ideal-*type* may be abstracted, can naturally take on a considerable number of different forms. The main point to be observed is that *in principle* they are both fundamentally different things," *ibid.*, p. 95.

Cf. also Talcott Parsons' introduction to Max Weber's *The Theory of Social and Economic Organization*, trans. by A. M. Henderson and Talcott Parsons, Glencoe, Ill., The Free Press of Glencoe, 1947, pp. 13–17.

For an emphasis on Weber's substantive work, intended to balance the recent widespread interest in his methodology, see also Reinhard Bendix, *Max Weber: An Intellectual Portrait*, New York, Doubleday, 1960. For a discussion of Weber's method, see *ibid.*, pp. 276–286.

16. For Max Weber's last comprehensive formulation of his basic concepts from the years 1918–1920, including notably his notion of "ideal types," see the chapter on "Soziologische Grundbegriffe" in his *Wirtschaft und Gesellschaft: Grundriss der Verstehenden Soziologie*, 4th ed., J. Winckelmann, ed., Tübingen, Mohr, 1956, I, 1–11. Cf. also his essay "The Meaning of 'Ethical Neutrality' in Sociology and Economics" in *The Methodology of the Social Sciences*, pp. 1–47, esp. 34–37; and Talcott Parsons' introduction to Weber, *The Theory of Social and Economic Organization*, pp. 15–17.

17. Max Weber, "Die sozialen Gründe des Untergangs der antiken Kultur," in Weber, *Gesammelte Aufsätze zur Sozial- und Wirtschaftsgeschichte*, Tübingen, Mohr, 1924, pp. 289–311, esp. 289–299.

18. Robert K. Merton, *Social Theory and Social Structure*, rev. and enlarged ed., Glencoe, Ill., The Free Press of Glencoe, 1957; and Talcott Parsons and Edward A. Shils, eds., *Toward a General Theory of Action*, Cambridge, Harvard University Press, 1951.

19. Talcott Parsons' introduction to Weber, *The Theory of Social and Economic Organization*, pp. 18–20.

20. Merton, *op. cit.*, p. 49.

21. I am obligated to Dr. Louis H. Nahum, Lecturer in Physiology at the Yale Medical School, for information on this point.

22. Merton, *op. cit.*, p. 36.

23. This difference in emphasis remains, even if one recalls Max

273

Weber's interest in a possible probabilistic approach to the analysis of political and historical decisions between alternative possible outcomes. Cf. Weber's essay "Critical Studies in the Logic of the Cultural Sciences" in *The Methodology of the Social Sciences*, pp. 113–188, esp. pp. 164–167, 180–181, 183–185.

CHAPTER 4

1. John von Neumann and Oskar Morgenstern, *Theory of Games and Economic Behavior*, 2nd ed., Princeton, Princeton University Press, 1947, p. 42. Cf. also R. Duncan Luce and Howard Raiffa, *Games and Decisions*, New York, Wiley, 1957, pp. 204–206, 229–230.

2. Von Neumann and Morgenstern, *op. cit.*, pp. 44–45.

3. For examples of such an approach, see Patrick Suppes and Richard C. Atkinson, *Markov Learning Models for Multiperson Interactions*, Stanford, Stanford University Press, 1960; Anatol Rapoport, *Mathematical Models of Social Interaction*, Ann Arbor, Mental Health Research Institute, University of Michigan, April, 1961, Preprint No. 58, pp. 95–100 (lithoprinted). Cf. Luce and Raiffa, eds., *Games and Decisions*, Appendix 8, "Sequential Compounding of Two-Person Games," pp. 457–484, and esp. pp. 458–461.

4. Cf. A. Rapoport, *Fights, Games and Debates*, pp. 227–231; and see also Thomas C. Schelling, *The Strategy of Conflict*, Cambridge, Harvard University Press, 1960.

5. John McDonald, *Strategy in Poker, Business and War*, New York, Norton, 1950; J. D. Williams, *The Compleat Strategyst*, New York, McGraw-Hill, 1954. It seems characteristic that recent discussions of military policy have made only peripheral use of game theory, and have mainly relied on more traditional forms of argument. Cf. Herman Kahn, *On Thermonuclear War*, Princeton, Princeton University Press, 1960; Oskar Morgenstern, *The Question of National Defense*, New York, Random House, 1959.

6. Von Neumann and Morgenstern, *op. cit.*, p. 164.

7. *Ibid.*, p. 30. Italics supplied.

8. This strategy differs significantly from the familiar one of keeping one's opponent "off balance." To keep an adversary off balance may mean, among other things, to prevent him from committing himself thoroughly to any course of action. The Russian chess strategy, like the warfare of the ancient Parthians, would on the contrary encourage him to make such a commitment, in the hope of turning this commitment later to his (opponent's) disadvantage. The latter strategy, unlike the former, can employ deliberate pauses of activity, as well as positive action. The

274

difference between the two strategies resembles thus, in some respects, the difference between boxing and jujitsu.

9. Jacob Marschak, "Efficient and Viable Organizational Forms," in Mason Haire, ed., *Modern Organization Theory*, New York, Wiley, 1959, pp. 307–320, esp. pp. 317–318. For other possible developments, see also Martin Shubik, *Towards a Theory of Threats*, Yorktown Heights, N.Y., I.B.M. Research Paper RC-687, May 24, 1962, lithoprint, pp. 13–18.

10. Luce and Raiffa, *Games and Decisions*, pp. 220–236.

11. For some appraisals of this prospect, and an interesting application, see Martin Shubik, "Introduction to the Nature of Game Theory" and "Does the Fittest Necessarily Survive?" in Martin Shubik, ed., *Readings in Game Theory and Political Behavior*, New York, Random, 1954, pp. 1–11, and 43–46; as well as Richard C. Snyder, "Game Theory and the Analysis of Political Behavior," in Stephen K. Bailey *et. al.*, *Research Frontiers in Politics and Government: Brookings Lectures 1955*, Washington, D.C., Brookings, 1955, pp. 70–103.

12. Cf. Morton A. Kaplan, *System and Process in International Politics*, New York, Wiley, 1957, pp. 36–45, with further distinctions between "tight" and "loose" bipolar systems.

13. Cf. Thomas C. Schelling, *The Strategy of Conflict*, and also O. Morgenstern, *The Question of National Defense*, pp. 3–158; K. Boulding, *Conflict and Defense*, pp. 41–57; Kaplan, *System and Process in International Politics*, pp. 207–241.

14. Schelling, *op. cit.*, pp. 142–143.

15. *Ibid.*, pp. 142, 197–200.

16. *Ibid.*, pp. 16–18.

17. *Ibid.*, p. 13, n. 6.

18. E.g., *ibid.*, pp. 164–165.

19. Accidental war might result from the misinterpretation of radar signals; catalytic war from the deliberate but possibly clandestine provocation of some third country; insubordinate war from the act even of one officer such as the southern officer who ordered the first shots fired on the United States flag at Fort Sumter, or from the act of an organization, such as the O.A.S. in Algeria.

CHAPTER 5

1. N. Wiener, *Cybernetics*, 2nd ed., New York, Wiley, 1961, and *The Human Use of Human Beings*, Boston, Houghton Mifflin, 1950; cf. also W. Ross Ashby, *An Introduction to Cybernetics*, New York, Wiley, 1956; and, for a brief account, G. T. Guilbaud, *What Is Cybernetics?* tr. Valerie MacKay, New York, Grove, 1960.

2. *Science and Common Sense*, New Haven, Yale University Press, 1961, pp. 47–49. Cf. also Conant, *On Understanding Science*, New Haven, Yale University Press, 1947, pp. 16–20, 23–28.

3. Wiener, Communication, M.I.T., 1955.

4. Cf. Wiener, *Cybernetics* and *The Human Use of Human Beings*, both *passim;* Colin Cherry, *On Human Communication*, Cambridge-New York, M.I.T. Press-Wiley, 1957; and J. Ruesch and G. Bateson, *Communication: The Social Matrix of Psychiatry*, New York, Norton, 1951.

5. Cf. G. Polya, "Analogy," in *How to Solve It*, Princeton, Princeton University Press, 1946, pp. 37–46.

6. On this whole subject, see also A. Rosenblueth, N. Wiener, and J. Bigelow, "Behavior, Purpose and Teleology," *Philosophy of Science*, X, January, 1943, 18–24; W. S. McCulloch and W. Pitts, "A Logical Calculus of the Ideas Immanent in Nervous Activity," *Bulletin of Mathematical Biophysics*, V, 1943, pp. 115–133; F. S. C. Northrop, "The Neurological and Behavioristic Psychological Basis of the Ordering of Society by Means of Ideas," *Science*, 107, No. 2782, April 23, 1948, pp. 411–416; J. Ruesch and G. Bateson, "Structure and Process in Social Relations," *Psychiatry*, XII, 2, May, 1949, pp. 105–124. On the learning aspects, cf. also Wiener, *Cybernetics*, 2nd ed., pp. 169–180; W. Ross Ashby, *Design for a Brain*, 2nd ed., New York, Wiley, 1960, pp. 11, 113, 234. Cf. also the essays in Peter Laslett, ed., *The Physical Basis of Mind*, Oxford, Blackwell, 1957, and W. Russell Brain, *Mind, Perception and Science*, Oxford, Blackwell, 1951.

7. K. W. Deutsch, "Higher Education and the Unity of Knowledge," in L. Bryson *et al.*, eds., *Goals for American Education*, New York, Harper, 1950, pp. 110–111.

8. Somewhat differently phrased, a communications *network* is "a system of physical objects interacting with each other in such a manner that a change in the state of some elements is followed by a determinate pattern of changes in other related elements, in such a manner that the changes remain more or less localized, and independent of changes in the system from other sources" (W. Pitts); a communication *channel* is a "physical system within which a pattern (or *message*) is more or less isolated from other changes in the system" (Norbert Wiener); "A *state description* of a network or part of it" (Pitts); or again, somewhat differently stated, "a message is a reproducible pattern regularly followed by determinate processes depending on that pattern" (Wiener). Oral Communication, M.I.T. (Spring, 1949). Cf. also Claude E. Shannon and Warren Weaver, *The Mathematical Theory of Communication*, Urbana, Ill., University of Illinois Press, 1949, pp. 99–106 ("Information").

9. For a discussion of this entire subject, see N. Wiener, *Cybernetics*,

Shannon and Weaver, *op. cit.*; for a much simplified account, cf. E. C. Berkeley, *Giant Brains*, New York, Wiley, 1949.

10. On "Information" and "Matter," see also John E. Burchard, ed., *Mid-Century: The Social Implications of Scientific Progress*, Cambridge-New York, M.I.T. Press-Wiley, 1950, p. 228, n. 52.

11. Peter B. Neiman, "The Operational Significance of Recognition," B.S. thesis, M.I.T., 1949 (unpublished). Cf. also Cherry, *On Human Communication*, pp. 256–273.

12. Cf. S. E. Cairncross and L. B. Sjöström, "Flavor Profiles—A New Approach to Flavor Problems," *Food Technology*, 4:8, 1950, pp. 308–311; Sjöström, Cairncross, and Jean F. Caul, "Methodology of the Flavor Profile," *ibid.*, 11:9, 1957, pp. 20–25; Caul, Cairncross, and Sjöström, "The Flavor Profile in Review," *Perfumery and Essential Oil Record*, 49, pp. 130–133, London, March, 1958; "Physicochemical Research on Flavor," *Analytical Chemistry*, 30, Feb., 1958, pp. 17A–21A; Caul, "Geruchs- und Geschmacksanalysen mit der Profilmethode, II. Welche Rolle spielt der Geschmack bei Verbrauchsgütern," *Die Ernährungswirtschaft*, 7:9, 1960, pp. 398–402.

13. For this last topic, cf. W. N. Locke and A. D. Booth, eds., *Machine Translation of Languages*, Cambridge-New York, M.I.T. Press-Wiley, 1955.

14. Neiman, *op. cit.*; Cherry, *loc. cit.*

15. Cf. the essays in Daniel Lerner, ed., *Quantity and Quality*, New York, The Free Press of Glencoe, 1961.

16. Rosenblueth-Wiener-Bigelow, *op. cit.*, p. 19. A more refined definition would put "output information" in place of "output energy," in accordance with the distinction between "communications engineering" and "power engineering." Cf. Wiener, *Cybernetics*, 2nd ed., pp. 39, 42.

17. Rosenblueth-Wiener-Bigelow, *op. cit.*, p. 18. There is also another kind of feedback, different from the negative feedback discussed in the text: "The feedback is . . . positive [if] the fraction of the output which reenters the object has the same sign as the original input signal. Positive feedback adds to the input signals, it does not correct them. . . ." *Ibid.*, p. 19; see also Wiener, *Cybernetics*, 2nd ed., pp. 95–115. Only self-correcting, i.e., negative, feedback is discussed here.

18. Wiener, *loc. cit.*

19. Harry G. Johnson, Review of Norbert Wiener's *Cybernetics*, in the *Economic Journal*, Vol. LIX, N. 236, London, December, 1949, pp. 573–575. For an early attempt to apply feedback analysis to economics, see A. Tustin, *The Mechanism of Economic Systems*, Cambridge, Harvard University Press, 1953. Cf. also the special issue on "automatic control" of *Scientific American*, 187:3, September, 1952.

20. Cf. John Dollard, "The Acquisition of New Social Habits," in Ralph Linton, *The Science of Man in the World Crisis*, New York, Columbia University Press, 1945, p. 442; with further references. "Drives . . . are 'rewarded' that is . . . they are reduced in intensity . . ." A. Irving Hallowell, "Sociopsychological Aspects of Acculturation," in Linton, *op. cit.*, p. 183; cf., in the same volume, Clyde Kluckhohn and William H. Kelly, "The Concept of Culture," pp. 84–86; and E. R. Hilgard, *Theories of Learning*, New York, Appleton-Century-Crofts, 1948. Cf. also the references to Wiener and Ashby in Note 6, above.

21. Rosenblueth-Wiener-Bigelow, *op. cit.*, p. 18. "By behavior is meant any change of an entity with respect to its surroundings. . . . Accordingly any modification of an object, detectable externally, may be denoted as behavior."—*Ibid.*

22. The performance of a human goal seeker who strives for new goals on reaching each old one has been immortalized in Goethe's *Faust:*

"Im Weiterschreiten find't er Qual und Glueck
Er, unbefriedigt jeden Augenblick."

Analytical understanding of this process need not diminish its sublimity, and its emotional impact on us in our experience of recognition. *Faust* becomes no more trivial by our knowledge of goal-changing feedbacks than a sunrise becomes trivial by our knowledge of the laws of refraction.

23. The nature of "self" to be preserved by this order of purposes will be discussed in a later chapter. See pp. 128–142, below.

24. Vannevar Bush, "As We May Think," *Atlantic Monthly*, 176, July, 1945, pp. 101–108.

25. An automatic telephone exchange capable of opening new channels in response to its own traffic counts was reported under construction by the Phillips Company of Eyndthove, Holland (*Science News Letter*, Washington, D.C., April 10, 1948, p. 233). A telephone exchange that would install such a channel control itself would represent one more extension of the same principle.

26. "Man is the only organism normally and inevitably subject to psychological conflict" (J. S. Huxley, *Man Stands Alone*, New York, Harper, 1941, pp. 22–26, with examples).

CHAPTER 6

1. "By 'culture' we mean those historically created selective processes which channel men's reactions both to internal and to external stimuli."— Clyde Kluckhohn and William H. Kelly, "The Concept of Culture," in R.

Linton, *The Science of Man in the World Crisis*, New York, Columbia University Press, 1945, p. 84.

2. For a description of this experience of "sudden insight," and of its unreliability, see Bertrand Russell, *History of Western Philosophy*, New York, Simon and Schuster, 1945, pp. 123–124, and 289–290. Cf. also W. B. Cannon, *The Way of an Investigator*, New York, Norton, 1945, pp. 57–67; G. Polya, *How to Solve It*, Princeton, Princeton University Press, 1945, pp. 56–58; W. James, *Varieties of Religious Experience*, New York, Modern Library, n.d., pp. 370–413; and J. Rosett, *The Mechanism of Thought, Imagery and Hallucination*, New York, Columbia University Press, 1939, *passim*.

3. The importance of consciousness in the growth of nationalism is stressed, without defining consciousness itself, in Hans Kohn, *The Idea of Nationalism*, New York, Macmillan, 1944, pp. 6–16.

4. Louis L. Sutro, "Emergency Simulation of the Duties of the President of the United States," *Proceedings of the Western Joint Computer Conference*, San Francisco, Calif., March, 1959, pp. 314–323.

5. Cf. Norbert Wiener, *Cybernetics*, 2nd ed., pp. 175–177.

6. *New York Times*, April 2, 1962, p. 4:3–4; and April 4, 1962, p. 13:1.

7. Gardner Murphy, *Personality*, New York, Harper, 1947, p. 981. "Consciousness" and "awareness" are referred to in the text, but do not appear in the elaborate glossary and subject index. A similar view is taken by W. Ross Ashby, *Design for a Brain*, London, Chapman & Hall, 1952, pp. 11–12.

8. Kohn, *op. cit.*; Harold D. Lasswell, *The Analysis of Political Behaviour*, London, Oxford University Press, 1949, pp. 22, 108, 116, 215, 240, 284, etc.

9. Clyde Kluckhohn and Henry A. Murray, eds., *Personality in Nature, Society, and Culture*, New York, Knopf, 1948, p. 9; italics omitted.

10. For a discussion of consciousness in physiological as well as psychological terms, see D. O. Hebb, *The Organization of Behavior*, New York, Wiley, 1949, pp. 144–146; and for a suggestive survey of much earlier literature on this topic, C. R. Noyes, *Economic Man in Relation to His Natural Environment*, New York, Columbia University Press, 1948, I, 98 ff.; II, 1138 ff. Both works indicate a return of interest to a crucial topic, but they also show the difficulties of analyzing consciousness with none but physiological and psychological material that usually is hard to take apart or reassemble. Here the aid of structural data from the theory and practice of communications, as developed in engineering, mathematics, and the social sciences, might show its usefulness.

11. E.g., in the pressing of a key or a signal in N. Ach's experiment where "at the very instant of action no consciousness of will need ap-

pear," but "such a consciousness was none the less present as a 'determining tendency' prior to the action and governing it." Richard Müller-Freienfels, *The Evolution of Modern Psychology*, New Haven, Yale University Press, 1935, pp. 109 f.; cf. also pp. 41, 69, 236.

12. Or at least we expect it so to follow. Cf. Rosenblueth-Wiener-Bigelow, *op. cit.*, p. 19; cf. also Warren S. McCulloch, *Finality and Form in Nervous Activity*, Fifteenth James Arthur Lecture, American Museum of Natural History, New York, May 2, 1946, Springfield, Ill., Thomas, 1952, pp. 23–25, 31.

13. McCulloch, *loc. cit.*

14. W. Grey Walter, *The Living Brain*, New York, Norton, 1953, pp. 136–137.

15. On the importance of "will" in nationalism and nationality, see again Kohn, *loc. cit.*

16. *Receptors* are elements of a network whose state may be influenced from outside, i.e., which is not altogether determined by the previous states of other elements. Communication from W. Pitts, M.I.T., April 6, 1948. "Outside the network" need not refer to physical location. Any element influenced by any process *other than those in the other elements of the network*—for instance, an inner element varying randomly—counts as a receptor under this definition. It is this last type of arrangement that I have called "internal receptor" in the text. It would differ from ordinary "external" receptors in that it might be largely independent from most other processes acting on the other receptors of the net.

17. There are two kinds of "new" information for a network. The first is outside information not previously present in the net. The second is an internal recombination of symbols not previously *recognized*, that is, not previously matched in this configuration by a new secondary symbol or symbols. See the discussion on the concept of *novelty* in the section on "mind," below.

18. The importance of memory and cumulative learning—including learning from opponents—is stressed in the recent work by Wiener, but the significance of random sources for initiative is not. Cf. Norbert Wiener, *Cybernetics*, 2nd. ed., pp. 171–172, and his 1962 Terry Lectures at Yale University, "Prolegomena to Theology," publication forthcoming.

19. This view of moral responsibility would exclude those determinate elements of behavior that are not freely learned through the intake of information, but are the results of heredity, mutilation, organic disease, or functional mental illness, after these have disrupted significantly the processes of learning or decision-making.

In imputing criminal responsibility to a lawbreaker, it is usually assumed that he is capable of learning from his punishment, or that he is a representative sample of other persons with undisrupted learning capacity who are expected to be deterred by his fate. The experience that these assumptions may be mistaken, and that traditional punishments often fail to have the intended effects, even where they hold, have contributed to demands for penal reform.

CHAPTER 7

1. For important discussions of current concepts of power in political science, see Harold D. Lasswell and Abraham Kaplan, *Power and Society*, New Haven, Yale University Press, 1950; Robert A. Dahl, "The Concept of Power," *Behavioral Science*, 2:3, July, 1957, pp. 201–215; Hans Morgenthau, *Politics Among Nations*, 3rd ed., New York, Knopf, 1960, pp. 27–37; Richard Rosecrance, "Categories, Concepts and Reasoning in the Study of International Relations," *Behavioral Science*, 6:3, July, 1961, pp. 221–231; and the forthcoming work by Carl J. Friedrich, *Systematic Politics*.

2. Cf. A. M. Guhl, *Social Behavior of the Domestic Fowl*, Technical Bulletin 73, June, 1953, Manhattan Agricultural Experiment Station, Kansas State College, 1953, esp. pp. 4–13.

3. Cf. Bruce M. Russett, "Cause, Surprise, and No Escape," *Journal of Politics*, 24:1, February, 1962, pp. 3–22.

4. For an initial tentative discussion, see my *Nationalism and Social Communication*, *op. cit.*, Chap. 3, pp. 46–59.

5. Dahl uses the example of presidential endorsement for the first test (the greater frequency of passing of bills so endorsed), and the example of a senator's voting record for the second (the frequency of his having voted for bills that passed). If one uses senators for both examples, the fundamental identity of the two tests, or rather the two formulations of the same test, becomes apparent. Cf. Dahl, *op. cit.*

6. In the draft of a forthcoming book, Dahl stresses the need to count not only the frequency with which the commands of an actor seem to be obeyed, but also the likelihood that the behavior called for would have occurred in any case for other reasons. Cf. Robert A. Dahl, "The Analysis of Power," in his *The Analysis of Politics*, New York, Prentice-Hall, forthcoming.

7. Lasswell and Kaplan, *op. cit.*, pp. 74–75.

8. Carl Friedrich has pointed out that "power hides" and that the most strongly entrenched power is the one that does not have to be used and that can be inferred only indirectly from the account taken by the weak of the anticipated reactions of the strong.

9. Lasswell and Kaplan, *op. cit.*, pp. 74–102, and esp. Table 2 on p. 87.

10. See Note 6, above. The notion of the cost of power was suggested by the author in *Nationalism and Social Communication, loc. cit.* (note 4 above). For a recent discussion of the "opportunity costs of power" and for an interesting link to game theory, see John C. Harsanyi, "Measurement of Social Power, Opportunity Costs, and the Theory of Two-Person Bargaining Games," *Behavioral Science*, 7:1, January, 1962, pp. 67–80, especially pp. 69–70.

11. Arnold J. Toynbee, *A Study of History*, 2nd ed., New York, Oxford University Press, 1935, III, 50–112.

12. Cf. Talcott Parsons and Neil E. Smelser, *Economy and Society*, Glencoe, Ill., The Free Press of Glencoe, 1956. The interesting notion of "power inputs" and "power investments," proposed by George Modelski, points in the same direction of political solvency and interchange. Cf. George Modelski, *A Theory of Foreign Policy*, New York, Praeger, 1962, pp. 150–152.

13. From data in International Monetary Fund, *International Financial Statistics*, 15:4, April, 1962, pp. 268–271. Professor Robert Triffin points out that it is well known that the proportion of money to national income rises in the early stages of economic development and that this proportion may again decline somewhat in highly developed countries. It would be interesting to investigate whether a similar change holds for the proportion of those human affairs that are carried on with a heavy use of influence, or of power, or even of force, to the total volume of social activities in the society in question. Do, in short, "monetization ratios" and "politicization ratios" vary together, and if so, to what extent?

14. Cf. Erich Roll, *A History of Economic Thought*, 3rd. ed., Englewood Cliffs, N.J., Prentice-Hall, 1956, pp. 68–85.

15. Some relevant passages from Marx and Engels are discussed in V. I. Lenin, *The State and Revolution*, New York, Vanguard, 1929, pp. 122–123, 166–171, 181–186, 189–206. Cf. also Herbert Marcuse, *Soviet Marxism*, New York, Columbia University Press, 1958; and K. W. Deutsch, "Anarchism," *Encyclopædia Britannica*, Vol. I, Chicago, 1962, pp. 867–869. H. G. Wells, *Men Like Gods*, London, Fisher Unwin, 1927 (*Works*, Vol. 28), pp. 62–63, 80, 284–285, pictures a world free from politics, governments, and crowds, three thousand years in the future; but other utopian constructs by the same author, imagined for an alternative present or the very near future, stress the need for considerable concentrations of power and authority, together with elaborate governmental organizations, as in Wells's *A Modern Utopia*, New York, Scribner's, 1905, pp. 142, 164, 212, 219–220, 261–264, 272, 310–312; and in his *The New World Order*, London, Secher and Warburg, 1940, pp. 182–183.

16. The point is strongly stated, and perhaps somewhat overstated, through underestimating the crosscurrents and contradictions in Soviet

ideology and politics, by Erich Fromm, *May Man Prevail? An Inquiry into the Facts and Fictions of Foreign Policy*, Garden City, New York, Doubleday, 1961, pp. 67–85, and generally 31–138.

17. K. W. Deutsch, "Social Mobilization and Political Development," *American Political Science Review*, 55:3, September, 1961, pp. 493–514.

18. Computed by Charles Taylor, Yale Political Data Program, from figures in Statistical Office of the United Nations, *Yearbook of National Accounts Statistics, 1958*, New York, 1959.

CHAPTER 8

1. On some possibilities for such research, see K. W. Deutsch, "A Note on the History of Entrepreneurship, Innovation and Decision-Making," *Explorations in Entrepreneurial History*, May, 1949, pp. 8–16; and "Mass Communications and the Loss of Freedom in National Decision-Making," *Conflict Resolution*, 1:2, July, 1957, pp. 200–211.

2. A. J. Toynbee, *A Study of History*, III, 126, 217, and 112–217, *passim*.

3. Cf. the passages on learning capacity, above, and Toynbee, *op. cit.*, III, 112–217.

4. Norbert Wiener, Communication, M.I.T., April 11, 1949.

5. On the connection between openness to the universe and the possibility of "intelligence amplification," see W. Ross Ashby's chapters on "Amplifying Regulation" and "Amplifying Adaptation" in his *Introduction to Cybernetics*, pp. 265–272, and *Design for a Brain*, pp. 231–237, respectively.

6. Beyond the minimum necessary for bare channel maintenance itself.

7. Or channel replacement, as discussed above. Our present calculating machines owe what efficiency they have to the fact that almost all their facilities can be devoted to the treatment of information, while maintenance of the machines is left to human beings.

8. Wiener, *Cybernetics*, 2nd ed., pp. 121, 146.

9. Toynbee, *A Study of History*, 2nd ed., III, 217.

10. *Ibid*. IV, 303–422. For the categories of Talcott Parsons, see Chapter 7, pp. 116–118, above, and the references given there.

CHAPTER 9

1. George A. Miller states the same point in somewhat different language:

"The 'amount of information' is exactly the same concept that we have talked about for years under the name of 'variance.' The equations are different, but if we hold tight to the idea that anything that increases the variance also increases the amount of information we cannot go far astray.

"The advantages of this new way of talking about variance are simple enough. Variance is always stated in terms of the unit of measurement—inches, pounds, volts, etc.—whereas the amount of information is a dimensionless quantity. Since the information in a discrete statistical distribution does not depend upon the unit of measurement, we can extend the concept to situations where we have no metric and we would not ordinarily think of using the variance. And it also enables us to compare results obtained in quite different experimental situations where it would be meaningless to compare variances based on different metrics. So there are some good reasons for adopting the newer concept.

"The similarity of variance and amount of information might be explained this way: When we have a large variance, we are very ignorant about what is going to happen. If we are very ignorant, then when we make the observation it gives us a lot of information. On the other hand, if the variance is very small, we know in advance how our observation must come out, so we get little information from making the observation.

"If you will now imagine a communication system, you will realize that there is a great deal of variability about what goes into the system and also a great deal of variability about what comes out. The input and the output can therefore be described in terms of their variance (or their information). If it is a good communication system, however, there must be some systematic relation between what goes in and what comes out. That is to say, the output will depend upon the input, or will be correlated with the input. If we measure this correlation, then we can say how much of the output variance is attributable to the input and how much is due to random fluctuations or 'noise' introduced by the system during transmission. So we see that the measure of transmitted information is simply a measure of the input-output correlation.

"There are two simple rules to follow. Whenever I refer to 'amount of information,' you will understand 'variance.' And whenever I refer to 'amount of transmitted information,' you will understand 'covariance' or 'correlation.'

"The situation can be described graphically by two partially overlapping circles. Then the left circle can be taken to represent the variance of the input, the right circle the variance of the output, and the overlap the covariance of input and output. I shall speak of the left circle as the 'amount of transmitted information,' you will understand 'covariance' or formation, and the overlap as the amount of transmitted information."

George A. Miller, "The Magical Number Seven, Plus or Minus Two: Some Limits on Our Capacity for Processing Information" *Psychological Review*, 63 (March, 1956), pp. 81–82.

2. Y. W. Lee, *Statistical Theory of Communication*, New York, Wiley, 1960.

3. G. W. Allport and L. J. Postman, "The Basic Psychology of Rumor," *Transactions of the New York Academy of Science*, Ser. II, VIII, 1945, pp. 61–81, reprinted in Wilbur Schramm, ed., *The Process and Effects of Mass Communication*, Urbana: University of Illinois Press, 1954, pp. 141–155. Cf. also F. C. Bartlett, "Social Factors in Recall" in T. M. Newcomb and E. L. Hartley, eds., *Readings in Social Psychology*, New York, Holt, 1947, pp. 69–76, especially on "The Method of Serial Reproduction," *ibid.*, p. 72; C. I. Hovland, I. L. Janis, and H. H. Kelley, *Communication and Persuasion*, New Haven, Yale University Press, 1953, pp. 245–249; and C. I. Hovland, "Human Learning and Retention" in S. S. Stevens, ed., *Handbook of Experimental Psychology*, New York, Wiley, 1951, pp. 613–689.

4. K. W. Deutsch, *Nationalism and Social Communication*, Cambridge-New York, M.I.T. Press-Wiley, 1953, pp. 70–74.

5. For efforts to include some data on elite attitudes and personnel at this middle level, see K. W. Deutsch and L. J. Edinger, *Germany Rejoins the Powers: Mass Opinion, Interest Groups, and Elites in Contemporary German Foreign Policy*, Stanford, Stanford University Press, 1959, pp. 60–144, 195–216. On this broad problem of political communication, see also Gabriel A. Almond, "A Functional Approach to Comparative Politics," in G. A. Almond and J. S. Coleman, eds., *The Politics of the Developing Areas*, Princeton, Princeton University Press, 1960, pp. 3–64, particularly pp. 45–52. Cf. also Charles Y. Glock, "The Comparative Study of Communication and Opinion Formation," in Schramm, *op. cit.*, pp. 469–479, and particularly the section on "Informal Channels of Communication," pp. 474–476. For the general elite problem, see also G. A. Almond, *The American People and Foreign Policy*, New York, Praeger, 1960, XXIV and 136–157.

6. Daniel Lerner, *The Passing of Traditional Society*, Glencoe, Ill., The Free Press of Glencoe, 1958, pp. 43–75.

7. Cf. James S. Coleman, "The Political Systems of Developing Areas," in Almond and Coleman, *op. cit.*, pp. 532–576, particularly pp. 544–547; Selig S. Harrison, *India: The Most Dangerous Decades*, Princeton, Princeton University Press, 1960; Lucian W. Pye, *Politics, Personality, and Nation Building: Burma's Search for Identity*, New Haven, Yale University Press, 1962.

8. Toynbee, *A Study of History*, IV, 119–133.

9. For an outstanding example, see E. A. Shils and M. Janowitz, "Cohesion and Disintegration in the Wehrmacht in World War II" in Schramm, *op. cit.*, pp. 501–516.

10. For an extremely informative summary of recent research on communications overload in biological systems and in small groups, see the forthcoming book by James Grier Miller, *Living Systems*, Ann Arbor, Mental Health Research Institute, 1962, preprint, Chapter 4.

CHAPTER 10

1. D. O. Hebb, *The Organization of Behavior*, New York, Wiley, 1949, pp. 109–134.

2. *Ibid.*

3. Karl W. Deutsch, "Innovation, Entrepreneurship and the Learning Process," in A. H. Cole, ed., *Change and the Entrepreneur: Postulates and Patterns for Entrepreneurial History*, Cambridge, Harvard University Press, 1949, pp. 24–29; citations are from pp. 25–27.

4. Gregory Bateson, "Social Planning and the Concept of 'Deutero-Learning,' " in T. M. Newcomb and E. L. Hartley, eds., *Readings in Social Psychology*, New York, Holt, 1st ed., 1947, pp. 121–128. This article was omitted from later editions of this work because these were limited increasingly to empirical material. Oral communication, T. M. Newcomb, Ann Arbor, Mich., March 20, 1962.

5. A. J. Toynbee, *Reconsiderations, A Study of History*, Vol. 12, New York, Oxford University Press, 1961, pp. 252, 254, 257, with reference to H. W. B. Joseph, *An Introduction to Logic*, 2nd ed., Oxford, Clarendon Press, 1916, pp. 406–408.

6. In addition to the works by N. Wiener, and D. O. Hebb, cited earlier, see, e.g., Lawrence S. Kubie, "The Fostering of Creative Scientific Productivity," *Daedalus: Journal of the American Academy of Arts and Sciences*, 91:2, Spring, 1962, pp. 294–309, esp. 305–306; Gordon S. Brown, "New Horizons in Engineering Education," *ibid.*, pp. 341–361, esp. 346–348; Gerald Holton, "Scientific Research and Scholarship: Notes Toward the Design of Proper Scales," *ibid.*, pp. 362–399; K. W. Deutsch, "The Way Our Children Grow," *Child Study*, 36:3, Summer, 1959, pp. 20–28; and "Creativity in a Scientific Civilization," in Associates of Bank Street College of Education, *Changing Attitudes in a Changing World*, New York, Bank Street College, 1958, pp. 29–36. Cf. also the essays in Harold H. Anderson, ed., *Creativity and Its Cultivation*, New York, Harper, 1959.

7. E.g., Almond and Coleman, *op. cit.*; Daniel Lerner, *op. cit.*; K. W. Deutsch, *et al.*, *Political Community and the North Atlantic Area*, Princeton, Princeton University Press, 1957; K. W. Deutsch, *et al.*, *Backgrounds for Political Community* (forthcoming); Ernst Haas, *The Uniting of Europe*, Stanford, Stanford University Press, 1958; Raymond Lindgren, *Norway-Sweden: Union, Disunion, and Scandinavian Integration*, Princeton, Princeton University Press, 1959; K. W. Deutsch and Herman Weilenmann, *Community for Diversity: The Political Integration of Switzerland* (in progress); Bruce M. Russett, *Community and Contention: Britain and America in the Twentieth Century*, Cambridge, M.I.T. Press, 1963; Richard L. Merritt, *Symbols of American Community, 1735-1775* (forthcoming).

CHAPTER 11

1. Norbert Wiener, *The Human Use of Human Beings*, Boston, Houghton Mifflin, 1950, pp. 12–15 (italics in original).

2. For the continued interest in equilibrium models see, e.g., George Liska, *International Equilibrium*, Cambridge, Harvard University Press, 1957, and the criticism in Stanley H. Hoffman, ed., *Contemporary Theory in International Relations*, Englewood Cliffs, N.J., Prentice-Hall, 1960, pp. 50–52. For a critical discussion of the limits of "the analogy between a market and a balance of power situation," cf. also Charles P. Kindleberger, "International Political Theory from Outside," in William T. R. Fox, ed., *Theoretical Aspects of International Relations*, Notre Dame, Ind., Notre Dame University, 1959, pp. 69–82. For other examples of the use of concepts of equilibrium or the balance of power, cf. Charles de Visscher, *Theory and Reality in Public International Law*, trans. Percy E. Corbett, Princeton, Princeton University Press, 1957, p. 92; Kenneth W. Thompson, *Political Realism and the Crisis of World Politics*, Princeton, Princeton University Press, 1960, pp. 144–166; and George Modelski, *A Theory of Foreign Policy*, New York, Praeger, 1962, p. 129. For another critical discussion of balance-of-power theory and its limitations, see Hans Morgenthau, *Politics Among Nations*, 3rd ed., New York, Knopf, 1960, pp. 167–216. It is interesting to note that both Thompson and Morgenthau compensate for some of the limitations and rigidities of the equilibrium and balance-of-power model by stressing heavily the need for normative theories of international morality. Cf. Thompson, *loc. cit.*, and pp. 166–173; Morgenthau, *op. cit.*, pp. 216–223.

3. Cf. the use of the concept by Anatol Rapoport, *Fights, Games, and Debates*, Ann Arbor, University of Michigan Press, 1960, pp. 25–43.

4. Cf. W. S. McCulloch: "Feedback was defined as an alteration of input by output; gain was defined as ratio of output to input; feedback was said to be negative or inverse if the return decreased the output, say by subtracting from the input. The same term, inverse or negative feedback, was used for a similar effect but dissimilar mechanism, wherein the return decreased the gain. The transmission of signals requires time, and gain depends on frequency; consequently, circuits inverse for some frequencies may be regenerative for others. All become regenerative when gain exceeds one."—"Summary of the Points of Agreement Reached in the Previous Nine Conferences on Cybernetics," Appendix I, in Heinz von Foerster, ed., *Cybernetics: Circular Causal and Feedback Mechanisms in Biological Social Systems*, New York, Macy Foundation, 1955, p. 71.

5. Cf. Russett, "Cause, Surprise, and No Escape," *Journal of Politics*, 24:1, February, 1962, pp. 3–22. A larger study of the 1914 crisis is currently being conducted by Professor Robert C. North and his associates at Stanford University.

6. *New York Times*, March 3, 1962, pp. 1–2.

7. E.g., Rapoport, *op. cit.*; Morton A. Kaplan, *The Strategy of Limited Retaliation*, Policy Memorandum No. 19, The Center for International Studies, Princeton, Princeton University Press, 1959; Thomas C. Schelling, *The Strategy of Conflict*, Cambridge, Harvard University Press, 1960; and Herman Kahn, *On Thermonuclear War*, Princeton, Princeton University Press, 1960. Cf. also the discussion in the last section of Chapter 4, above.

8. Cf. also David M. Potter, *People of Plenty: Economic Abundance and the American Character*, Chicago, University of Chicago Press, 1954, pp. 3–72; Alex Inkeles and Daniel J. Levinson, "National Character: The Study of Modal Personality and Sociocultural Systems," in Gardner Lindzey, ed., *Handbook of Social Psychology*, Reading, Mass., Addison-Wesley, 1954, II, 977–1020; and Margaret Mead, "National Character" in A. L. Kroeber, ed., *Anthropology Today*, Chicago, University of Chicago Press, 1953, pp. 642–667. Cf. also David Riesman, Nathan Glazer, and Rueul Denny, *The Lonely Crowd: A Study of the Changing American Character*, New Haven, Yale University Press, 1950, esp. pp. 17–31; and Washington Platt, *National Character in Action*, New Brunswick, N.J., Rutgers University Press, 1961.

9. For a thoughtful study of an important case—the employment of atomic bombs against Japanese cities—see Robert C. Batchelder, *The Irreversible Decision, 1939–1950*, Boston, Houghton Mifflin, 1962, esp. pp. 190–210.

10. Riesman, *op. cit.*, pp. 199–209.

CHAPTER 12

1. Cf. K. W. Deutsch, *Nationalism and Social Communication*, pp. 144–151.
2. For the influence of French historians on the reputation of Napoleon, see Stanley Mellon, *The Political Uses of History: A Study of Historians in the French Restoration*, Stanford, Stanford University Press, 1958, pp. 35, 46, 99, 109–112, 193–195.

CHAPTER 13

1. For a discussion of self-reference and the "self-reference effect," see Harold D. Lasswell, *The World Revolution of Our Time: A Framework for Basic Policy Research*, Stanford, Stanford University Press, 1951, pp. 30–32.
2. Cf. Hans Morgenthau, *Politics Among Nations*, 3rd ed., New York, Knopf, 1960, pp. 10–11; Reinhold Niebuhr, *Christian Realism and Political Problems*, New York, Scribner's, 1953 ("St. Augustine's Political Realism"), pp. 119–146; and George Kennan, *American Diplomacy, 1900–1950*, New York, New American Library, 9th printing, 1960, p. 87. For a critical view, see Franz Neumann, "Approaches to the Study of Political Power," *Political Science Quarterly*, 65:2, June 1950, pp. 161–180.
3. Cf. W. S. McCulloch: " 'Traffic jams' of brains become increasingly probable with increase in volume, for the number of long distance connections cannot be expanded to keep pace with the number of relays to be connected, except by increasing cable-space disproportionately."—"Summary of the Points of Agreement Reached in the Previous Nine Conferences on Cybernetics," Appendix I, in von Foerster, ed., *Cybernetics*, New York, Macy Foundation, 1955, p. 71.

CHAPTER 14

1. Cf. for example, Henry A. Kissinger, *Nuclear Weapons and Foreign Policy*, Garden City, L.I., Doubleday, 1958, pp. 3, 14, 144, 149, 159, etc.; Thomas C. Schelling, *The Strategy of Conflict*, Cambridge, Harvard University Press, 1960, p. 14, 40, etc.; Hans Kohn, *Nationalism, Its Meaning and History*, Princeton, Van Nostrand, 1955, p. 10.
2. Julian Huxley, *Evolution, the Modern Synthesis*, New York and

London, Harper, 1943, pp. 556–578; Huxley, *Man in the Modern World,* New York, New American Library, 1951, pp. 7–27.

3. C. Northcote Parkinson, *Parkinson's Law, and Other Studies in Administration,* Boston, Houghton Mifflin, 1957.

4. For a stimulating discussion of psychological and other aspects of growth and innovation; cf. David C. McClelland, *The Achieving Society,* Princeton, Van Nostrand, 1961, esp. Chapter 10, "Accelerating Economic Growth," pp. 391–437.

INDEX

Index

294

Date Due